Design Patterns in Java

From Basics to Expert Proficiency

Contents

Introduction

Design patterns form an essential part of software engineering, shaping the way developers approach complex design problems. By defining a reusable solution to common design issues, design patterns offer a structured approach to software development. This book, *Design Patterns in Java: From Basics to Expert Proficiency*, aims to provide a detailed exploration of these patterns, tailored specifically for Java programming.

The concept of design patterns was popularized by the seminal work "Design Patterns: Elements of Reusable Object-Oriented Software" by Erich Gamma, Richard Helm, Ralph Johnson, and John Vlissides, often referred to as the "Gang of Four" (GoF). Their work categorized and described 23 patterns, divided into Creational, Structural, and Behavioral patterns, each offering unique solutions to recurring design problems. Understanding these categorisations not only aids in recognizing suitable patterns but also enhances one's ability to communicate complex design concepts clearly.

In the realm of Java programming, the importance of design patterns cannot be overstressed. Java's object-oriented nature makes it a fertile ground for the application of design patterns. As you progress through this book, you will gain a thorough understanding of how each pattern can be implemented in Java, along with best practices and common pitfalls.

The initial chapters will introduce you to the foundational concepts surrounding design patterns, detailing their history, evolution, and the rationale behind their adoption. This theoretical groundwork will equip you with the necessary context to understand the more intricate details that follow. Subsequent chapters will delve into the specifics of Creational, Structural, and Behavioral patterns, offering practical examples and explanations to illustrate their application.

As we explore each pattern, emphasis will be placed on real-world use cases, demonstrating how design patterns can resolve actual software design issues. This practical approach ensures that the knowledge gained is not merely theoretical but can be directly applied to improve the quality and maintainability of your code.

In addition to detailed explanations and examples, this book will guide you through best practices to adopt and common mistakes to avoid. Such guidance is crucial as misuse or overuse of design patterns can lead to over-engineering and complicate otherwise simple solutions. The aim is to instill a balanced understanding, enabling you to judiciously apply design patterns where they are most effective.

By the end of this text, you will have a comprehensive understanding of design patterns and their implementation in Java. Whether you are a beginner or an experienced developer, the insights provided will enhance your design skills and prepare you for more complex software development challenges. This book aims to be a definitive resource in your journey towards mastering design patterns in Java, equipping you with the knowledge to harness their full potential in your software projects.

Chapter 1

Introduction to Design Patterns

Design patterns are essential solutions to commonly occurring problems in software design. This chapter covers what design patterns are, their historical evolution, and their significance in software development, specifically in Java programming. It introduces the three main categories of design patterns—Creational, Structural, and Behavioral—and outlines their roles. The chapter also explains the principles behind the Gang of Four (GoF) patterns, offers guidelines on selecting appropriate patterns, discusses best practices for implementation, and provides real-world examples to illustrate their application.

1.1 What Are Design Patterns?

Design patterns are established solutions to recurring problems in software design. These patterns provide a template that developers can utilize to solve specific problems in a structured and efficient manner. A design pattern is not a finished design that can be directly transformed into code; rather, it is a description or template for how to solve a problem that can be used in many different situations. The core objective of design patterns is to increase the productivity of developers and to promote code reuse, leading to more maintainable and scalable software.

Design patterns facilitate the communication of complex concepts in software engineering. They serve as a common language between developers, enabling them to avoid misunderstandings and to share solutions more effectively. When a design pattern is recognized and adopted, it reduces the effort required to find a solution because the pattern's structure, participants, and interactions already define the solution space.

The recognition of patterns is crucial in creative software design. By recognizing where a particular pattern might fit within the context of a problem, developers can leverage proven strategies rather than reinventing the wheel. This consideration significantly reduces the risk of making design errors and provides a reliable starting point for problem solving.

There are several common elements found in each pattern, which include:

- **Name**: The pattern's name provides a concise reference to the pattern and its intent.
- **Problem**: This component specifies the problem and context in which the pattern is applicable.
- **Solution**: The pattern's solution represents the design structures and the relationships between its elements.
- **Consequences**: This considers the results and trade-offs of applying the pattern. Here, the pros and cons of the pattern are discussed to help determine when the pattern is suitable.

Let's consider a practical example using the Singleton pattern. The Singleton design pattern ensures a class has only one instance and provides a global point of access to that instance. This is particularly useful when exactly one object is needed to coordinate actions across the system.

Consider the following Java implementation of the Singleton pattern:

```
public class Singleton {
    // private static instance of the class
    private static Singleton singleInstance = null;

    // private constructor to prevent instantiation
    private Singleton() {
        // initialization logic
    }
```

```
    // public static method to provide access to the instance
    public static Singleton getInstance() {
        if (singleInstance == null) {
            singleInstance = new Singleton();
        }
        return singleInstance;
    }

    // other methods for the class
    public void showMessage() {
        System.out.println("Hello World from Singleton!");
    }
}
```

In this example, the Singleton class enforces a single instance through a private static variable, singleInstance, and a private constructor. Access to the single instance is provided via the getInstance() method, which ensures that only one instance of the class is created. The implementation effectively prevents the creation of multiple instances, thus avoiding issues related to global state.

Executing the following code demonstrates the Singleton pattern:

```
public class SingletonDemo {
    public static void main(String[] args) {
        // get the singleton instance
        Singleton instance = Singleton.getInstance();

        // call method of singleton instance
        instance.showMessage();
    }
}
```

The output of the program is:

```
Hello World from Singleton!
```

This example illustrates the application of the Singleton design pattern. It showcases how design patterns provide boilerplate implementations that adhere to best practices, thereby streamlining development and reducing error frequencies.

Understanding and applying design patterns in Java require familiarity with both the problem domain and the nuances of the pattern itself. Learning to discern when to utilize a particular pattern demands practice and experience. Design patterns are not one-size-fits-all solutions; their efficacy depends on the specific context and requirements of the problem being addressed.

By mastering design patterns, developers can write code that is not only effective and efficient but also easier to understand, maintain, and expand. This chapter will further explore various types of design patterns, laying a foundation for their effective use in Java programming.

1.2 History and Evolution of Design Patterns

The concept of design patterns in software engineering has its roots in the field of architecture, credited primarily to Christopher Alexander. His seminal works, *A Pattern Language: Towns, Buildings, Construction* and *The Timeless Way of Building*, were instrumental in introducing the idea of "patterns" as a means of capturing and reusing solutions to recurrent problems. In the late 1980s, software engineers began adapting these principles to the realm of software design.

The formal adoption of design patterns within software development burgeoned through the work of the "Gang of Four" (GoF): Erich Gamma, Richard Helm, Ralph Johnson, and John Vlissides. Their 1994 book, *Design Patterns: Elements of Reusable Object-Oriented Software*, established a catalog of 23 classic design patterns and provided the foundation for the formal study and application of design patterns within the field.

Before the GoF patterns gained prominence, practitioners already applied nascent forms of these principles without formal acknowledgment. The common use of certain composition and inheritance techniques in languages like Smalltalk and C++ exemplifies this. However, the publication of the GoF's work offered a common vocabulary and a set of well-defined paradigms, facilitating a more structured approach to software development.

As object-oriented programming (OOP) matured, the necessity for reusable, flexible, and efficient software design became apparent, catalyzing the widespread adoption of design patterns. In the 1990s, with the rise of languages such as Java and C++, the integration of these patterns became more prevalent. The nature of Java, with its emphasis on portability and its strong type system, made it particularly suited to the implementation of these patterns. This period also saw the conceptual broadening of the design pattern field, with additional patterns and variants being documented and disseminated by the developer community and in academic research.

The evolutionary trajectory of design patterns has continued into the 21st century, with the focus expanding beyond purely object-oriented environments. Patterns now address issues pertinent to different paradigms and domains, such as functional programming, concurrent systems, and cloud computing. The advent of agile methodologies and DevOps practices has also influenced the way patterns are utilized, emphasizing adaptability, continuous integration, and delivery.

Modern development environments and tools often come with built-in support for common design patterns, enhancing productivity and reducing error. Integrated Development Environments (IDEs) such as Eclipse or IntelliJ IDEA offer features like automated refactoring tools which implicitly apply some design pattern principles. Likewise, various software frameworks and libraries embed patterns to promote standardized, efficient, and scalable application development.

The expansive evolution of design patterns is also exemplified in the proliferation of pattern languages and catalogs by numerous authors and researchers following the GoF. These include "Pattern-Oriented Software Architecture" by Frank Buschmann et al., "Enterprise Integration Patterns" by Gregor Hohpe and Bobby Woolf, and others addressing specialized contexts like security and cloud-native architectures.

Given these historical and evolutionary perspectives, it is evident that design patterns are integral to the modern software engineering discipline. They offer structured solutions to manage complexity and variability, advocate best practices in design, and ensure that software systems are robust and maintainable.

To illustrate the adaptability and enduring relevance of design patterns, consider the Singleton pattern. Initially conceived to ensure a class has only one instance and provide a global point of access to it, its application has adapted with the rise of multithreading and distributed systems. In contemporary Java, implementing a thread-safe Singleton might leverage the Double-Checked Locking idiom or the more modern Initialization-on-demand Holder pattern, showcasing how core design principles are continually refined.

```
public class Singleton {
    private Singleton() { }

    private static class Holder {
        private static final Singleton INSTANCE = new Singleton();
    }

    public static Singleton getInstance() {
        return Holder.INSTANCE;
    }
}
```

The code demonstrates the implementation of an *Initialization-on-demand Holder* pattern to ensure thread safety while maintaining lazy initialization.

As we delve deeper into the taxonomy of design patterns through this chapter, it is beneficial to recognize their historical context and evolution. This awareness not only enriches our understanding but also empowers us to innovate and adapt these solutions to contemporary challenges.

1.3 Importance of Design Patterns in Software Development

Design patterns play a crucial role in software development due to their ability to provide time-tested solutions to recurring problems. These patterns, identified and catalogued by experienced developers over years of practice, bring several advantages that enhance the overall efficiency, maintainability, and scalability of software projects.

Design patterns serve as a common language among developers, simplifying communication and collaboration within development teams. When a developer refers to a design pattern, the entire team understands the context and structure of the solution, reducing complexity and promoting a shared understanding. For example, when a team decides to use the Singleton pattern to manage the lifecycle of a resource, all members recognize that only one instance of a class will exist throughout the application lifecycle.

Moreover, design patterns help in achieving software design principles such as SOLID (Single Responsibility, Open-Closed, Liskov Substitution, Interface Segregation, and Dependency Inversion). By adhering to these principles, design patterns contribute to the creation of robust and flexible codebases, thus enhancing software quality. Consider the Strategy Pattern, which promotes the Open-Closed Principle by allowing algorithms to be selected at runtime without modifying the client code.

Code reusability is another significant benefit of design patterns. These patterns encapsulate best practices that can be reused across multiple projects. This reduces redundancy and promotes the reuse of proven solutions, leading to faster development cycles and more reliable software. For instance, the Factory Method Pattern abstracts the instantiation process, allowing a class to defer the instantiation of objects to its subclasses.

Additionally, design patterns provide a blueprint for solving complex design problems, thereby reducing the learning curve for new developers. When patterns are properly documented and integrated into the development process, they can guide less experienced developers in understanding and implementing effective design solutions. A well-documented Observer Pattern, for example, can quickly teach developers how to establish a one-to-many dependency relationship, wherein multiple observers are notified of changes to a subject's state.

Design patterns also aid in the maintainability of software by promoting cleaner and more organized code. They encapsulate variations that might occur in future requirements, thus making the code easier to extend and modify. The Decorator Pattern illustrates this by allowing behavior to be added to individual objects, without affecting the behavior of other objects from the same class. This makes it easier to add or change functionalities as requirements evolve.

Performance optimization is another area where design patterns prove valuable. Certain patterns, such as Flyweight and Proxy, are specifically geared towards optimizing resource management and improving application performance. The Flyweight Pattern minimizes memory usage by sharing as much data as possible with similar objects, which can be particularly effective in applications with a large number of similar objects.

To illustrate the practical application of design patterns, consider a scenario within a Java-based application where object creation is a resource-intensive operation. Using the Prototype Pattern, developers can clone existing objects, thus reducing the overhead associated with object creation. The following Java code demonstrates the implementation of the Prototype Pattern:

```
import java.util.HashMap;
import java.util.Map;

interface Prototype extends Cloneable {
    Prototype clone();
}

class ConcretePrototypeA implements Prototype {
    private String name;

    public ConcretePrototypeA(String name) {
        this.name = name;
    }

    @Override
    public Prototype clone() {
        return new ConcretePrototypeA(this.name);
    }
```

```
    @Override
    public String toString() {
        return "PrototypeA: " + name;
    }
}

class PrototypeRegistry {
    private Map<String, Prototype> registry = new HashMap<>();

    public void addPrototype(String key, Prototype prototype) {
        registry.put(key, prototype);
    }

    public Prototype getPrototype(String key) {
        return registry.get(key).clone();
    }
}

public class PrototypePatternDemo {
    public static void main(String[] args) {
        PrototypeRegistry registry = new PrototypeRegistry();

        ConcretePrototypeA prototypeA = new ConcretePrototypeA("Object A");
        registry.addPrototype("A", prototypeA);

        Prototype clonedObject = registry.getPrototype("A");
        System.out.println(clonedObject);
    }
}
```

The above example showcases how the Prototype Pattern allows objects to be cloned efficiently, bypassing the need for expensive instantiation process.

Reusability, maintainability, and optimization are core advantages brought by design patterns in software development. By integrating these patterns into development practices, teams can build adaptable and high-performing applications that stand the test of time and continue to evolve gracefully with changing requirements.

Understanding and implementing design patterns effectively can transform the development process, turning it into a structured and predictable endeavor. The cumulative experience encoded in these patterns aids in tackling design challenges systematically, ensuring robust and maintainable software architectures.

1.4 Types of Design Patterns: Creational, Structural, and Behavioral

Design patterns are categorized into three primary types: Creational, Structural, and Behavioral patterns. Each category addresses a specific aspect of software design and problem-solving in object-oriented programming. Understanding these categories enables developers to select the most appropriate pattern for a given problem. This section elaborates on these categories and presents key patterns within each.

Creational Patterns deal with object creation mechanisms, optimizing the instantiation process. They abstract the instantiation process and help make the system independent of how its objects are created, composed, and represented. The principal intent is to manage the complexity of the object creation process.

Key Creational Patterns include:

- **Singleton**: Ensures a class has only one instance and provides a global point of access to it. This is useful for scenarios where exactly one object is needed to coordinate actions across the system.

```
// Singleton Pattern in Java
public class Singleton {
    private static Singleton uniqueInstance;

    private Singleton() { }

    public static synchronized Singleton getInstance() {
        if (uniqueInstance == null) {
            uniqueInstance = new Singleton();
        }
        return uniqueInstance;
    }
}
```

- **Factory Method**: Defines an interface for creating objects, but lets subclasses alter the type of objects that will be created. This pattern enables a class to defer instantiation to subclasses.

```
// Factory Method Pattern in Java
public interface Product {
    void use();
}

public class ConcreteProduct implements Product {
    public void use() {
        System.out.println("Using ConcreteProduct");
    }
```

```
}

public abstract class Creator {
    public abstract Product factoryMethod();

    public void anOperation() {
        Product product = factoryMethod();
        product.use();
    }
}

public class ConcreteCreator extends Creator {
    public Product factoryMethod() {
        return new ConcreteProduct();
    }
}
```

- **Abstract Factory**: Provides an interface for creating families of related or dependent objects without specifying their concrete classes. It is useful when a system needs to be independent of the way products are created or composed.

```
// Abstract Factory Pattern in Java
public interface GUIFactory {
    Button createButton();
    Checkbox createCheckbox();
}

public class MacOSFactory implements GUIFactory {
    public Button createButton() {
        return new MacOSButton();
    }
    public Checkbox createCheckbox() {
        return new MacOSCheckbox();
    }
}

public class WindowsFactory implements GUIFactory {
    public Button createButton() {
        return new WindowsButton();
    }
    public Checkbox createCheckbox() {
        return new WindowsCheckbox();
    }
}
```

Structural Patterns deal with object composition and typically identify simple ways to realize relationships between different objects. These patterns help ensure that if one part of a system changes, the entire system does not need to be altered.

Key Structural Patterns include:

- **Adapter**: Allows incompatible interfaces to work together. It acts as a bridge between two incompatible interfaces by converting the interface of a class into another interface clients expect.

```
// Adapter Pattern in Java
public interface Target {
    void request();
}

public class Adaptee {
    public void specificRequest() {
        System.out.println("Called specificRequest()");
    }
}

public class Adapter implements Target {
    private Adaptee adaptee;

    public Adapter(Adaptee adaptee) {
        this.adaptee = adaptee;
    }

    public void request() {
        adaptee.specificRequest();
    }
}
```

- **Decorator**: Adds behavior to individual objects, dynamically and transparently, without affecting other objects. It uses object composition instead of inheritance to add responsibilities to objects.

```
// Decorator Pattern in Java
public interface Component {
    void operation();
}

public class ConcreteComponent implements Component {
    public void operation() {
        System.out.println("ConcreteComponent operation");
    }
}

public abstract class Decorator implements Component {
    protected Component component;

    public Decorator(Component component) {
        this.component = component;
    }

    public void operation() {
        component.operation();
    }
}

public class ConcreteDecorator extends Decorator {
    public ConcreteDecorator(Component component) {
        super(component);
    }

    public void operation() {
        super.operation();
        addedBehavior();
    }
```

```
    private void addedBehavior() {
        System.out.println("ConcreteDecorator addedBehavior");
    }
}
```

- **Facade**: Simplifies the interface of a complex system, providing a single point of access to its functionality. This pattern hides the complexities of the system and provides a more straightforward interface.

```
// Facade Pattern in Java
public class Facade {
    private Subsystem1 subsystem1;
    private Subsystem2 subsystem2;

    public Facade() {
        subsystem1 = new Subsystem1();
        subsystem2 = new Subsystem2();
    }

    public void operation() {
        subsystem1.operation();
        subsystem2.operation();
    }
}

public class Subsystem1 {
    public void operation() {
        System.out.println("Subsystem1 operation");
    }
}

public class Subsystem2 {
    public void operation() {
        System.out.println("Subsystem2 operation");
    }
}
```

Behavioral Patterns focus on communication between objects, identifying common interaction patterns and improving the flexibility and clarity in carrying out communication.

Key Behavioral Patterns include:

- **Observer**: Defines a one-to-many dependency between objects so when one object changes state, all its dependents are notified and updated automatically. This pattern is essential for implementing distributed event-handling systems.

```
// Observer Pattern in Java
public interface Observer {
    void update();
}
```

```
public class ConcreteObserver implements Observer {
    public void update() {
        System.out.println("ConcreteObserver has been notified.");
    }
}

public interface Subject {
    void attach(Observer observer);
    void detach(Observer observer);
    void notifyObservers();
}

public class ConcreteSubject implements Subject {
    private List<Observer> observers = new ArrayList<>();

    public void attach(Observer observer) {
        observers.add(observer);
    }

    public void detach(Observer observer) {
        observers.remove(observer);
    }

    public void notifyObservers() {
        for (Observer observer : observers) {
            observer.update();
        }
    }

    public void changeState() {
        // Some change in state
        notifyObservers();
    }
}
```

- **Strategy**: Enables selecting an algorithm's behavior at runtime. It defines a family of algorithms, encapsulates each one, and makes them interchangeable.

```
// Strategy Pattern in Java
public interface Strategy {
    void execute();
}

public class ConcreteStrategyA implements Strategy {
    public void execute() {
        System.out.println("ConcreteStrategyA strategy");
    }
}

public class ConcreteStrategyB implements Strategy {
    public void execute() {
        System.out.println("ConcreteStrategyB strategy");
    }
}

public class Context {
    private Strategy strategy;
```

```
    public Context(Strategy strategy) {
        this.strategy = strategy;
    }

    public void setStrategy(Strategy strategy) {
        this.strategy = strategy;
    }

    public void executeStrategy() {
        strategy.execute();
    }
}
```

- **Command**: Encapsulates a request as an object, thereby allowing parameterization of clients with queues, requests, and operations. It also supports undoable operations.

```
// Command Pattern in Java
public interface Command {
    void execute();
}

public class Light {
    public void on() {
        System.out.println("Light is ON");
    }

    public void off() {
        System.out.println("Light is OFF");
    }
}

public class LightOnCommand implements Command {
    private Light light;

    public LightOnCommand(Light light) {
        this.light = light;
    }

    public void execute() {
        light.on();
    }
}

public class LightOffCommand implements Command {
    private Light light;

    public LightOffCommand(Light light) {
        this.light = light;
    }

    public void execute() {
        light.off();
    }
}

public class RemoteControl {
    private Command command;

    public void setCommand(Command command) {
```

```
        this.command = command;
    }

    public void pressButton() {
        command.execute();
    }
}
```

Creational patterns address the process of object creation, structural patterns deal with the composition of classes or objects, and behavioral patterns focus on effective communication between objects. Each category offers patterns that can significantly simplify and improve software design. Understanding and applying these patterns appropriately can lead to more maintainable, scalable, and robust software systems.

1.5 Role of Design Patterns in Java Programming

Design patterns serve as proven solutions to routine design problems that software developers encounter regularly. Their role in Java programming is multifaceted and significant. Java, as an object-oriented programming (OOP) language, inherently supports many of the principles that design patterns encapsulate, making these patterns indispensable tools for Java developers.

A key role of design patterns in Java programming is fostering code reusability. By using a well-established pattern, developers can avoid reinventing the wheel. For instance, using the Singleton pattern ensures that a class has only one instance and provides a global point of access to it. This is particularly useful when exactly one object is needed to coordinate actions across the system. In Java, this can be implemented as follows:

```
public class Singleton {
    private static Singleton instance;

    private Singleton() {
        // private constructor
    }

    public static Singleton getInstance() {
        if (instance == null) {
            instance = new Singleton();
        }
        return instance;
    }
}
```

Another crucial role of design patterns is to enhance the maintainability and readability of code. Patterns encapsulate best practices and solutions that are easily recognizable to experienced developers, making the code easier to understand and modify. For example, the Observer pattern is pivotal in scenarios where an object (the subject) needs to notify other objects (observers) about changes in its state. This pattern is widely used in Java's event handling mechanisms, such as in Swing:

```
import java.util.ArrayList;
import java.util.List;

interface Observer {
    void update(String message);
}

class Subject {
    private List<Observer> observers = new ArrayList<>();

    public void addObserver(Observer observer) {
        observers.add(observer);
    }

    public void notifyObservers(String message) {
        for (Observer observer : observers) {
            observer.update(message);
        }
    }
}

class ConcreteObserver implements Observer {
    private String name;

    public ConcreteObserver(String name) {
        this.name = name;
    }

    @Override
    public void update(String message) {
        System.out.println(name + " received: " + message);
    }
}

// Usage
public class ObserverPatternDemo {
    public static void main(String[] args) {
        Subject subject = new Subject();
        ConcreteObserver observer1 = new ConcreteObserver("Observer 1");
        ConcreteObserver observer2 = new ConcreteObserver("Observer 2");

        subject.addObserver(observer1);
        subject.addObserver(observer2);

        subject.notifyObservers("Notification");
    }
}
```

Moreover, design patterns support scalability in Java application development by offering flexible solutions that can evolve with the system requirements. For instance, the Factory Method pattern helps create objects without specifying the exact class of object that will be created, promoting loose coupling. This is especially useful when integrating new functionalities:

```
abstract class Product {
    public abstract void use();
}

class ConcreteProductA extends Product {
    public void use() {
        System.out.println("Product A used.");
    }
}

class ConcreteProductB extends Product {
    public void use() {
        System.out.println("Product B used.");
    }
}

abstract class Creator {
    public abstract Product factoryMethod();

    public void anOperation() {
        Product product = factoryMethod();
        product.use();
    }
}

class ConcreteCreatorA extends Creator {
    public Product factoryMethod() {
        return new ConcreteProductA();
    }
}

class ConcreteCreatorB extends Creator {
    public Product factoryMethod() {
        return new ConcreteProductB();
    }
}

// Usage
public class FactoryMethodPatternDemo {
    public static void main(String[] args) {
        Creator creatorA = new ConcreteCreatorA();
        Creator creatorB = new ConcreteCreatorB();

        creatorA.anOperation();
        creatorB.anOperation();
    }
}
```

Design patterns also play a role in leveraging Java's built-in features and libraries. For instance, the Adapter pattern allows objects with incompatible interfaces to work together. This pattern is useful when leveraging existing third-party libraries or when working with legacy codebases:

```
interface Target {
    void request();
}

class Adaptee {
    public void specificRequest() {
        System.out.println("Specific request.");
    }
}

class Adapter implements Target {
    private Adaptee adaptee;

    public Adapter(Adaptee adaptee) {
        this.adaptee = adaptee;
    }

    public void request() {
        adaptee.specificRequest();
    }
}

// Usage
public class AdapterPatternDemo {
    public static void main(String[] args) {
        Adaptee adaptee = new Adaptee();
        Target target = new Adapter(adaptee);
        target.request();
    }
}
```

Interfacing with the extensive Java APIs becomes more manageable and intuitive using design patterns. For example, Java's inheritance and interface-based design heavily leverage the Decorator pattern to extend classes with additional responsibilities dynamically and transparently:

```
interface Component {
    void operation();
}

class ConcreteComponent implements Component {
    public void operation() {
        System.out.println("ConcreteComponent operation");
    }
}

abstract class Decorator implements Component {
    protected Component component;

    public Decorator(Component component) {
        this.component = component;
    }

    public void operation() {
        component.operation();
    }
}
```

```
class ConcreteDecoratorA extends Decorator {
    public ConcreteDecoratorA(Component component) {
        super(component);
    }

    public void operation() {
        super.operation();
        System.out.println("ConcreteDecoratorA additional operation");
    }
}

// Usage
public class DecoratorPatternDemo {
    public static void main(String[] args) {
        Component component = new ConcreteComponent();
        Component decorated = new ConcreteDecoratorA(component);
        decorated.operation();
    }
}
```

Using design patterns in Java also contributes to enhanced performance by promoting efficient design paradigms. Applying patterns like the Flyweight can lead to significant memory savings in high-volume applications by sharing objects that are costly to instantiate but frequently used:

```
import java.util.HashMap;
import java.util.Map;

interface Flyweight {
    void operation(String extrinsicState);
}

class ConcreteFlyweight implements Flyweight {
    private String intrinsicState;

    public ConcreteFlyweight(String intrinsicState) {
        this.intrinsicState = intrinsicState;
    }

    public void operation(String extrinsicState) {
        System.out.println("Intrinsic: " + intrinsicState + ", Extrinsic: " +
                extrinsicState);
    }
}

class FlyweightFactory {
    private Map<String, Flyweight> flyweights = new HashMap<>();

    public Flyweight getFlyweight(String key) {
        if (!flyweights.containsKey(key)) {
            flyweights.put(key, new ConcreteFlyweight(key));
        }
        return flyweights.get(key);
    }
}

// Usage
public class FlyweightPatternDemo {
    public static void main(String[] args) {
```

```
        FlyweightFactory factory = new FlyweightFactory();
        Flyweight flyweight1 = factory.getFlyweight("state1");
        Flyweight flyweight2 = factory.getFlyweight("state2");

        flyweight1.operation("extrinsic1");
        flyweight2.operation("extrinsic2");
    }
}
```

In Java programming, design patterns significantly enhance coding efficiency, maintainability, scalability, and performance, making them indispensable tools for both novice and experienced developers.

1.6 Understanding the Gang of Four (GoF) Patterns

The Gang of Four (GoF) comprises Erich Gamma, Richard Helm, Ralph Johnson, and John Vlissides, who authored the seminal book, *Design Patterns: Elements of Reusable Object-Oriented Software*. This book is foundational in the field of software engineering and introduced twenty-three design patterns, categorized into Creational, Structural, and Behavioral patterns.

Creational patterns focus on object creation mechanisms, enhancing flexibility and reuse of code. They abstract the instantiation process and make a system independent of how its objects are created, composed, and represented. The most commonly encountered Creational patterns include the Singleton, Factory Method, Abstract Factory, Builder, and Prototype patterns. For instance, the Singleton pattern ensures a class has only one instance, and provides a global point of access to it.

```
// Singleton Pattern in Java
public class Singleton {
    private static Singleton instance;

    private Singleton() {
        // Private constructor to prevent instantiation
    }

    public static Singleton getInstance() {
        if (instance == null) {
            instance = new Singleton();
        }
        return instance;
    }
}
```

In the above example, instance is a static private member variable of the Singleton class. The private constructor prevents any external class from instantiating a new object. The getInstance method ensures that only one instance of the Singleton class exists.

Structural patterns focus on class and object composition. These patterns use inheritance to compose interfaces and define ways to compose objects to obtain new functionalities. Key Structural patterns include Adapter, Bridge, Composite, Decorator, Facade, Flyweight, and Proxy.

The Adapter pattern allows incompatible interfaces to work together. It acts as a bridge between two incompatible interfaces by wrapping an existing class with a new interface.

```
// Adapter Pattern in Java
public interface MediaPlayer {
    public void play(String audioType, String fileName);
}

public class AudioPlayer implements MediaPlayer {
    MediaAdapter mediaAdapter;

    @Override
    public void play(String audioType, String fileName) {
        if (audioType.equalsIgnoreCase("mp3")) {
            System.out.println("Playing mp3 file. Name: " + fileName);
        } else if (audioType.equalsIgnoreCase("vlc") || audioType.equalsIgnoreCase("
            mp4")) {
            mediaAdapter = new MediaAdapter(audioType);
            mediaAdapter.play(audioType, fileName);
        } else {
            System.out.println("Invalid media. " + audioType + " format not supported
                ");
        }
    }
}

// Adapter class
public class MediaAdapter implements MediaPlayer {
    AdvancedMediaPlayer advancedMusicPlayer;

    public MediaAdapter(String audioType) {
        if (audioType.equalsIgnoreCase("vlc")) {
            advancedMusicPlayer = new VlcPlayer();
        } else if (audioType.equalsIgnoreCase("mp4")) {
            advancedMusicPlayer = new Mp4Player();
        }
    }

    @Override
    public void play(String audioType, String fileName) {
        if (audioType.equalsIgnoreCase("vlc")) {
            advancedMusicPlayer.playVlc(fileName);
        } else if (audioType.equalsIgnoreCase("mp4")) {
            advancedMusicPlayer.playMp4(fileName);
        }
    }
```

```
}
```

In this example, MediaPlayer is an interface implemented by AudioPlayer. The MediaAdapter class allows AudioPlayer to play formats not natively supported by converting requests into compatible formats.

Behavioral patterns are concerned with algorithms and the assignment of responsibilities between objects. These patterns describe not only the patterns of objects or classes but also their communication. Examples include Chain of Responsibility, Command, Interpreter, Iterator, Mediator, Memento, Observer, State, Strategy, Template Method, and Visitor patterns.

The Observer pattern defines a one-to-many relationship between objects such that when one object changes state, all its dependents are notified and updated automatically.

```
// Observer Pattern in Java
import java.util.ArrayList;
import java.util.List;

public class Subject {
    private List<Observer> observers = new ArrayList<Observer>();
    private int state;

    public int getState() {
        return state;
    }

    public void setState(int state) {
        this.state = state;
        notifyAllObservers();
    }

    public void attach(Observer observer){
        observers.add(observer);
    }

    public void notifyAllObservers(){
        for (Observer observer : observers) {
            observer.update();
        }
    }
}

public abstract class Observer {
    protected Subject subject;
    public abstract void update();
}

public class BinaryObserver extends Observer{
    public BinaryObserver(Subject subject){
        this.subject = subject;
        this.subject.attach(this);
    }

    @Override
```

```
    public void update() {
        System.out.println("Binary String: " + Integer.toBinaryString(subject.getState()
            ));
    }
}

public class OctalObserver extends Observer{
    public OctalObserver(Subject subject){
        this.subject = subject;
        this.subject.attach(this);
    }

    @Override
    public void update() {
        System.out.println("Octal String: " + Integer.toOctalString(subject.getState()));
    }
}

public class HexaObserver extends Observer{
    public HexaObserver(Subject subject){
        this.subject = subject;
        this.subject.attach(this);
    }

    @Override
    public void update() {
        System.out.println("Hex String: " + Integer.toHexString(subject.getState()));
    }
}

// Using the Observer pattern
public class ObserverPatternDemo {
    public static void main(String[] args) {
        Subject subject = new Subject();

        new HexaObserver(subject);
        new OctalObserver(subject);
        new BinaryObserver(subject);

        System.out.println("First state change: 15");
        subject.setState(15);
        System.out.println("Second state change: 10");
        subject.setState(10);
    }
}
```

In this example, the Subject class maintains a list of Observer objects and notifies them when its state changes. BinaryObserver, OctalObserver, and HexaObserver are concrete implementations of the Observer class, reacting to changes in the Subject by converting the state to different numeral systems.

Understanding the GoF patterns involves recognizing the distinct roles these patterns play in tackling recurrent software development problems. Each pattern provides a template solution that can be adapted and implemented in specific contexts, enhancing code reuse, flexibility, and maintainability. The patterns also promote best practices in object-oriented design, such as encapsulation, polymorphism, and delegation, ensuring robust and scalable software architectures.

1.7 How to Choose the Right Pattern for the Job

The process of selecting an appropriate design pattern for a given problem involves careful consideration of several factors, including the context of the problem, the intent and applicability of the pattern, and the consequences of applying the pattern. This section outlines a structured approach to guide you in making informed and effective choices when integrating design patterns into your Java projects.

Understanding Pattern Intent:

Each design pattern addresses a specific problem and provides a standardized solution. Begin by clearly understanding the intent of the pattern. The intent describes the goal or the problem that the pattern aims to solve. For example, the Singleton pattern ensures that a class has only one instance and provides a global point of access to that instance. Ask yourself: what precise issue am I tackling? Does the intent of a candidate pattern align well with this issue?

Analyze the Context:

The context includes the environment in which the pattern will be applied. This involves examining the software architecture, existing codebase, dependencies, and the framework in use. Evaluate how a pattern fits within the current design constraints and objectives. A Factory Method pattern, for instance, is well-suited for situations where there is a need to create objects without specifying the exact class of object that will be created. Consider how existing structures will interact with the new pattern.

Pattern Applicability:

After understanding the intent and context, determine the applicability of the pattern. Patterns usually contain specific prerequisites and assumptions about how the solution should be applied. Not every pattern is suitable for every scenario. The Adapter pattern, for instance, is applicable when there is a need to integrate incompatible interfaces without altering their existing code. Ensure that your chosen pattern does not violate any applied constraints.

```
interface Target {
    void request();
}

class Adaptee {
    public void specificRequest() {
        System.out.println("Called specificRequest()");
    }
}

class Adapter implements Target {
    private Adaptee adaptee;

    public Adapter(Adaptee adaptee) {
        this.adaptee = adaptee;
    }

    @Override
    public void request() {
        adaptee.specificRequest();
    }
}
```

Identify Consequences:

Analyze the consequences of applying the pattern in terms of both benefits and potential downsides. Each pattern introduces some form of trade-off. For instance, the Decorator pattern enhances or extends the functionality of objects but can introduce complexity to the system. Create a balance sheet of advantages and disadvantages. Review memory overhead, runtime performance impacts, maintainability, and coherence with coding standards.

Evaluate Pattern Collaboration:

Patterns do not exist in isolation; they frequently interact with other patterns. Consider how applying one pattern might affect or be supported by other patterns. For example, the Composite and Iterator patterns often work together to traverse complex structures like tree hierarchies. Think holistically about how adopting a pattern could influence overall system architecture.

Prototype and Refine:

Implement a small prototype to evaluate the pattern's efficacy in solving your problem. This allows you to experiment with different patterns and see their practical implications before committing to significant changes in your codebase. Use the prototype to identify any unforeseen issues or limitations early in the development process.

```
public class Singleton {
    private static Singleton instance;
```

```
    private Singleton() {
        // Private constructor to prevent instantiation
    }

    public static Singleton getInstance() {
        if (instance == null) {
            instance = new Singleton();
        }
        return instance;
    }

    public void showMessage(){
        System.out.println("Hello World!");
    }
}
```

Test Output:
Hello World!

Consult Pattern Catalogs and References:

Refer to established pattern catalogs and literature for comprehensive descriptions and real-world usage scenarios. The Gang of Four (GoF) book is an authoritative reference providing detailed insights into the implementation and context of 23 classic design patterns. Online resources, communities, and frameworks documentation also offer valuable information and practical examples.

Collaborative Discussion:

Engage with other developers through code reviews, design discussions, and collaborative meetings. Gaining multiple perspectives can bring to light potential issues or alternative solutions that you might not have considered. Utilize systems such as design walkthroughs, where peer review helps scrutinize the applicability and consequences of selected design patterns.

Document Decisions:

Thoroughly document your decision-making process, rationale behind selecting a specific pattern, and any trade-offs considered. This documentation serves as a valuable resource for future maintenance and for team members to understand the architectural choices made. Include diagrams and code snippets to illustrate how the pattern is implemented and interacts with other parts of the system.

By methodically evaluating pattern intent, context, applicability, and consequences, and by leveraging collaborative and reference resources, you can make informed decisions that enhance the maintainability, scalability, and functionality of your Java applications.

1.8 Applying Design Patterns: Best Practices

Applying design patterns effectively requires a thoughtful understanding of the context in which they are used, as well as an appreciation for the intent and structure of the pattern itself. This section explores the best practices for applying design patterns, with particular focus on maintaining code readability, ensuring scalability, fostering reusability, and avoiding over-engineering.

When choosing a design pattern, the primary consideration should be the problem it aims to solve. Different patterns are designed to address specific types of issues, and understanding the nature of the problem is crucial for selecting an appropriate solution.

- **Understand the Problem Domain:** Before selecting a design pattern, ensure that the problem domain is clearly understood. This involves identifying the requirements, constraints, and expected behaviors of the system.
- **Familiarize with Pattern Intent:** Each design pattern has an intended purpose it aims to fulfill. For instance, the Singleton pattern ensures a class has only one instance, while the Observer pattern defines a one-to-many dependency. Being familiar with these intents helps in making informed decisions.
- **Leverage Existing Patterns:** Instead of creating new patterns from scratch, it is often beneficial to use established patterns. The Gang of Four (GoF) patterns are well-documented and widely used, offering proven solutions for common design problems.

Once an appropriate pattern has been selected, the next step is to implement it in a way that aligns with best practices. This includes maintaining clean code, adhering to principles of object-oriented design, and ensuring the pattern integrates seamlessly into the existing architecture.

- **Write Clean and Readable Code:** Design patterns should make the codebase more understandable, not more complex. Use meaningful names for classes and methods, and provide comments to explain the intent and functioning of the pattern within the context of the application.

- **Adhere to SOLID Principles:** The SOLID principles of object-oriented design—Single Responsibility, Open/Closed, Liskov Substitution, Interface Segregation, and Dependency Inversion—are fundamental to creating robust and maintainable systems. Design patterns should be applied in a manner that respects these principles.
- **Ensure Scalability:** Design patterns should facilitate scalability. For example, the Factory Method pattern can help manage the creation of objects in a manner that allows for easy extension.

It is also essential to consider the broader impact of introducing a design pattern into a codebase. While patterns can provide powerful solutions, they can also lead to over-engineering if not used judiciously.

- **Avoid Over-Engineering:** Not every problem requires a design pattern. Over-engineering occurs when patterns are applied unnecessarily, leading to increased complexity without proportional benefits. Evaluate whether a pattern truly adds value before implementing it.
- **Refactor When Necessary:** As systems evolve, previously implemented patterns may no longer be the best solution. Refactoring allows for continuous improvement and adaptation to changing requirements.
- **Test Extensively:** Design patterns should enhance the testability of a system, not hinder it. Thorough testing ensures that the pattern has been correctly implemented and integrates well with other components.

The following Java code example demonstrates the application of the Factory Method pattern, which provides an interface for creating objects but allows subclasses to alter the type of objects that will be created:

```
abstract class Creator {
    public abstract Product createProduct();

    public void someOperation() {
        Product product = createProduct();
        // Further operations on the product
    }
}

class ConcreteCreatorA extends Creator {
    public Product createProduct() {
```

```
        return new ConcreteProductA();
    }
}

class ConcreteCreatorB extends Creator {
    public Product createProduct() {
        return new ConcreteProductB();
    }
}

interface Product {
    void someMethod();
}

class ConcreteProductA implements Product {
    public void someMethod() {
        System.out.println("ConcreteProductA method implementation");
    }
}

class ConcreteProductB implements Product {
    public void someMethod() {
        System.out.println("ConcreteProductB method implementation");
    }
}

public class FactoryMethodExample {
    public static void main(String[] args) {
        Creator creator = new ConcreteCreatorA();
        creator.someOperation();

        creator = new ConcreteCreatorB();
        creator.someOperation();
    }
}
```

Output:

```
ConcreteProductA method implementation
ConcreteProductB method implementation
```

In this example, the Creator class defines an abstract method createProduct() that subclasses ConcreteCreatorA and ConcreteCreatorB override to instantiate their respective Product types. This design allows the code to be flexible and scalable, as new product types can be added with minimal changes to the existing code. Ensuring that object creation is encapsulated in this manner adheres to the Single Responsibility and Open/Closed principles, thereby adhering to best practices in design pattern application.

1.9 Common Pitfalls and Misconceptions

When employing design patterns in Java, developers may encounter several pitfalls and misconceptions that can undermine the effectiveness of these patterns. Recognizing and understanding these pitfalls is crucial for applying design patterns effectively.

One common misconception is that design patterns are universally applicable solutions. While design patterns provide generalized solutions to recurring design problems, they are not a one-size-fits-all remedy. Misapplying a design pattern to a problem it was not intended to solve can lead to inefficient, cumbersome, or overly complex code. Developers must carefully analyze the specific requirements and context of their problems before choosing an appropriate design pattern.

Another pitfall is pattern overuse. Inexperienced developers may introduce numerous design patterns into their projects, driven by enthusiasm or a misunderstanding of their necessity. Overuse can result in "design pattern mania," where the code becomes convoluted and difficult to manage. Design patterns should be applied judiciously, only when their benefits clearly outweigh the added complexity they introduce.

Incorrect implementation of design patterns can also pose significant issues. Misinterpretation of the pattern's structure or intent can deviate the solution from its purpose, leading to suboptimal design. To mitigate this risk, developers should thoroughly understand the design pattern's principles and refer to reputable sources or documentation for guidance. Proper implementation often includes implementing all the key components that define the design pattern and ensuring they interact as intended.

A specific example of incorrect implementation is evident in the Singleton pattern. The goal of the Singleton pattern is to ensure that a class has only one instance and provides a global point of access to it. An often overlooked aspect is handling multithreading. Without proper synchronization, multiple instances may be created when accessed by multiple threads concurrently. This can be illustrated with the following Java code example:

```
public class Singleton {
    private static Singleton instance;

    private Singleton() {}

    public static Singleton getInstance() {
```

```
        if (instance == null) {
            instance = new Singleton();
        }
        return instance;
    }
}
```

In a multithreaded environment, the above implementation can fail, allowing multiple Singleton instances to be created. To address this, developers must use synchronization:

```
public class Singleton {
    private static Singleton instance;
    private static final Object lock = new Object();

    private Singleton() {}

    public static Singleton getInstance() {
        if (instance == null) {
            synchronized (lock) {
                if (instance == null) {
                    instance = new Singleton();
                }
            }
        }
        return instance;
    }
}
```

Another misconception is that design patterns are a silver bullet that guarantees improved design. While they do promote design principles such as modularity, reusability, and flexibility, blindly applying design patterns without careful consideration of their impact on the overall system can lead to overengineering. Each pattern introduces its own complexities, and the balance between simplicity and flexibility must be maintained.

In addition, developers might fall into the trap of focusing too much on individual design patterns rather than the relationships between them. Real-world applications often require combining multiple design patterns to address complex requirements. For instance, the Composite pattern can be employed in conjunction with the Iterator pattern to provide a way to iterate over composite structures uniformly.

Understanding the evolving nature of software requirements is also essential. A design pattern that fits today's requirements may not be suitable as the software evolves. Flexibility and adaptability are key principles that developers should consider when using design patterns, ensuring that their design can accommodate future changes with minimal disruption.

Another area of concern is the lack of understanding of the underlying principles behind design patterns. Merely knowing the names and structures of patterns without grasping the design principles such as encapsulation, delegation, and separation of concerns can lead to improper usage. Developers should focus on mastering these principles, as they form the foundation upon which design patterns are built.

Inadequate documentation and code comments also contribute to the difficulties faced when applying design patterns. Sparse or unclear documentation can make it challenging for other developers to understand the rationale behind the use of specific patterns, leading to maintenance issues. Comprehensive documentation, including diagrams and commentary, is essential to communicate the design intent clearly.

Lastly, developers may misinterpret design patterns as solutions only meant for large-scale, complex systems. This misconception can limit the potential benefits in smaller projects where design patterns can equally improve the quality and maintainability of the codebase. Design patterns are applicable across various project scales and understanding this can help in leveraging their full potential.

By recognizing these common pitfalls and misconceptions, developers can better navigate the challenges of applying design patterns. A mindful approach to pattern selection, implementation, and documentation will foster more effective and maintainable software designs.

1.10 Real-World Examples of Design Patterns in Java

This section demonstrates the application of various design patterns within the context of real-world Java programming. By examining practical examples, learners can better understand the utility and implementation of these patterns. This section focuses on three design patterns: Singleton, Observer, and Strategy.

Singleton Pattern Example:

The Singleton pattern ensures that a class has only one instance and provides a global point of access to that instance. This is particularly useful for managing shared resources like configurations, logging, or database connections.

Consider the following code to implement a Singleton pattern for a configuration manager:

```
public class ConfigurationManager {
    private static ConfigurationManager instance;
    private Properties properties;

    // Private constructor to prevent instantiation
    private ConfigurationManager() {
        properties = new Properties();
        // Load properties from a configuration file or other sources
    }

    // Public method to provide access to the instance
    public static synchronized ConfigurationManager getInstance() {
        if (instance == null) {
            instance = new ConfigurationManager();
        }
        return instance;
    }

    public String getProperty(String key) {
        return properties.getProperty(key);
    }

    public void setProperty(String key, String value) {
        properties.setProperty(key, value);
    }
}
```

This code ensures that only one instance of ConfigurationManager is created and provides thread-safe access through the synchronized keyword.

Observer Pattern Example:

The Observer pattern defines a one-to-many dependency between objects so that when one object changes state, all its dependents are notified and updated automatically.

Here is an example involving a simple weather station application:

```
import java.util.ArrayList;
import java.util.List;

// Subject
class WeatherStation {
    private List<WeatherObserver> observers = new ArrayList<>();
    private float temperature;

    public void addObserver(WeatherObserver observer) {
        observers.add(observer);
    }

    public void removeObserver(WeatherObserver observer) {
        observers.remove(observer);
    }

    public void setTemperature(float temperature) {
        this.temperature = temperature;
```

```
        notifyAllObservers();
    }

    private void notifyAllObservers() {
        for (WeatherObserver observer : observers) {
            observer.update(temperature);
        }
    }
}

// Observer interface
interface WeatherObserver {
    void update(float temperature);
}

// Concrete Observer
class Display implements WeatherObserver {
    private String name;

    public Display(String name) {
        this.name = name;
    }

    @Override
    public void update(float temperature) {
        System.out.println(name + " display: Temperature updated to " + temperature
                + " degrees.");
    }
}

// Usage
public class WeatherStationApp {
    public static void main(String[] args) {
        WeatherStation station = new WeatherStation();
        Display display1 = new Display("Display1");
        Display display2 = new Display("Display2");

        station.addObserver(display1);
        station.addObserver(display2);

        station.setTemperature(25.0f);
        station.setTemperature(27.0f);
    }
}
```

The WeatherStation class represents the subject containing a list of WeatherObserver objects. The Display class implements WeatherObserver and updates the display whenever the temperature changes.

Strategy Pattern Example:

The Strategy pattern defines a family of algorithms, encapsulates each one, and makes them interchangeable. Strategy allows the algorithm to vary independently from clients that use it.

Consider a payment system that supports multiple payment methods using the Strategy pattern:

```
interface PaymentStrategy {
```

```
    void pay(int amount);
}

class CreditCardPayment implements PaymentStrategy {
    private String cardNumber;

    public CreditCardPayment(String cardNumber) {
        this.cardNumber = cardNumber;
    }

    @Override
    public void pay(int amount) {
        System.out.println("Paid " + amount + " using credit card " + cardNumber);
    }
}

class PayPalPayment implements PaymentStrategy {
    private String email;

    public PayPalPayment(String email) {
        this.email = email;
    }

    @Override
    public void pay(int amount) {
        System.out.println("Paid " + amount + " using PayPal account " + email);
    }
}

class PaymentContext {
    private PaymentStrategy paymentStrategy;

    public void setPaymentStrategy(PaymentStrategy paymentStrategy) {
        this.paymentStrategy = paymentStrategy;
    }

    public void executePayment(int amount) {
        paymentStrategy.pay(amount);
    }
}

// Usage
public class PaymentSystem {
    public static void main(String[] args) {
        PaymentContext context = new PaymentContext();

        context.setPaymentStrategy(new CreditCardPayment("1234-5678-9012-3456"));
        context.executePayment(100);

        context.setPaymentStrategy(new PayPalPayment("user@example.com"));
        context.executePayment(200);
    }
}
```

The PaymentContext class is configured with a PaymentStrategy, and the payment method can be changed at runtime without modifying the PaymentContext or client code.

These examples illustrate the practical application of the Singleton, Observer, and Strategy patterns in Java. By understanding these real-world implementations, one can appreciate the power and flexibility that design patterns bring to software development.

Chapter 2

Creational Patterns: Fundamentals and Use Cases

This chapter delves into Creational Patterns, which are responsible for object creation mechanisms that increase flexibility and reuse of existing code. It provides an overview of various creational patterns including Singleton, Factory Method, Abstract Factory, Builder, and Prototype. Each pattern is examined in terms of its implementation in Java, the scenarios where it is most applicable, and the benefits and drawbacks it introduces. The chapter concludes with best practices, common mistakes to avoid, and real-world use cases to solidify understanding.

2.1 Introduction to Creational Patterns

Creational patterns abstract the instantiation process, making systems independent of how their objects are created, composed, and represented. These patterns enable a system to be designed more flexibly by allowing for easy exchange, extension, and management of classes. In Java, creational patterns leverage the language's capabilities to provide reusable and consistent methods of object creation, ensuring a clean and maintainable codebase.

Creational patterns fall into five primary categories: Singleton, Factory Method, Abstract Factory, Builder, and Prototype. Each pattern offers specific benefits and is suited to particular scenarios that address different aspects of object creation, often solving similar problems in diverse ways.

To understand the need for creational patterns, consider the basic approach to object instantiation in Java, which typically involves direct calls to constructors. Such an approach can lead to issues regarding flexibility and reuse. Directly instantiating classes binds a client to specific implementations, making the code less modular and harder to extend or modify.

Creational patterns solve these issues by providing a higher level of abstraction. For instance, instead of directly using the `new` operator, a class might delegate the instantiation to another object that follows a specified pattern. This ensures that the instantiation logic can change without affecting the client's code, enhancing maintainability and scalability.

Benefits of Creational Patterns:

- **Increased Flexibility**: By decoupling the instantiation process, it becomes simpler to introduce new classes or extend existing ones with minimal changes.
- **Enhanced Reusability**: Creational patterns promote code that is more readable and easier to understand, which can be reused across different parts of a system.
- **Improved Design**: These patterns contribute to a more organized and modular code structure, simplifying the maintenance of large systems.

Common Creational Patterns in Java:

The following sections briefly introduce the five primary creational patterns:

Singleton Pattern: Ensures a class has only one instance and provides a global point of access to it. The Singleton pattern is often used in resource management scenarios, such as managing database connections or configuration settings.

Factory Method Pattern: Defines an interface for creating an object, but allows subclasses to alter the type of object that will be created. This pattern is beneficial when a class cannot anticipate the class of objects it must create.

Abstract Factory Pattern: Provides an interface for creating families of related or dependent objects without specifying their concrete classes. This pattern is advantageous when the system needs to be independent of how its objects are created and represented.

Builder Pattern: Separates the construction of a complex object from its representation so that the same construction process can create different representations. The Builder pattern is especially useful for constructing objects with many parameters or composite objects.

Prototype Pattern: Specifies the kind of objects to create using a prototypical instance, and creates new objects by copying this prototype. This pattern is particularly useful when the cost of creating an object is high.

Each pattern is discussed in further sections, illustrating its implementation and use cases in Java with example code and explanations.

By understanding and applying creational patterns, Java developers can create more maintainable, scalable, and flexible code. The following code snippet demonstrates a basic application of the Factory Method pattern in Java:

```
abstract class Product {
    abstract void use();
}

class ConcreteProductA extends Product {
    @Override
    void use() {
        System.out.println("Using product A");
    }
}

class ConcreteProductB extends Product {
    @Override
    void use() {
        System.out.println("Using product B");
    }
}

abstract class Creator {
    abstract Product factoryMethod(String type);
}

class ConcreteCreator extends Creator {
    @Override
    Product factoryMethod(String type) {
        switch(type) {
            case "A":
                return new ConcreteProductA();
            case "B":
```

```
            return new ConcreteProductB();
        default:
            throw new IllegalArgumentException("Unknown type");
        }
    }
}

public class FactoryMethodDemo {
    public static void main(String[] args) {
        Creator creator = new ConcreteCreator();
        Product productA = creator.factoryMethod("A");
        productA.use();

        Product productB = creator.factoryMethod("B");
        productB.use();
    }
}
```

Output:
Using product A
Using product B

In this example, the ConcreteCreator's factoryMethod determines which Product subclass to instantiate based on the input type. This abstraction allows the client code (in FactoryMethodDemo) to remain the same regardless of the specific subclass being instantiated, demonstrating the flexibility provided by the Factory Method pattern.

The goal of this chapter is to explore each creational pattern in detail, deepening your understanding of their implementation and application in Java to solve common software design problems effectively.

2.2 The Singleton Pattern

The Singleton Pattern is a design pattern that restricts the instantiation of a class to a single instance and provides a global point of access to that instance. This pattern is useful when exactly one object is needed to coordinate actions across the system. The Singleton Pattern ensures that a class has only one instance and that the instance is easily accessible. This pattern is suitable for scenarios such as logging, configuration settings, or resource management where a single instance is desired.

To implement the Singleton Pattern in Java, it is essential to control the instantiation of the class and ensure thread safety. Below is an exemplary implementation of the Singleton Pattern in Java:

```
public class Singleton {
```

```
    // Private static variable to hold the single instance of the class
    private static Singleton instance;

    // Private constructor to prevent direct instantiation
    private Singleton() {}

    // Public method to provide the singleton instance
    public static Singleton getInstance() {
        if (instance == null) {
            instance = new Singleton();
        }
        return instance;
    }

    // Other methods of the Singleton class
    public void showMessage() {
        System.out.println("Hello from Singleton!");
    }
}
```

In this implementation:

- instance is a private static variable that holds the single instance of the Singleton class.
- The constructor of the class is private, which prevents the instantiation of the class using the new keyword from outside the class.
- The getInstance() method is public and static, providing a global point of access to the instance. It initializes the instance on the first call and returns the same instance on subsequent calls.

This basic implementation, however, is not thread-safe. In a multi-threading environment, it is possible for multiple threads to create separate instances of the Singleton class simultaneously. Thus, additional measures are needed to ensure thread safety. One such approach is the use of synchronized blocks:

```
public class Singleton {

    private static Singleton instance;
    private static final Object lock = new Object();

    private Singleton() {}

    public static Singleton getInstance() {
        if (instance == null) {
            synchronized (lock) {
                if (instance == null) {
                    instance = new Singleton();
                }
            }
        }
```

```
        return instance;
    }

    public void showMessage() {
        System.out.println("Hello from Singleton!");
    }
}
```

This implementation ensures that only one thread can execute the critical section of code at a time. The use of the lock object ensures that the block of code that initializes the Singleton instance is mutually exclusive.

For an even more efficient initialization, the Singleton Pattern can utilize the Bill Pugh Singleton Design, which capitalizes on the class loader mechanism to ensure that the instance is created only when required:

```
public class Singleton {

    private Singleton() {}

    private static class SingletonHelper {
        private static final Singleton INSTANCE = new Singleton();
    }

    public static Singleton getInstance() {
        return SingletonHelper.INSTANCE;
    }

    public void showMessage() {
        System.out.println("Hello from Singleton!");
    }
}
```

In this implementation:

- The SingletonHelper nested class contains the instance of the Singleton class.
- The INSTANCE is created when the SingletonHelper class is loaded into memory, providing a thread-safe, lazy-initialized Singleton instance.

To illustrate the usage of the Singleton Pattern, consider the following example:

```
public class SingletonDemo {
    public static void main(String[] args) {
        // Illegal construct
        // Compile Time Error: The constructor Singleton() is not visible
        // Singleton instance = new Singleton();

        // Get the only object available
```

```
        Singleton singleInstance = Singleton.getInstance();

        // Show the message
        singleInstance.showMessage();
    }
}
```

```
Hello from Singleton!
```

In this use case, the Singleton instance is accessed using the getInstance() method, ensuring that only one instance exists.

The Singleton Pattern provides several benefits:

- Controlled access to a single instance.
- Reduced namespace conflicts by encapsulating the instance.
- Flexibility in changing the instantiation process.

However, there are also some drawbacks:

- Singleton instances can be challenging to unit test as they hide dependencies.
- They may introduce global state into an application, which can be complex to manage.

Being mindful of these considerations can aid in the effective application of the Singleton Pattern, promoting the creation of a more maintainable and robust application.

2.3 The Factory Method Pattern

The Factory Method Pattern is a creational design pattern that provides an interface for creating objects in a super class but allows subclasses to alter the type of objects that will be created. This pattern delegates the instantiation logic to child classes, offering greater extensibility without modifying the super class.

Factory Method falls under the category of creational patterns and promotes loose coupling in the system. It is particularly useful when the exact type of object to be created cannot be anticipated beforehand or when the creation process encompasses logic that cannot be centralized.

Intent: The primary intention of the Factory Method Pattern is to define an interface for creating an object, but let subclasses decide which class to instantiate. The Factory Method lets a class defer instantiation to subclasses.

Structure: The Factory Method Pattern can be exemplified with the following UML class diagram and summarized in terms of its participants:

- Product: Defines the interface of objects that the factory method creates.
- ConcreteProduct: Implements the Product interface.
- Creator: Declares the factory method, which returns an object of type Product. Creator might also define a default implementation of the factory method that returns a default ConcreteProduct object.
- ConcreteCreator: Overrides the factory method to change the resulting product.

Implementation in Java: We illustrate the Factory Method Pattern using the example of a logistics application that manages different kinds of transport vehicles:

```
// Product interface
public interface Transport {
    void deliver();
}

// ConcreteProduct implementations
public class Truck implements Transport {
    @Override
    public void deliver() {
        System.out.println("Deliver by land in a box.");
    }
}

public class Ship implements Transport {
    @Override
    public void deliver() {
        System.out.println("Deliver by sea in a container.");
    }
}

// Creator abstract class
public abstract class Logistics {
    // Factory method
    public abstract Transport createTransport();

    public void planDelivery() {
        // Call the factory method to create a Transport object
        Transport transport = createTransport();
```

```
        transport.deliver();
    }
}

// ConcreteCreator implementations
public class RoadLogistics extends Logistics {
    @Override
    public Transport createTransport() {
        return new Truck();
    }
}

public class SeaLogistics extends Logistics {
    @Override
    public Transport createTransport() {
        return new Ship();
    }
}
```

In the code example above, Transport is the product interface. Truck and Ship are concrete products implementing the Transport interface. Logistics is an abstract creator class which declares the factory method createTransport(). Subclasses like RoadLogistics and SeaLogistics override this method to create specific transport objects.

Applicability: The Factory Method Pattern is useful in scenarios where:

- A class cannot anticipate the class of objects it must create.
- A class wants its subclasses to specify the objects it creates.
- Classes delegate responsibility to one of several helper sub-classes, and you want to localize the knowledge of which helper subclass is the delegate.

Consequences: Utilizing the Factory Method Pattern offers several benefits:

- Flexibility: It allows for more flexible and reusable code by delegating the object creation to subclasses.
- Encapsulation: The Factory Method promotes encapsulation by hiding the specifics of instantiation and allowing subclasses to handle creation.
- Decoupling: By deferring instantiation to sub-classes, the dependency between creator classes and concrete products is reduced.

Conversely, there are some downsides to consider:

- Complexity: Implementing factory methods can introduce complexity into the code base due to the hierarchy of classes required.
- Maintenance Overhead: If subclass count increases, managing these subclasses could become cumbersome, making the application harder to extend and maintain.

Example Use Case: A graphical application framework that needs to instantiate different types of UI components like buttons, check-boxes, and text-fields can benefit considerably from the Factory Method Pattern. Each platform (Windows, Mac, Linux) might require a different look and feel, where the factory methods in subclasses would instantiate the appropriate components per platform without altering the existing framework.

In implementing the Factory Method Pattern, one should aim to strike a balance between the gained flexibility and any introduced complexity, ensuring the architecture remains maintainable and scalable.

2.4 The Abstract Factory Pattern

The Abstract Factory Pattern is one of the creational patterns that provides an interface for creating families of related or dependent objects without specifying their concrete classes. This pattern encapsulates a group of individual factories within a class to have a more complex hierarchy. Through this pattern, we can ensure that a system is independent of how its objects are created, composed, and represented.

Implementation in Java:

To understand the implementation of the Abstract Factory Pattern, let's consider a scenario where we want to create a family of GUI elements like buttons and checkboxes. We will start by defining interfaces for products and their factories.

```
public interface Button {
    void paint();
}
```

```
public interface Checkbox {
    void paint();
}
```

Next, we create concrete implementations of the Button and Checkbox interfaces for different types of GUI elements.

```
public class WindowsButton implements Button {
    @Override
    public void paint() {
        System.out.println("Windows Button");
    }
}
```

```
public class MacButton implements Button {
    @Override
    public void paint() {
        System.out.println("Mac Button");
    }
}
```

```
public class WindowsCheckbox implements Checkbox {
    @Override
    public void paint() {
        System.out.println("Windows Checkbox");
    }
}
```

```
public class MacCheckbox implements Checkbox {
    @Override
    public void paint() {
        System.out.println("Mac Checkbox");
    }
}
```

We then define an Abstract Factory interface that declares creation methods for all the abstract products.

```
public interface GUIFactory {
    Button createButton();
    Checkbox createCheckbox();
}
```

Concrete factory classes implement this interface to produce a family of products.

```
public class WindowsFactory implements GUIFactory {
    @Override
    public Button createButton() {
        return new WindowsButton();
    }

    @Override
    public Checkbox createCheckbox() {
        return new WindowsCheckbox();
    }
}
```

```
public class MacFactory implements GUIFactory {
    @Override
    public Button createButton() {
        return new MacButton();
    }
```

```
    @Override
    public Checkbox createCheckbox() {
        return new MacCheckbox();
    }
}
```

Finally, the client code uses instances of the factory classes to create objects. This decouples the client code from the concrete classes of products, promoting code reuse and flexibility.

```
public class Application {
    private Button button;
    private Checkbox checkbox;

    public Application(GUIFactory factory) {
        button = factory.createButton();
        checkbox = factory.createCheckbox();
    }

    public void paint() {
        button.paint();
        checkbox.paint();
    }
}
```

```
public class Demo {
    private static Application configureApplication() {
        Application app;
        GUIFactory factory;
        String osName = System.getProperty("os.name").toLowerCase();
        if (osName.contains("mac")) {
            factory = new MacFactory();
        } else {
            factory = new WindowsFactory();
        }
        app = new Application(factory);
        return app;
    }

    public static void main(String[] args) {
        Application app = configureApplication();
        app.paint();
    }
}
```

Executing the Program:

Upon executing the demo class, depending on the operating system detected by the code, the output will be different.

```
# On a Windows system:
Windows Button
Windows Checkbox

# On a Mac system:
Mac Button
Mac Checkbox
```

Applicability:

The Abstract Factory Pattern is applicable in scenarios where:

- A system needs to be independent of how its products are created, composed, and represented.
- A system should be configured with one of multiple families of products.
- A family of related product objects is designed to be used together, and this constraint should be enforced.
- We want to provide a library of products, and only reveal their interfaces, not their implementations.

Benefits and Drawbacks:

The Abstract Factory Pattern comes with several benefits:

- **Consistency among products:** Ensures that the created products are compatible with each other.
- **Flexibility in changing product families:** Makes exchanging one product family with another easy.
- **Encapsulation of creation logic:** Hides the creation logic from the client.

However, it also presents some drawbacks:

- **Complexity increase:** Adding a new family of products requires changes in all the factory classes.
- **Hard to extend for new products:** Introducing new kinds of products involves significant changes across the abstract factory and all its implementations.

To sum up, despite the associated complexity, the Abstract Factory Pattern is valuable for systems requiring a high degree of decoupling and consistency across families of related objects. Understanding its implementation deeply can significantly enhance the design and flexibility of software systems.

2.5 The Builder Pattern

The Builder Pattern is a design pattern aimed at separating the construction of a complex object from its representation, enabling the same construction process to create various representations. This pattern is particularly useful when an object requires numerous parameters for its construction, making it difficult to manage their order or when an object's construction process must allow intermediate steps to ensure its proper state. The Builder Pattern falls under the category of Creational Patterns and plays a crucial role in object creation mechanisms by providing control over the object instantiation process.

Implementing the Builder Pattern in Java typically involves four main components: the Product, the Builder, the ConcreteBuilder, and the Director.

Product: The complex object to be constructed. It can contain various parts that need to be built in a specific sequence or manner.

Builder: The abstract interface that defines the process of building the parts that make up the Product.

ConcreteBuilder: The class that implements the Builder interface, constructing and assembling parts of the Product.

Director: The class responsible for managing the construction process, calling the appropriate builder methods to build the parts in the correct sequence.

Below is an example of how the Builder Pattern can be implemented in Java to construct a House object:

```
public class House {
    private String foundation;
    private String structure;
    private String roof;
    private boolean furnished;
    private boolean painted;

    private House(HouseBuilder builder) {
        this.foundation = builder.foundation;
        this.structure = builder.structure;
        this.roof = builder.roof;
        this.furnished = builder.furnished;
        this.painted = builder.painted;
    }

    public static class HouseBuilder {
        private String foundation;
        private String structure;
        private String roof;
        private boolean furnished;
```

```
        private boolean painted;

        public HouseBuilder setFoundation(String foundation) {
            this.foundation = foundation;
            return this;
        }

        public HouseBuilder setStructure(String structure) {
            this.structure = structure;
            return this;
        }

        public HouseBuilder setRoof(String roof) {
            this.roof = roof;
            return this;
        }

        public HouseBuilder setFurnished(boolean furnished) {
            this.furnished = furnished;
            return this;
        }

        public HouseBuilder setPainted(boolean painted) {
            this.painted = painted;
            return this;
        }

        public House build() {
            return new House(this);
        }
    }

    @Override
    public String toString() {
        return "House [foundation=" + foundation + ", structure=" + structure +
                ", roof=" + roof + ", furnished=" + furnished + ", painted=" + painted
                    + "]";
    }
}

public class Director {
    private HouseBuilder builder;

    public Director(HouseBuilder builder) {
        this.builder = builder;
    }

    public House constructLuxuryHouse() {
        return builder.setFoundation("Concrete")
                    .setStructure("Wood and Brick")
                    .setRoof("Concrete and Clay")
                    .setFurnished(true)
                    .setPainted(true)
                    .build();
    }

    public House constructSimpleHouse() {
        return builder.setFoundation("Wood")
                    .setStructure("Wood")
                    .setRoof("Thatch")
                    .setFurnished(false)
                    .setPainted(false)
```

```
                .build();
    }
}

public class BuilderPatternDemo {
    public static void main(String[] args) {
        HouseBuilder builder = new House.HouseBuilder();
        Director director = new Director(builder);

        House luxuryHouse = director.constructLuxuryHouse();
        System.out.println(luxuryHouse);

        House simpleHouse = director.constructSimpleHouse();
        System.out.println(simpleHouse);
    }
}
```

Executing the above Java code will produce the following output:

```
House [foundation=Concrete, structure=Wood and Brick, roof=Concrete and Clay, furnished=true, painted=true]
House [foundation=Wood, structure=Wood, roof=Thatch, furnished=false, painted=false]
```

The Builder Pattern offers several notable benefits:

- **Controlled Construction Process**: By breaking down the construction process into discrete steps, the Builder Pattern ensures encapsulation and control over the creation process, leading to more maintainable and readable code.
- **Flexibility and Extensibility**: Different concrete builders can share the same construction process managed by the director, offering flexibility in object representation.
- **Improved Object State Integrity**: Ensures that the complex object is created step-by-step in a proper state, adhering to any constraints or intermediate validations.
- **Simplified Client Code**: Helps reduce the complexity of client code by abstracting the intricate construction logic within builders.

However, the Builder Pattern also has some drawbacks:

- **Increased Number of Classes**: It requires creating several additional classes, potentially increasing the complexity of the codebase.
- **Indirection**: The use of a director introduces an additional level of indirection which might complicate debugging or maintenance efforts.

Understanding the strengths and limitations of the Builder Pattern is crucial for effectively utilizing it in software applications. When employed appropriately, the Builder Pattern can significantly enhance the flexibility and robustness of the object creation process.

2.6 The Prototype Pattern

The Prototype Pattern is a creational design pattern that is used to create new objects by copying an existing object, known as the prototype. This pattern is particularly useful in situations where creating an object from scratch is expensive or complex. Instead of instantiating a new object from a class, an existing object is cloned, ensuring that the newly created object has the same properties as the original.

The Prototype Pattern involves defining a prototype interface, which declares a method for cloning objects. Concrete classes implementing the prototype interface will override the cloning method to return a copy of the object. In Java, this is often achieved through the Cloneable interface and the clone method.

Implementation in Java

To implement the Prototype Pattern in Java, the following steps are typically followed:

- Define a prototype interface with a method to clone objects.
- Implement the prototype interface in concrete classes.
- Utilize the clone method to create copies of objects.

Here is an example implementation of the Prototype Pattern in Java:

```
public interface Prototype {
    Prototype clone();
}
```

The Prototype interface declares a single method, clone, which will be implemented by concrete classes to return a copy of the object.

```
public class ConcretePrototype implements Prototype {
    private String field;

    public ConcretePrototype(String field) {
        this.field = field;
    }
```

```
    @Override
    public Prototype clone() {
        return new ConcretePrototype(this.field);
    }

    public String getField() {
        return field;
    }

    public void setField(String field) {
        this.field = field;
    }
}
```

In ConcretePrototype, the clone method is overridden to return a new instance of ConcretePrototype with the same value for the field variable as the existing instance.

To demonstrate the Prototype Pattern in use, consider the following client code:

```
public class PrototypeDemo {
    public static void main(String[] args) {
        ConcretePrototype original = new ConcretePrototype("Original");
        ConcretePrototype copy = (ConcretePrototype) original.clone();

        System.out.println("Original: " + original.getField());
        System.out.println("Copy: " + copy.getField());

        copy.setField("Modified Copy");
        System.out.println("Original after modification: " + original.getField());
        System.out.println("Copy after modification: " + copy.getField());
    }
}
```

The execution of this client code would produce the following output:

```
Original: Original
Copy: Original
Original after modification: Original
Copy after modification: Modified Copy
```

This output demonstrates that the cloned object is a distinct instance with the same initial state as the original but can be modified independently.

Advantages and Disadvantages

The Prototype Pattern offers several advantages:

- It can be more efficient than creating a new object from scratch, especially if the object's initialization is costly.
- It allows for the creation of complex object structures that would be cumbersome to instantiate otherwise.

- It provides a way to add or remove products at runtime by cloning existing instances.

However, the Prototype Pattern also has some drawbacks:

- It may require careful implementation of the clone method to ensure that cloned objects are deep copies, not shallow copies, which can be error-prone.
- It relies on having well-defined and manageable prototypical instances, which may not always be feasible.
- The Java Cloneable interface and the clone method can be restrictive and do not support exception handling, necessitating extra care in their use.

Real-World Use Cases

The Prototype Pattern is typically used in scenarios where object creation is computationally expensive or complex. Some practical applications include:

- **Graphic Editing Applications:** Complex shapes or characters can be duplicated to create new instances without re-initiating the creation process.
- **Distributed Systems:** Objects across different systems can be replicated or restored without needing to transport detailed creation instructions.
- **Game Development:** Characters, environments, or other game elements can be cloned to maintain consistency while allowing for individual modifications.

The Prototype Pattern, while powerful, requires a disciplined approach to ensure that objects are correctly cloned and manage their state independently. Applying this pattern effectively enhances the flexibility and efficiency of object creation, contributing significantly to building robust and maintainable systems. When integrating this pattern, consider the overall architecture and specific requirements to determine if cloning is suitable for the application domain.

2.7 Comparing Creational Patterns

Understanding the nuances and comparative advantages of various creational patterns is crucial for designing robust, maintainable, and flexible object-oriented systems. The patterns covered in this chapter—Singleton, Factory Method, Abstract Factory, Builder, and Prototype—serve different purposes and are suitable for specific scenarios. We will examine these patterns based on several criteria: intent, structure, applicability, consequences, and implementation.

Intent

Each creational pattern addresses a different need in the object creation process:

- Singleton: Ensures a class has only one instance and provides a global access point to this instance.
- Factory Method: Defines an interface for creating an object, but allows subclasses to alter the type of objects that will be created.
- Abstract Factory: Provides an interface for creating families of related or dependent objects without specifying their concrete classes.
- Builder: Separates the construction of a complex object from its representation, allowing the same construction process to create various representations.
- Prototype: Specifies the kinds of objects to create using a prototypical instance, creating new objects by copying this prototype.

Structure

The structure of each pattern often dictates its use and flexibility:

- Singleton involves a single class which is responsible for creating and managing its instance.
- Factory Method uses inheritance and relies on subclasses to specify the objects that the base class's method will create.
- Abstract Factory typically uses composition and delegation to create families of related objects without tight coupling.

- Builder involves multiple classes: a Builder class that constructs the complex object step by step and a Director class that orchestrates the construction process.

- Prototype involves a prototype interface that declares a clone method and a concrete prototype class that implements this interface.

Applicability

Different scenarios justify the use of different creational patterns:

- Singleton is used when exactly one instance of a class is needed, such as for logging, driver objects, thread pools, and configuration settings.

- Factory Method is suited to scenarios where a class cannot anticipate the class of objects it must create. It is useful when a class wants its subclasses to specify the creation of objects.

- Abstract Factory is appropriate for systems that involve multiple families of products and need to ensure that the products are coupled appropriately.

- Builder is ideal for constructing complex objects with many optional parts or configurations, such as constructing a multi-component product Car or House.

- Prototype is beneficial in contexts that require the creation of objects that are costly to create new, such as when objects are initialized with a series of configurations.

Consequences

Each pattern comes with its own set of benefits and liabilities:

- Singleton restricts instantiation to a single instance but can lead to issues in unit testing and excessive strictness in object management.

- Factory Method enhances flexibility and reusability by decoupling object creation from the client but can introduce complexity due to the inheritance structure.

- Abstract Factory ensures consistency among products and abstracts instantiation logic but can lead to a proliferation of classes and increased complexity.
- Builder provides fine control over the construction process and isolates the complex construction code but necessitates the creation of multiple new classes.
- Prototype facilitates object creation by cloning, leading to performance improvement but requiring a careful approach to object copying.

Implementation

Considering the practical implementation of each pattern:

```
public class Singleton {
    private static Singleton uniqueInstance;

    private Singleton() {}

    public static synchronized Singleton getInstance() {
        if (uniqueInstance == null) {
            uniqueInstance = new Singleton();
        }
        return uniqueInstance;
    }
}
```

```
public abstract class Product {}

public class ConcreteProductA extends Product {}
public class ConcreteProductB extends Product {}

public abstract class Creator {
    public abstract Product factoryMethod();
}

public class ConcreteCreatorA extends Creator {
    public Product factoryMethod() {
        return new ConcreteProductA();
    }
}

public class ConcreteCreatorB extends Creator {
    public Product factoryMethod() {
        return new ConcreteProductB();
    }
}
```

```
public interface AbstractFactory {
    ProductA createProductA();
    ProductB createProductB();
}

public class ConcreteFactory1 implements AbstractFactory {
```

```
    public ProductA createProductA() {
        return new ProductA1();
    }

    public ProductB createProductB() {
        return new ProductB1();
    }
}

public class ConcreteFactory2 implements AbstractFactory {
    public ProductA createProductA() {
        return new ProductA2();
    }

    public ProductB createProductB() {
        return new ProductB2();
    }
}
```

```
public class Product {
    private String partA;
    private String partB;

    // Getters and setters
}

public abstract class Builder {
    protected Product product;

    public void createNewProduct() {
        product = new Product();
    }

    public Product getProduct() {
        return product;
    }

    public abstract void buildPartA();
    public abstract void buildPartB();
}

public class ConcreteBuilder extends Builder {
    public void buildPartA() {
        product.setPartA("Built Part A");
    }

    public void buildPartB() {
        product.setPartB("Built Part B");
    }
}

public class Director {
    private Builder builder;

    public void setBuilder(Builder builder) {
        this.builder = builder;
    }

    public Product construct() {
        builder.createNewProduct();
        builder.buildPartA();
        builder.buildPartB();
```

```
        return builder.getProduct();
    }
}
```

```
public class Prototype implements Cloneable {
    private String field;

    public Prototype(String field) {
        this.field = field;
    }

    @Override
    public Object clone() {
        try {
            return super.clone();
        } catch (CloneNotSupportedException e) {
            return null;
        }
    }
}
```

Evaluating the patterns based on these criteria provides a clearer picture of their appropriate application contexts and their impact on system architecture. Decisions regarding which pattern to implement should consider the specific requirements and constraints of the software project at hand, aiming to maximize code reuse, maintainability, and flexibility. Each pattern offers a unique strategy for managing object creation, fostering better design practices and system architecture.

2.8 Use Cases for Creational Patterns

Creational patterns provide solutions to instantiating objects. Each pattern is uniquely suited to certain scenarios, offering ways to control the complexity and flexibility of object creation. Understanding the appropriate use cases for each pattern can facilitate optimal design choices.

Singleton Pattern is appropriate when exactly one instance of a class is needed to coordinate actions throughout the system. This is beneficial in the following scenarios:

- **Logging**: A single logging instance manages the logging mechanism.
- **Configuration Settings**: A single object that holds configuration data for an application.
- **Cache**: A singleton cache to store frequently accessed data.

- **Thread Pool**: Managing a pool of threads to control resource allocation.

Consider the implementation of a Singleton in Java:

```
public class Singleton {
    private static Singleton instance;

    private Singleton() {}

    public static Singleton getInstance() {
        if (instance == null) {
            instance = new Singleton();
        }
        return instance;
    }
}
```

Factory Method Pattern is suitable when a class cannot anticipate the class of objects it must create or when a class wants its subclasses to specify the objects it creates. Use cases include:

- **Framework Design**: When designing a framework that should allow extended functionalities (e.g., document readers).
- **Dependency Injection**: Creating objects to reduce the coupling between classes and their dependencies.
- **Testing**: Facilitating testing by creating mock objects or stub implementations.

The Factory Method pattern can be implemented as follows:

```
abstract class Creator {
    public abstract Product factoryMethod();

    public void someOperation() {
        Product product = factoryMethod();
        // Operate on the product
    }
}

class ConcreteCreator extends Creator {
    @Override
    public Product factoryMethod() {
        return new ConcreteProduct();
    }
}
```

Abstract Factory Pattern is employed when there is a need to create families of related or dependent objects without specifying their concrete classes. Ideal use cases include:

- **User Interface Themes**: Supporting different themes with varying components like buttons, menus, etc.
- **Cross-Platform Applications**: Creating UI components for various operating systems that handle system-specific implementations.
- **Product Variants**: Manufacturing systems requiring different products created in uniform ways.

A Java implementation of the Abstract Factory Pattern might look like this:

```
interface GUIFactory {
    Button createButton();
    Checkbox createCheckbox();
}

class WinFactory implements GUIFactory {
    public Button createButton() {
        return new WinButton();
    }
    public Checkbox createCheckbox() {
        return new WinCheckbox();
    }
}

class MacFactory implements GUIFactory {
    public Button createButton() {
        return new MacButton();
    }
    public Checkbox createCheckbox() {
        return new MacCheckbox();
    }
}
```

Builder Pattern is used when creating complex objects requiring multiple steps or configurations. Use cases encompass:

- **Complex Objects**: Objects that need not be created in a single constructor call (e.g., vehicles, house plans).
- **Immutable Objects**: Building objects where the final state must be immutable and defined in a step-by-step manner.
- **Fluent Interface**: Easier readability of chains of method calls.

Builder Pattern implementation in Java can be as follows:

```
public class House {
    private final String walls;
    private final String roof;
```

```
    private final int windows;

    private House(Builder builder) {
        this.walls = builder.walls;
        this.roof = builder.roof;
        this.windows = builder.windows;
    }

    public static class Builder {
        private String walls;
        private String roof;
        private int windows;

        public Builder setWalls(String walls) {
            this.walls = walls;
            return this;
        }

        public Builder setRoof(String roof) {
            this.roof = roof;
            return this;
        }

        public Builder setWindows(int windows) {
            this.windows = windows;
            return this;
        }

        public House build() {
            return new House(this);
        }
    }
}
```

Prototype Pattern is optimal when the cost of creating a new object is prohibitive or when an object's state is a crucial factor in object creation. Ideal use cases are:

- **Performance Optimization**: Cloning objects to avoid the overhead of costly operations.
- **Stateful Objects**: When an object includes several configurations that frequently change.
- **Document Templates**: Using prototypes for standard document templates that can be cloned and modified.

Prototype Pattern implementation is typically seen as follows:

```
public abstract class Shape implements Cloneable {
    private String id;
    protected String type;

    abstract void draw();

    public String getType() {
```

```
        return type;
    }

    public String getId() {
        return id;
    }

    public void setId(String id) {
        this.id = id;
    }

    public Object clone() {
        Object clone = null;
        try {
            clone = super.clone();
        } catch (CloneNotSupportedException e) {
            e.printStackTrace();
        }
        return clone;
    }
}

public class Circle extends Shape {
    public Circle() {
        type = "Circle";
    }

    public void draw() {
        System.out.println("Inside Circle::draw() method.");
    }
}
```

Effective application of these design patterns enables developers to solve common object creation problems with reusable and maintainable solutions.

2.9 Best Practices in Applying Creational Patterns

The implementation of Creational Patterns in Java development requires a nuanced understanding of both the patterns themselves and the context in which they are applied. Adhering to best practices ensures that the flexibility, maintainability, and efficiency intended by the creation mechanisms are fully realized.

Understand the Problem Domain: Before selecting a creational pattern, it is crucial to thoroughly understand the problem and the requirements. Evaluate whether the primary concern is object creation complexity, performance, or potential future scalability. The choice of pattern should address these specific concerns.

Leverage Polymorphism: Creational patterns often rely on inheritance and interfaces to provide a flexible and reusable object creation mechanism. For example, the Factory Method pattern uses an interface or abstract class for the product objects, allowing for a polymorphic approach to object creation. This should be utilized to ensure that objects can be created without specifying their exact class.

Data: An interface Shape with methods draw() and erase()
Result: A concrete class Circle that implements Shape

```
begin
    Shape shape = ShapeFactory.getShape("Circle");
    shape.draw();
```

Encapsulate Construction Logic: Ensure that the object creation logic is encapsulated within the factory or builder class rather than scattered throughout the client code. This abstraction not only simplifies the client code but also adheres to the Single Responsibility Principle by isolating the construction process.

```
public class ShapeFactory {
    public Shape getShape(String shapeType) {
        if(shapeType == null){
            return null;
        }
        if(shapeType.equalsIgnoreCase("CIRCLE")){
            return new Circle();
        } else if(shapeType.equalsIgnoreCase("RECTANGLE")){
            return new Rectangle();
        }
        return null;
    }
}
```

Lazy Initialization: When employing the Singleton pattern, lazy initialization is a common practice to delay the creation of the instance until it is actually required. This can improve performance and resource utilization.

```
public class LazySingleton {
    private static LazySingleton instance;

    private LazySingleton() { }

    public static LazySingleton getInstance() {
        if (instance == null) {
            instance = new LazySingleton();
        }
        return instance;
    }
}
```

Thread Safety: In multi-threaded applications, it is essential to ensure that creational patterns remain thread-safe. For Singleton implementations, double-checked locking can be employed.

```
public class ThreadSafeSingleton {
    private volatile static ThreadSafeSingleton instance;

    private ThreadSafeSingleton() { }

    public static ThreadSafeSingleton getInstance() {
        if (instance == null) {
            synchronized (ThreadSafeSingleton.class) {
                if (instance == null) {
                    instance = new ThreadSafeSingleton();
                }
            }
        }
        return instance;
    }
}
```

Avoid Overuse of Patterns: While creational patterns are powerful tools, their overuse can complicate the code rather than simplify it. It is important to apply patterns judiciously and only when they solve a specific problem that simpler techniques cannot.

Use Abstract Factories for Families of Related Objects: When dealing with families of related objects, Abstract Factory is a suitable pattern as it provides an interface for creating related objects without specifying their concrete classes.

```
public interface GUIFactory {
    public Button createButton();
    public Checkbox createCheckbox();
}

public class WindowsFactory implements GUIFactory {
    public Button createButton() {
        return new WindowsButton();
    }
    public Checkbox createCheckbox() {
        return new WindowsCheckbox();
    }
}

public class MacFactory implements GUIFactory {
    public Button createButton() {
        return new MacButton();
    }
    public Checkbox createCheckbox() {
        return new MacCheckbox();
    }
}
```

Prototype for Cloning: If an object's creation is resource-intensive, consider using the Prototype pattern to clone objects. Ensure that the clone method performs a deep copy of the object if necessary.

```
public class Prototype implements Cloneable {
    private String field;

    @Override
    protected Object clone() throws CloneNotSupportedException {
        Prototype clone = (Prototype) super.clone();
        clone.field = new String(this.field);
        return clone;
    }
}
```

Builder for Complex Objects: When constructing an object that requires numerous parameters or complex initialization, the Builder pattern can manage the construction process effectively. It facilitates the creation of immutable objects and separates the construction logic from the object's representation.

```
public class House {
    private final int windows;
    private final int doors;
    private final boolean hasGarage;
    private final boolean hasSwimmingPool;

    private House(HouseBuilder builder) {
        this.windows = builder.windows;
        this.doors = builder.doors;
        this.hasGarage = builder.hasGarage;
        this.hasSwimmingPool = builder.hasSwimmingPool;
    }

    public static class HouseBuilder {
        private int windows;
        private int doors;
        private boolean hasGarage;
        private boolean hasSwimmingPool;

        public HouseBuilder setWindows(int windows) {
            this.windows = windows;
            return this;
        }

        public HouseBuilder setDoors(int doors) {
            this.doors = doors;
            return this;
        }

        public HouseBuilder setHasGarage(boolean hasGarage) {
            this.hasGarage = hasGarage;
            return this;
        }

        public HouseBuilder setHasSwimmingPool(boolean hasSwimmingPool) {
            this.hasSwimmingPool = hasSwimmingPool;
            return this;
        }
```

```
        public House build() {
            return new House(this);
        }
    }
}
```

Ensuring these best practices are integrated into the design and implementation phases not only leverages the full potential of creational patterns but also guarantees robust, scalable, and maintainable code.

2.10 Common Mistakes and How to Avoid Them

When implementing creational patterns, certain pitfalls can undermine the benefits they offer. By recognizing these common mistakes, developers can actively avoid them and ensure robust, maintainable, and scalable code. We will explore frequent mistakes encountered in various creational patterns and provide guidance on how to avoid them.

- **Overuse of Singleton Pattern**
  A frequent mistake while applying the Singleton pattern is its overuse. Developers sometimes perceive Singleton as a universal design pattern for any class requiring a single instance. This can lead to several issues, such as hindering unit testing due to hidden dependencies and creating a global state in the application which can be difficult to manage and debug.

  To avoid this, restrict the use of Singleton only to classes where it is essential to have one and only one instance. Additionally, consider using Dependency Injection to handle instances which can enhance testability and maintainability. For instance:

```
// Overused Singleton Pattern
public class ConfigurationManager {
    private static ConfigurationManager instance;
    private String config;

    private ConfigurationManager() {
        // Constructor
    }

    public static ConfigurationManager getInstance() {
        if (instance == null) {
            instance = new ConfigurationManager();
        }
        return instance;
    }
```

```
    public String getConfig() {
        return config;
    }
}

// Better approach with Dependency Injection
public class ConfigurationManager {
    private String config;

    public ConfigurationManager() {
        // Constructor
    }

    public String getConfig() {
        return config;
    }
}

// Dependency Injection
public class App {
    private ConfigurationManager configurationManager;

    public App(ConfigurationManager configurationManager) {
        this.configurationManager = configurationManager;
    }
}
```

- **Factory Method Pattern Complexity**
  Another common mistake is overcomplicating the Factory Method pattern. While the Factory Method aims to provide a way to delegate the instantiation logic to subclasses, developers can make this pattern overly complex by introducing unnecessary levels of inheritance and abstract classes which complicate the design.

  To avoid this mistake, keep the hierarchy as simple as possible and always evaluate if the complexity added aligns with the simplicity goal of design patterns. Here's an example showing sensible use of the Factory Method pattern:

```
abstract class Vehicle {
    public abstract void create();
}

class Car extends Vehicle {
    @Override
    public void create() {
        System.out.println("Car created");
    }
}

class Motorcycle extends Vehicle {
    @Override
    public void create() {
        System.out.println("Motorcycle created");
    }
}
```

```
abstract class VehicleFactory {
    public abstract Vehicle createVehicle();
}

class CarFactory extends VehicleFactory {
    @Override
    public Vehicle createVehicle() {
        return new Car();
    }
}

class MotorcycleFactory extends VehicleFactory {
    @Override
    public Vehicle createVehicle() {
        return new Motorcycle();
    }
}
```

- **Misuse of Abstract Factory Pattern**
  Utilizing the Abstract Factory pattern incorrectly by having a single concrete factory class that violates the abstraction principle can lead to a hardcoded and less flexible design. Abstract Factory should define interfaces for creating families of related or dependent objects without specifying their concrete classes.

  To avoid this mistake, ensure that the client interacts only with interfaces without knowing about the concrete implementations. This promotes a decoupled design and easy scalability for new components.

```
// Interface for Engines
interface Engine {
    void design();
}

// Interface for Tires
interface Tire {
    void manufacture();
}

// Concrete implementation for Car Engine
class CarEngine implements Engine {
    @Override
    public void design() {
        System.out.println("Designing Car Engine");
    }
}

// Concrete implementation for Motorcycle Engine
class MotorcycleEngine implements Engine {
    @Override
    public void design() {
        System.out.println("Designing Motorcycle Engine");
    }
}

// Abstract Factory Interface
interface VehicleFactory {
```

```
    Engine createEngine();
    Tire createTire();
}

// Concrete Factory for Car
class CarFactory implements VehicleFactory {
    @Override
    public Engine createEngine() {
        return new CarEngine();
    }

    @Override
    public Tire createTire() {
        // return Tire Implementation
    }
}

// Concrete Factory for Motorcycle
class MotorcycleFactory implements VehicleFactory {
    @Override
    public Engine createEngine() {
        return new MotorcycleEngine();
    }

    @Override
    public Tire createTire() {
        // return Tire Implementation
    }
}
```

- **Builder Pattern Inconsistencies**
  Misusing the Builder pattern by not following a consistent approach or creating incomplete builders can result in unreliable construction processes. The purpose of the Builder pattern is to separate the construction of a complex object from its representation, ensuring that the same construction process can produce different representations.

  To avoid inconsistencies, ensure that the Builder interface provides all necessary methods to construct the object fully and that the construction process is systematic. An example follows demonstrating a consistent Builder pattern:

```
class House {
    private final String foundation;
    private final String structure;
    private final String roof;

    private House(Builder builder) {
        this.foundation = builder.foundation;
        this.structure = builder.structure;
        this.roof = builder.roof;
    }

    public static class Builder {
        private String foundation;
        private String structure;
```

```
        private String roof;

        public Builder withFoundation(String foundation) {
            this.foundation = foundation;
            return this;
        }

        public Builder withStructure(String structure) {
            this.structure = structure;
            return this;
        }

        public Builder withRoof(String roof) {
            this.roof = roof;
            return this;
        }

        public House build() {
            return new House(this);
        }
    }
}
// Usage
House house = new House.Builder()
                .withFoundation("Concrete")
                .withStructure("Wood")
                .withRoof("Shingles")
                .build();
```

- **Improper Cloning in Prototype Pattern**
  In the Prototype pattern, improper implementation of cloning can lead to issues such as shallow copies where deep copies are necessary. Improper cloning may result in unintended sharing of references, which can cause bugs that are hard to trace.

  To avoid improper cloning, ensure careful implementation of the clone() method. For deep copies, clone objects referenced by the fields as well. Here's an example showing both shallow and deep cloning:

```
class Address implements Cloneable {
    private String city;
    private String street;

    // Constructor, getters, setters

    @Override
    protected Object clone() throws CloneNotSupportedException {
        return super.clone(); // shallow copy for simplicity
    }
}

class Person implements Cloneable {
    private String name;
    private Address address;

    // Constructor, getters, setters
```

```
    @Override
    protected Object clone() throws CloneNotSupportedException {
        Person cloned = (Person) super.clone();
        cloned.address = (Address) address.clone(); // deep copy of address
        return cloned;
    }
}
```

These insights into common mistakes and their solutions aim to foster better utilization of creational patterns, thereby, enhancing the overall design of software systems.

Chapter 3

Structural Patterns: Building Flexible Structures

This chapter explores Structural Patterns, which facilitate the design of flexible and efficient class and object structures. It covers key patterns such as Adapter, Bridge, Composite, Decorator, Facade, Flyweight, and Proxy. Each pattern is discussed in terms of its implementation in Java, its utility in various scenarios, and the architectural advantages it offers. The chapter also provides comparisons between patterns, guidelines for effective use, common pitfalls, and practical examples to demonstrate their application in real-world software design.

3.1 Introduction to Structural Patterns

Structural design patterns are pivotal in the construction of flexible and efficient software architectures. These patterns ease the design and implementation of class and object structures, providing a cohesive and organized approach to achieving desired functionalities. By allowing developers to compose objects and classes into larger structures, they facilitate the creation of complex software systems that are both manageable and extensible.

The core objective of structural patterns is to identify simple ways to realize relationships between entities. Unlike creational patterns that deal with object creation mechanisms or behavioral patterns that focus on object interaction, structural patterns define the composition of classes or objects.

One of the primary categories within structural patterns is the class pattern. These patterns leverage inheritance to structure interfaces and define relationships within classes. They enhance the functionality of a class by wrapping it with another class. An example of this is the Adapter pattern.

The other major category is the object pattern. These patterns use object composition, which involves composing objects to achieve new functionalities rather than inheriting from a parent class. Object patterns promote greater flexibility because the composition can be altered at runtime. Examples of object patterns include the Proxy and Decorator patterns.

Java, being an object-oriented programming language, is conducive to the implementation of these structural patterns. The following section will delve into each pattern with practical Java examples to illustrate the concepts.

Adapter Pattern: The Adapter pattern bridges the gap between incompatible interfaces, allowing classes to work together that otherwise could not. This pattern is particularly useful when integrating legacy code with newer systems.

```
public interface TargetInterface {
    void request();
}

public class Adaptee {
    public void specificRequest() {
        System.out.println("Called specificRequest()");
    }
}

public class Adapter implements TargetInterface {
    private Adaptee adaptee;

    public Adapter(Adaptee adaptee) {
        this.adaptee = adaptee;
    }

    @Override
    public void request() {
        adaptee.specificRequest();
    }
}

// Usage
```

```
Adaptee adaptee = new Adaptee();
TargetInterface target = new Adapter(adaptee);
target.request();
```

Output:
Called specificRequest()

Bridge Pattern: The Bridge pattern decouples an abstraction from its implementation, enabling both to vary independently. This is achieved by creating a bridge between them.

```
public interface Implementor {
    void operationImpl();
}

public class ConcreteImplementorA implements Implementor {
    @Override
    public void operationImpl() {
        System.out.println("ConcreteImplementorA operation");
    }
}

public abstract class Abstraction {
    protected Implementor implementor;

    protected Abstraction(Implementor implementor) {
        this.implementor = implementor;
    }

    public abstract void operation();
}

public class RefinedAbstraction extends Abstraction {
    public RefinedAbstraction(Implementor implementor) {
        super(implementor);
    }

    @Override
    public void operation() {
        implementor.operationImpl();
    }
}
// Usage
Implementor implementor = new ConcreteImplementorA();
Abstraction abstraction = new RefinedAbstraction(implementor);
abstraction.operation();
```

Output:
ConcreteImplementorA operation

Composite Pattern: The Composite pattern allows individual objects to be treated uniformly. It composes objects into tree structures to represent part-whole hierarchies. This significantly aids in constructing recursive tree structures wherein a single node and a group of nodes are treated uniformly.

```
public interface Component {
```

```
    void operation();
}

public class Leaf implements Component {
    @Override
    public void operation() {
        System.out.println("Leaf operation");
    }
}

public class Composite implements Component {
    private List<Component> children = new ArrayList<>();

    public void add(Component component) {
        children.add(component);
    }

    public void remove(Component component) {
        children.remove(component);
    }

    @Override
    public void operation() {
        for (Component child : children) {
            child.operation();
        }
    }
}

// Usage
Composite root = new Composite();
Composite branch = new Composite();
Leaf leaf = new Leaf();

branch.add(leaf);
root.add(branch);
root.operation();
```

Output:
Leaf operation

Decorator Pattern: The Decorator pattern provides a way to extend the functionalities of objects dynamically. It achieves this by wrapping the object with another object that adds new behaviors.

```
public interface Component {
    void operation();
}

public class ConcreteComponent implements Component {
    @Override
    public void operation() {
        System.out.println("ConcreteComponent operation");
    }
}

public abstract class Decorator implements Component {
    protected Component component;

    public Decorator(Component component) {
        this.component = component;
```

```
    }

    @Override
    public void operation() {
        component.operation();
    }
}

public class ConcreteDecorator extends Decorator {
    public ConcreteDecorator(Component component) {
        super(component);
    }

    @Override
    public void operation() {
        super.operation();
        addedBehavior();
    }

    public void addedBehavior() {
        System.out.println("ConcreteDecorator added behavior");
    }
}

// Usage
Component component = new ConcreteComponent();
Decorator decorator = new ConcreteDecorator(component);
decorator.operation();
```

Output:
ConcreteComponent operation
ConcreteDecorator added behavior

Facade Pattern: The Facade pattern provides a simplified interface to a complex subsystem. It defines a higher-level interface that makes the subsystem easier to use.

```
public class SubsystemClass1 {
    public void method1() {
        System.out.println("SubsystemClass1 method1");
    }
}

public class SubsystemClass2 {
    public void method2() {
        System.out.println("SubsystemClass2 method2");
    }
}

public class Facade {
    private SubsystemClass1 subsystem1 = new SubsystemClass1();
    private SubsystemClass2 subsystem2 = new SubsystemClass2();

    public void operation() {
        subsystem1.method1();
        subsystem2.method2();
    }
}

// Usage
Facade facade = new Facade();
```

```
facade.operation();
```

Output:
SubsystemClass1 method1
SubsystemClass2 method2

Flyweight Pattern: The Flyweight pattern reduces memory usage by sharing as much data as possible with similar objects. It is typically used in scenarios where a high number of objects are needed.

```
import java.util.HashMap;
import java.util.Map;

public interface Flyweight {
    void operation();
}

public class ConcreteFlyweight implements Flyweight {
    private String intrinsicState;

    public ConcreteFlyweight(String intrinsicState) {
        this.intrinsicState = intrinsicState;
    }

    @Override
    public void operation() {
        System.out.println("ConcreteFlyweight: " + intrinsicState);
    }
}

public class FlyweightFactory {
    private Map<String, Flyweight> flyweights = new HashMap<>();

    public Flyweight getFlyweight(String key) {
        if (!flyweights.containsKey(key)) {
            flyweights.put(key, new ConcreteFlyweight(key));
        }
        return flyweights.get(key);
    }
}

// Usage
FlyweightFactory factory = new FlyweightFactory();
Flyweight flyweight1 = factory.getFlyweight("A");
Flyweight flyweight2 = factory.getFlyweight("B");
flyweight1.operation();
flyweight2.operation();
```

Output:
ConcreteFlyweight: A
ConcreteFlyweight: B

Proxy Pattern: The Proxy pattern provides a surrogate or placeholder for another object to control access to it. This can be useful in implementing lazy initialization, access control, logging, etc.

```
public interface Subject {
    void request();
}
```

```
public class RealSubject implements Subject {
    @Override
    public void request() {
        System.out.println("RealSubject request");
    }
}

public class Proxy implements Subject {
    private RealSubject realSubject;

    @Override
    public void request() {
        if (realSubject == null) {
            realSubject = new RealSubject();
        }
        System.out.println("Proxy request");
        realSubject.request();
    }
}

// Usage
Subject proxy = new Proxy();
proxy.request();
```

```
Output:
Proxy request
RealSubject request
```

As demonstrated, structural patterns are essential for creating robust and flexible software architectures. They not only enable the integration of new features but also ensure the maintainability and scalability of the systems.

3.2 The Adapter Pattern

The Adapter Pattern is a structural design pattern that allows incompatible interfaces to work together. This pattern is used to wrap an existing class with a new interface, making it compatible with a specific client interface. The Adapter acts as a bridge between two incompatible interfaces by transforming the interface of a class into another interface that a client expects.

The Adapter Pattern can be implemented using two primary methods:

- **Class Adapter:** This approach uses inheritance to adapt one interface to another.
- **Object Adapter:** This approach uses composition to reference an instance of the adapted class.

In Java, the Adapter Pattern is typically implemented using the Object Adapter approach, leveraging composition to delegate requests to the existing class. This is generally preferred over the Class Adapter approach due to Java's single inheritance constraint, which limits the flexibility of using multiple adaptations.

Structure of the Adapter Pattern: The Adapter Pattern involves four key components:

- Target: Defines the domain-specific interface that the client uses.
- Client: Collaborates with objects conforming to the Target interface.
- Adaptee: Defines an existing interface that needs adaptation.
- Adapter: Implements the Target interface and maps calls from the Target interface to the Adaptee interface.

```
interface Target {
    void request();
}

class Adaptee {
    public void specificRequest() {
        System.out.println("Called SpecificRequest()");
    }
}

class Adapter implements Target {
    private Adaptee adaptee;

    public Adapter(Adaptee adaptee) {
        this.adaptee = adaptee;
    }

    @Override
    public void request() {
        adaptee.specificRequest();
    }
}
```

In the above example, the Target interface defines a standard method request() that the Client will use. The Adaptee class already exists with a different method, specificRequest(). The Adapter class implements the Target interface and uses the Adaptee to fulfill the request by translating the call to specificRequest().

Example Implementation in Java: Consider a scenario where we have a modern interface MediaPlayer and an existing incompatible interface AdvancedMediaPlayer. We can use an adapter to make the two interfaces compatible.

```
interface MediaPlayer {
    void play(String audioType, String fileName);
}

class Mp3Player implements MediaPlayer {
    @Override
    public void play(String audioType, String fileName) {
        if(audioType.equalsIgnoreCase("mp3")) {
            System.out.println("Playing mp3 file. Name: " + fileName);
        } else {
            System.out.println("Invalid media. " + audioType + " format not supported
                ");
        }
    }
}

interface AdvancedMediaPlayer {
    void playVlc(String fileName);
    void playMp4(String fileName);
}

class VlcPlayer implements AdvancedMediaPlayer {
    @Override
    public void playVlc(String fileName) {
        System.out.println("Playing vlc file. Name: " + fileName);
    }

    @Override
    public void playMp4(String fileName) {
        // do nothing
    }
}

class Mp4Player implements AdvancedMediaPlayer {
    @Override
    public void playVlc(String fileName) {
        // do nothing
    }

    @Override
    public void playMp4(String fileName) {
        System.out.println("Playing mp4 file. Name: " + fileName);
    }
}
class MediaAdapter implements MediaPlayer {
    AdvancedMediaPlayer advancedMusicPlayer;

    public MediaAdapter(String audioType) {
        if(audioType.equalsIgnoreCase("vlc")) {
            advancedMusicPlayer = new VlcPlayer();
        } else if(audioType.equalsIgnoreCase("mp4")) {
            advancedMusicPlayer = new Mp4Player();
        }
    }

    @Override
    public void play(String audioType, String fileName) {
        if(audioType.equalsIgnoreCase("vlc")) {
            advancedMusicPlayer.playVlc(fileName);
        } else if(audioType.equalsIgnoreCase("mp4")) {
            advancedMusicPlayer.playMp4(fileName);
```

```
        }
    }
}

class AudioPlayer implements MediaPlayer {
    MediaAdapter mediaAdapter;

    @Override
    public void play(String audioType, String fileName) {
        if(audioType.equalsIgnoreCase("mp3")) {
            System.out.println("Playing mp3 file. Name: " + fileName);
        } else if(audioType.equalsIgnoreCase("vlc") || audioType.equalsIgnoreCase("
            mp4")) {
            mediaAdapter = new MediaAdapter(audioType);
            mediaAdapter.play(audioType, fileName);
        } else {
            System.out.println("Invalid media. " + audioType + " format not supported
                ");
        }
    }
}

// Demonstration of Adapter Pattern
public class AdapterPatternDemo {
    public static void main(String[] args) {
        AudioPlayer audioPlayer = new AudioPlayer();

        audioPlayer.play("mp3", "beyond the horizon.mp3");
        audioPlayer.play("mp4", "alone.mp4");
        audioPlayer.play("vlc", "far far away.vlc");
        audioPlayer.play("avi", "mind me.avi");
    }
}
```

```
Playing mp3 file. Name: beyond the horizon.mp3
Playing mp4 file. Name: alone.mp4
Playing vlc file. Name: far far away.vlc
Invalid media. avi format not supported
```

The above example demonstrates how the MediaAdapter class implements the MediaPlayer interface and delegates calls to an AdvancedMediaPlayer instance based on the provided media type. The AudioPlayer class uses MediaAdapter to play different formats while maintaining a consistent interface for the client.

Advantages:

- Facilitates the reuse of existing classes whose interfaces are incompatible with the current system.
- Promotes the principle of least knowledge by reducing the amount of information needed by the client to use the service.
- Simplifies client code by providing a unified interface for diverse and complex subsystems.

The Adapter Pattern is particularly useful when integrating new features into an existing system or when a legacy component needs to interact with newer components.

3.3 The Bridge Pattern

The Bridge Pattern is a structural design pattern that decouples an abstraction from its implementation, allowing both to vary independently. This pattern is especially useful in scenarios where an abstraction can have multiple implementations, and it is desirable to avoid the explosion of class combinations.

In the Bridge Pattern, the abstraction is represented by two hierarchies: one for the abstraction and one for the implementation. These hierarchies are connected via composition, where the abstraction maintains a reference to the implementation. This provides the flexibility to change or extend the implementations without modifying the client code.

The implementation of the Bridge Pattern in Java involves creating an interface for the implementer and concrete classes for each implementation. The abstraction class will contain a reference to the implementer interface, and its methods will delegate the work to the implementer.

```
public interface Implementor {
    void operationImpl();
}

public class ConcreteImplementorA implements Implementor {
    @Override
    public void operationImpl() {
        System.out.println("ConcreteImplementorA: operationImpl");
    }
}

public class ConcreteImplementorB implements Implementor {
    @Override
    public void operationImpl() {
        System.out.println("ConcreteImplementorB: operationImpl");
    }
}

public abstract class Abstraction {
    protected Implementor implementor;

    protected Abstraction(Implementor implementor) {
        this.implementor = implementor;
    }

    public abstract void operation();
}

public class RefinedAbstraction extends Abstraction {
```

```
    public RefinedAbstraction(Implementor implementor) {
        super(implementor);
    }

    @Override
    public void operation() {
        implementor.operationImpl();
    }
}

// Usage
public class Client {
    public static void main(String[] args) {
        Implementor implementorA = new ConcreteImplementorA();
        Abstraction abstractionA = new RefinedAbstraction(implementorA);
        abstractionA.operation();

        Implementor implementorB = new ConcreteImplementorB();
        Abstraction abstractionB = new RefinedAbstraction(implementorB);
        abstractionB.operation();
    }
}
```

```
Output:
ConcreteImplementorA: operationImpl
ConcreteImplementorB: operationImpl
```

In the code above, Implementor defines the interface for the implementation classes. ConcreteImplementorA and ConcreteImplementorB provide specific implementations for the operationImpl method. The Abstraction class maintains a reference to the Implementor and delegates the operation to the Implementor through the operation method defined in RefinedAbstraction.

The Bridge Pattern brings several benefits:

- It enhances flexibility by enabling the separation of interface and implementation.
- It promotes strong encapsulation as the details of implementation are hidden from the client.
- It allows switching between different implementations dynamically at runtime.

However, the Bridge Pattern is not without its potential drawbacks. It can introduce complexity due to the increased number of classes and interfaces. Therefore, its use should be weighed against the complexity it introduces, particularly in simpler systems where fewer implementations are unlikely to change.

The Bridge Pattern is particularly useful in scenarios requiring:

- Platforms requiring different variations of an abstraction (e.g., different UI libraries or database drivers).
- Complex class hierarchies both on the abstraction and the implementation side.
- Situations where future extensions to both abstraction and implementation are anticipated independently.

A real-world analogy of the Bridge Pattern can be drawn from drawing APIs. Consider a drawing program that needs to draw shapes such as circles and squares on different platforms, such as Windows and Linux. Without the Bridge Pattern, you may end up with a class explosion like WindowsCircle, WindowsSquare, LinuxCircle, and LinuxSquare. With the Bridge Pattern, we can separate the shape hierarchy from the platform implementation.

```
public interface DrawingAPI {
    void drawCircle(double x, double y, double radius);
}

public class WindowsDrawingAPI implements DrawingAPI {
    @Override
    public void drawCircle(double x, double y, double radius) {
        System.out.println("Windows API drawing a circle at (" + x + ", " + y + ")
             with radius " + radius);
    }
}

public class LinuxDrawingAPI implements DrawingAPI {
    @Override
    public void drawCircle(double x, double y, double radius) {
        System.out.println("Linux API drawing a circle at (" + x + ", " + y + ") with
             radius " + radius);
    }
}

public abstract class Shape {
    protected DrawingAPI drawingAPI;

    protected Shape(DrawingAPI drawingAPI) {
        this.drawingAPI = drawingAPI;
    }

    public abstract void draw();
}

public class CircleShape extends Shape {
    private double x, y, radius;

    public CircleShape(double x, double y, double radius, DrawingAPI drawingAPI) {
        super(drawingAPI);
        this.x = x;
        this.y = y;
        this.radius = radius;
    }
```

```
    @Override
    public void draw() {
        drawingAPI.drawCircle(x, y, radius);
    }
}

// Usage
public class BridgePatternExample {
    public static void main(String[] args) {
        Shape circle1 = new CircleShape(1, 2, 3, new WindowsDrawingAPI());
        circle1.draw();

        Shape circle2 = new CircleShape(4, 5, 6, new LinuxDrawingAPI());
        circle2.draw();
    }
}
```

```
Output:
Windows API drawing a circle at (1.0, 2.0) with radius 3.0
Linux API drawing a circle at (4.0, 5.0) with radius 6.0
```

In this example, the DrawingAPI interface abstracts the drawing operations, while concrete implementations such as WindowsDrawingAPI and LinuxDrawingAPI provide platform-specific implementations. The Shape class leverages these drawing APIs to render a shape. The circle drawing can now be extended to different platforms without altering the shape abstraction, demonstrating the power and flexibility of the Bridge Pattern in software design.

3.4 The Composite Pattern

The Composite Pattern is a design pattern that enables the composition of objects into tree-like structures to represent part-whole hierarchies. It allows clients to treat individual objects and compositions of objects uniformly. This pattern is particularly useful when dealing with a hierarchy of objects where individual objects and composite objects are used in a similar manner. The Composite Pattern can simplify client code that would otherwise need to handle different classes of objects separately.

The key participants in the Composite Pattern include:

- **Component**: An abstract class or interface that declares the interface for objects in the composition.
- **Leaf**: A class that represents leaf objects in the composition. A leaf has no children.

- **Composite**: A class that represents composite objects, which may have children that are either leaves or other composites.

Here is a Java implementation of the Composite Pattern:

```
import java.util.ArrayList;
import java.util.List;

// Component
interface Graphic {
    void draw();
}

// Leaf
class Circle implements Graphic {
    @Override
    public void draw() {
        System.out.println("Circle");
    }
}

// Leaf
class Square implements Graphic {
    @Override
    public void draw() {
        System.out.println("Square");
    }
}

// Composite
class CompositeGraphic implements Graphic {
    // Collection of child graphics.
    private List<Graphic> childGraphics = new ArrayList<>();

    @Override
    public void draw() {
        for (Graphic graphic : childGraphics) {
            graphic.draw();
        }
    }

    // Adds the graphic to the composition.
    public void add(Graphic graphic) {
        childGraphics.add(graphic);
    }

    // Removes the graphic from the composition.
    public void remove(Graphic graphic) {
        childGraphics.remove(graphic);
    }
}
```

In this implementation, Graphic is the component interface that defines a method draw(). The Circle and Square classes implement this interface, making them leaves of the composition. The CompositeGraphic class implements the Graphic interface and contains a list of Graphic objects. It can add or remove Graphic objects to and from the list, and it delegates the draw() method to its children.

The main method demonstrates how to use the Composite Pattern:

```
public class CompositeDemo {
    public static void main(String[] args) {
        // Initialise leaf graphics
        Graphic circle1 = new Circle();
        Graphic square1 = new Square();
        Graphic circle2 = new Circle();

        // Initialise a composite graphic
        CompositeGraphic composite1 = new CompositeGraphic();
        composite1.add(circle1);
        composite1.add(square1);

        // Initialise another composite graphic
        CompositeGraphic composite2 = new CompositeGraphic();
        composite2.add(composite1);
        composite2.add(circle2);

        // Draw all graphics
        composite2.draw();
    }
}
```

The expected output of the program would be:

```
Circle
Square
Circle
```

This output demonstrates that the composite object composite2 correctly delegates the draw() method to its children and their children recursively.

The Composite Pattern generalizes the relationship between individual objects and composite objects. It is akin to a recursive tree structure where a composite can contain both primitives and other composites. This makes the pattern suitable for scenarios such as graphical component hierarchies, file system implementations, or any part-whole hierarchy.

To apply the Composite Pattern effectively:

- Ensure that composite objects and leaf objects implement the same interface, allowing them to be treated uniformly.
- Consider situations where you need to represent part-whole relationships, and ensure that your hierarchy does not require excessive navigation code in the client.
- Be mindful of the potential complexity added by the recursive structure, and use appropriate data structures and algorithms to manage the components.

Common pitfalls when implementing the Composite Pattern include:

- Over-complicating the design by including too many operations in the component interface, leading to a bloated interface.
- Assuming that leaf objects will never change to composite objects, which can break the uniformity if not managed properly.
- Ignoring the cost of operations in large hierarchies, as recursive operations can become expensive.

Understanding and correctly implementing the Composite Pattern can greatly enhance the flexibility and maintainability of object structures in software design. By leveraging this pattern, one can create systems that are both robust and adaptable, supporting the addition and removal of components with minimal impact on client code.

3.5 The Decorator Pattern

The Decorator Pattern is employed to dynamically extend the functionalities of objects at runtime without altering their structure. This pattern involves a set of decorator classes that are used to wrap concrete components. Decorators provide a flexible alternative to subclassing for extending functionality.

In adhering to the Open/Closed Principle, the Decorator Pattern ensures that classes remain open for extension but closed for modification. By wrapping objects, the pattern can dynamically add behavior without modifying the existing code. This is particularly beneficial in scenarios where future requirements might necessitate additional functionalities.

```
interface Component {
    void operation();
}

class ConcreteComponent implements Component {
    public void operation() {
        System.out.println("ConcreteComponent operation");
    }
}

abstract class Decorator implements Component {
    protected Component wrappee;

    Decorator(Component component) {
        this.wrappee = component;
```

```
    }

    public void operation() {
        wrappee.operation();
    }
}

class ConcreteDecoratorA extends Decorator {

    ConcreteDecoratorA(Component component) {
        super(component);
    }

    public void operation() {
        super.operation();
        addedBehaviorA();
    }

    private void addedBehaviorA() {
        System.out.println("ConcreteDecoratorA added behavior A");
    }
}

class ConcreteDecoratorB extends Decorator {

    ConcreteDecoratorB(Component component) {
        super(component);
    }

    public void operation() {
        super.operation();
        addedBehaviorB();
    }

    private void addedBehaviorB() {
        System.out.println("ConcreteDecoratorB added behavior B");
    }
}
```

In the provided example, Component defines a standard interface, while ConcreteComponent provides the base implementation. The Decorator class serves as the abstract base class for all decorators, maintaining a reference to a Component object, also known as the 'wrappee.' This class delegates original operation() calls to the wrapped object and introduces the potential for additional behavior by concrete decorators.

ConcreteDecoratorA and ConcreteDecoratorB add specific behaviors by extending the Decorator class and overriding the operation() method without altering the original ConcreteComponent. The additional behaviors addedBehaviorA() and addedBehaviorB() are included in these concrete decorators.

```
Component component = new ConcreteComponent();
Component decoratedComponentA = new ConcreteDecoratorA(component);
Component decoratedComponentB = new ConcreteDecoratorB(decoratedComponentA);
decoratedComponentB.operation();
```

The output of the execution is:

```
ConcreteComponent operation
ConcreteDecoratorA added behavior A
ConcreteDecoratorB added behavior B
```

It portrays a concrete example of the dynamic and flexible nature of the Decorator Pattern. The original operation from ConcreteComponent is executed, followed by additional behaviors introduced by ConcreteDecoratorA and ConcreteDecoratorB, demonstrating layered extensions.

The Decorator Pattern's utility extends to numerous use cases. One prevalent use is in graphical user interface (GUI) toolkits. For instance, the Java Swing library employs decorators to enhance visual components. Scrollbars, borders, and various effects can be added to GUI elements at runtime without modifying the core classes. Another common application is in I/O stream libraries, where decorators dynamically add buffering, filtering, and other functionalities to basic stream objects.

When implementing the Decorator Pattern, be cautious of certain pitfalls:

- **Overuse of Decorators:** Excessive layering of decorators can result in a complex and hard-to-debug system. Aim for a balanced approach to maintain clarity.
- **Performance Overhead:** As each decorator wraps another, the additional layers can introduce performance overhead due to the compounded calls to methods.
- **Object Creation Manageability:** Dynamic nature involves multiple objects and references, which might complicate memory management, especially in resource-constrained environments.

Applying this pattern strategically is crucial for leveraging its benefits while minimizing drawbacks. Endeavor to design your decorators with simplicity and clear separation of concerns to ensure they augment your system effectively.

3.6 The Facade Pattern

The Facade Pattern is a structural design pattern that provides a simplified interface to a complex subsystem. It aims to make a subsystem easier to use and understand by providing a higher-level interface that hides the system's complexities and inner workings. This pattern is particularly useful when dealing with large codebases or complex libraries requiring frequent interaction from client code.

Intent and Motivation

The primary intent of the Facade Pattern is to shield clients from complex subsystem interactions. By providing a single interface, the Facade simplifies the subsystem usage and reduces dependencies on multiple subsystem components. This encapsulated structure increases modularity and ensures easier maintenance.

Consider a case where an application needs to interact with a complex library, such as a multimedia framework or a financial transaction processing system. Without a Facade, client code would be tightly coupled with the various subsystem components, making the code hard to maintain and evolve. The Facade centralizes the interaction, making the client's code cleaner and less dependent on the subsystem's internal changes.

Implementation in Java

In Java, implementing a facade involves defining a class that wraps the interactions with the subsystem. This wrapper class exposes methods that correspond to high-level operations, internally managing the detailed interactions with the subsystem components.

Consider an example where a complex system of bank services includes multiple classes for managing accounts, processing loans, and handling customer support. Here's how a Facade could be implemented to simplify client interactions:

```
public class AccountService {
    public void openAccount(String accountHolder) {
        System.out.println("Account opened for " + accountHolder);
    }
}

public class LoanService {
    public void processLoan(String accountHolder, double amount) {
        System.out.println("Processing loan for " + accountHolder + " amount: " +
                amount);
    }
}

public class CustomerService {
    public void provideSupport(String accountHolder) {
        System.out.println("Providing support for " + accountHolder);
    }
}
```

We will now define a BankFacade class to encapsulate complex interactions.

```
public class BankFacade {
    private AccountService accountService;
    private LoanService loanService;
    private CustomerService customerService;

    public BankFacade() {
        this.accountService = new AccountService();
        this.loanService = new LoanService();
        this.customerService = new CustomerService();
    }

    public void createAccount(String accountHolder) {
        accountService.openAccount(accountHolder);
    }

    public void applyForLoan(String accountHolder, double amount) {
        loanService.processLoan(accountHolder, amount);
    }

    public void getSupport(String accountHolder) {
        customerService.provideSupport(accountHolder);
    }
}
```

Clients can use the BankFacade to perform operations without needing to interact with individual subsystem components.

```
public class Client {
    public static void main(String[] args) {
        BankFacade bankFacade = new BankFacade();

        bankFacade.createAccount("John Doe");
        bankFacade.applyForLoan("John Doe", 5000.00);
        bankFacade.getSupport("John Doe");
    }
}
```

```
Output:
Account opened for John Doe
Processing loan for John Doe amount: 5000.0
Providing support for John Doe
```

Benefits and Applicability

The Facade Pattern offers several advantages:

- **Simplifies Client Interaction**: Reduces the complexity for client classes, making the code more intuitive and less error-prone.
- **Loose Coupling**: Decouples the client from the subsystem, minimizing the impact of subsystem changes on the client code.
- **Improved Maintenance**: Centralizes subsystem interactions, making the system easier to maintain and evolve.

- **Enhances Readability**: High-level interfaces enhance the readability and comprehension of client code.

The Facade Pattern is applicable under the following scenarios:

- A system with many interdependent classes where a complex interaction is required.
- A legacy system with intricate and cumbersome APIs that need to be simplified for new development.
- Abstracting away complex or cluttered implementations for client convenience.
- Offering a consistent, high-level interface to different subsystems regardless of their internal implementations.

Key Considerations

While the Facade Pattern provides significant simplification, it is vital to consider the following aspects:

- **Over-simplification**: Avoid hiding too much functionality behind the Facade, as this could limit access to essential features.
- **Performance Overhead**: The Facade introduces an additional layer, which might lead to minimal performance overhead.
- **Design Consistency**: Ensure that the Facade accurately represents the subsystem's capabilities and constraints, maintaining consistent behavior.

The Facade Pattern serves as a strategic tool for managing complex systems and libraries by aligning with principles of modularity and encapsulation, offering structured and maintainable codebases.

3.7 The Flyweight Pattern

The Flyweight Pattern is a structural pattern designed to minimize memory usage by sharing common data between multiple objects. This pattern is particularly useful when dealing with a large number of objects that incur a significant memory cost, which can be reduced by storing shared parts of their state externally. In Java, this can be especially beneficial when creating applications that need to handle many similar objects simultaneously.

Flyweight Concept and Structure:

The core idea of the Flyweight Pattern is to use sharing to support large numbers of fine-grained objects efficiently. It achieves this by dividing the state of the objects into two categories: intrinsic and extrinsic. Intrinsic state is shared between multiple objects, whereas extrinsic state is unique to each object and must be maintained separately.

The structure of the Flyweight Pattern involves the following key components:

- Flyweight: An interface or abstract class that defines the methods for sharing.
- ConcreteFlyweight: Implements the Flyweight interface and adds storage for intrinsic state.
- FlyweightFactory: A factory that creates and manages Flyweight objects ensuring that flyweights are shared properly.
- Client: Maintains references to flyweights and computes or stores the extrinsic state.

Implementation in Java:

To illustrate this structural pattern, consider an example where we are working with a graphical application that draws a large number of similar shapes, such as circles, which have many common properties but also some that are unique to each instance.

First, we define the Flyweight interface:

```
public interface Flyweight {
    void draw(int x, int y, int color);
}
```

Next, we create a ConcreteFlyweight class that implements the Flyweight interface:

```
public class Circle implements Flyweight {
    private final String intrinsicState; // Shared state

    public Circle(String intrinsicState) {
        this.intrinsicState = intrinsicState;
    }
```

```
    @Override
    public void draw(int x, int y, int color) {
        System.out.println("Drawing Circle: " + intrinsicState +
            " at (" + x + ", " + y + ") with color " + color);
    }
}
```

Here, the Circle class has an intrinsic state representing shared properties of circles.

The FlyweightFactory is responsible for creating and managing instances of Flyweights:

```
import java.util.HashMap;
import java.util.Map;

public class FlyweightFactory {
    private static final Map<String, Flyweight> flyweights = new HashMap<>();

    public static Flyweight getFlyweight(String intrinsicState) {
        // Check if the flyweight already exists
        Flyweight flyweight = flyweights.get(intrinsicState);
        if (flyweight == null) {
            // Create new flyweight if not exists
            flyweight = new Circle(intrinsicState);
            flyweights.put(intrinsicState, flyweight);
        }
        return flyweight;
    }
}
```

The FlyweightFactory employs a map to store and retrieve existing flyweight instances, ensuring shared data is reused.

Finally, we showcase the client code interacting with the Flyweights:

```
public class Client {
    private static final int[] colors = {Color.RED, Color.GREEN, Color.BLUE};

    public static void main(String[] args) {
        for (int i = 0; i < 10; i++) {
            Flyweight flyweight = FlyweightFactory.getFlyweight("CircleType" + (i %
                3));
            flyweight.draw(i, i * 2, colors[i % colors.length]);
        }
    }
}
```

In this code, the client generates multiple instances of circles but ensures that common properties (intrinsic state) are shared to conserve memory.

Advantages and Disadvantages:

The Flyweight Pattern offers several advantages:

- **Memory Efficiency:** By sharing large portions of object state, memory consumption is significantly reduced.
- **Performance Improvement:** Lower memory use can lead to overall performance improvements, particularly in systems with limited resources.

However, it also introduces some trade-offs:

- **Increased Complexity:** Separating intrinsic and extrinsic state adds complexity to the system design.
- **Latency Costs:** Managing large numbers of objects and sharing states introduces a small overhead, which might impact system response times.

The Flyweight Pattern's ability to handle numerous similar objects efficiently, often at the cost of increased code complexity, makes it invaluable in memory-sensitive applications, such as those involving graphical elements or high-volume object instances.

3.8 The Proxy Pattern

The Proxy Pattern provides a surrogate or placeholder for another object to control access to it. In Java, this pattern plays a crucial role in situations where the real object is complicated or time-consuming to instantiate, or when additional operations like access control, lazy initialization, logging, or caching are needed.

The Proxy Pattern involves three key components: the Subject interface, the RealSubject class, and the Proxy class. The Subject interface declares the operations that are available on both the real and proxy objects. The RealSubject class defines the actual operations. The Proxy class controls access to the RealSubject by implementing the same interface as RealSubject and adding additional behavior where necessary.

To understand the practical implementation of the Proxy Pattern, consider the following example involving an image viewer application. Here, we want to load images only when required, to save memory and processing time.

```
public interface Image {
    void display();
}
```

The Image interface declares a single display() method which will be implemented by both the RealImage and the ProxyImage classes.

```
public class RealImage implements Image {
    private String fileName;

    public RealImage(String fileName) {
        this.fileName = fileName;
        loadFromDisk(fileName);
    }

    @Override
    public void display() {
        System.out.println("Displaying " + fileName);
    }

    private void loadFromDisk(String fileName) {
        System.out.println("Loading " + fileName);
    }
}
```

In this example, RealImage represents the object that requires intensive resources to instantiate. The loadFromDisk() method simulates the resource-intensive operation briefly.

```
public class ProxyImage implements Image {
    private RealImage realImage;
    private String fileName;

    public ProxyImage(String fileName) {
        this.fileName = fileName;
    }

    @Override
    public void display() {
        if (realImage == null) {
            realImage = new RealImage(fileName);
        }
        realImage.display();
    }
}
```

The ProxyImage class contains a reference to the RealImage. It initializes the RealImage only when the display() method is called. This ensures that the RealImage is loaded from disk only when it is actually needed.

```
public class ProxyPatternDemo {
    public static void main(String[] args) {
        Image image = new ProxyImage("test_image.jpg");

        // Image will be loaded from disk
```

```
        image.display();

        // Image will not be loaded from disk
        image.display();
    }
}
```

In the client code, we use the ProxyImage to display an image. On the first call to display(), the image is loaded from disk. On subsequent calls, the already loaded image is used without reloading, demonstrating the benefit of the Proxy Pattern in terms of performance optimization.

```
Output:
Loading test_image.jpg
Displaying test_image.jpg
Displaying test_image.jpg
```

Through this process, clients interact with the proxy rather than working directly with resource-intensive real objects. This approach enhances flexibility and control.

The Proxy Pattern can be categorized into different types:

- **Virtual Proxy**: Controls access to a resource that is expensive to create until it is needed. Our image example is a virtual proxy.
- **Remote Proxy**: Provides a local representation for an object that exists in a different address space (e.g., in remote method invocation).
- **Protection Proxy**: Controls access to resources based on access rights.
- **Smart Proxy**: Adds additional behavior when an object is accessed. For example, reference counting, logging, or access control.

Effective application of the Proxy Pattern can greatly improve system performance and scalability by managing resource-intensive objects more efficiently. Understanding the context and requirement is crucial for deciding when and how to deploy this pattern. The Proxy Pattern requires careful design to ensure that it does not introduce unnecessary complexity or performance bottlenecks.

3.9 Comparing Structural Patterns

Structural patterns play a vital role in developing flexible and maintainable object-oriented software. Each pattern addresses different aspects of structure and interactions between classes and objects. Understanding when and how to use these patterns effectively requires a detailed comparison that highlights their differences, similarities, and appropriate application contexts.

Adapter vs. Bridge

The Adapter and Bridge patterns both involve two interfacing hierarchies, but they serve different purposes.

The *Adapter Pattern* is primarily used to make incompatible interfaces work together. It does this by providing a wrapper that translates one interface to another, enabling integration of otherwise incompatible classes. This pattern is used when you need to integrate a class with a known interface into a different system without modifying the class itself.

```
class LegacyPrinter {
  public void print(String content) {
    // Print implementation
  }
}

interface Printer {
  void printDocument(String text);
}

class PrinterAdapter extends LegacyPrinter implements Printer {
  @Override
  public void printDocument(String text) {
    print(text);
  }
}
```

The *Bridge Pattern* focuses on separating an object's abstraction from its implementation, so that the two can vary independently. It is useful when you need to extend a single abstraction in multiple ways but also need to extend the implementation independently.

```
interface DrawingAPI {
  void drawCircle(double x, double y, double radius);
}

class DrawingAPI1 implements DrawingAPI {
  @Override
  public void drawCircle(double x, double y, double radius) {
    // Drawing implementation using API1
  }
```

```
}

class DrawingAPI2 implements DrawingAPI {
  @Override
  public void drawCircle(double x, double y, double radius) {
    // Drawing implementation using API2
  }
}

abstract class Shape {
  protected DrawingAPI drawingAPI;

  protected Shape(DrawingAPI drawingAPI) {
    this.drawingAPI = drawingAPI;
  }

  public abstract void draw();
}

class CircleShape extends Shape {
  private double x, y, radius;

  public CircleShape(double x, double y, double radius, DrawingAPI drawingAPI) {
    super(drawingAPI);
    this.x = x;
    this.y = y;
    this.radius = radius;
  }

  @Override
  public void draw() {
    drawingAPI.drawCircle(x, y, radius);
  }
}
```

Composite vs. Decorator

Both the Composite and Decorator patterns relate to object composition by allowing objects to be composed out of other objects. However, their purposes and structures differ.

The *Composite Pattern* is intended to allow individual objects and compositions of objects to be treated uniformly. It is commonly used to represent part-whole hierarchies, enabling clients to interact with single objects and compositions in a consistent manner.

```
interface Component {
  void operation();
}

class Leaf implements Component {
  @Override
  public void operation() {
    // Leaf-specific operation
  }
}

class Composite implements Component {
  private List<Component> children = new ArrayList<>();
```

```
  @Override
  public void operation() {
    for (Component child : children) {
      child.operation();
    }
  }

  public void add(Component component) {
    children.add(component);
  }

  public void remove(Component component) {
    children.remove(component);
  }
}
```

The *Decorator Pattern* is used to add responsibilities to objects dynamically. Decorators provide a flexible and reusable alternative to subclassing for extending functionality, making it particularly useful when object responsibilities need to be added or changed at runtime.

```
interface Coffee {
  double cost();
  String description();
}

class SimpleCoffee implements Coffee {
  @Override
  public double cost() {
    return 2.0;
  }

  @Override
  public String description() {
    return "Simple coffee";
  }
}

class CoffeeDecorator implements Coffee {
  protected Coffee coffee;

  public CoffeeDecorator(Coffee coffee) {
    this.coffee = coffee;
  }

  @Override
  public double cost() {
    return coffee.cost();
  }

  @Override
  public String description() {
    return coffee.description();
  }
}

class MilkDecorator extends CoffeeDecorator {
  public MilkDecorator(Coffee coffee) {
    super(coffee);
```

```
  }

  @Override
  public double cost() {
    return coffee.cost() + 0.5;
  }

  @Override
  public String description() {
    return coffee.description() + ", with milk";
  }
}
```

Facade vs. Proxy

The Facade and Proxy patterns might seem similar as they both use a single class to control access to others. However, their intents are distinct.

The *Facade Pattern* provides a simplified interface to a complex subsystem. It is designed to ease the usage and reduce the complexity of the subsystem by shielding the client from the intricate details.

```
class SubsystemA {
  public void operationA() {
    // Some operations
  }
}

class SubsystemB {
  public void operationB() {
    // Some operations
  }
}

class SubsystemC {
  public void operationC() {
    // Some operations
  }
}

class Facade {
  private SubsystemA subsystemA;
  private SubsystemB subsystemB;
  private SubsystemC subsystemC;

  public Facade() {
    subsystemA = new SubsystemA();
    subsystemB = new SubsystemB();
    subsystemC = new SubsystemC();
  }

  public void operation() {
    subsystemA.operationA();
    subsystemB.operationB();
    subsystemC.operationC();
  }
}
```

The *Proxy Pattern* provides a surrogate or placeholder for another object to control access to it, often to defer the full cost of its creation and initialization until it's needed (lazy initialization), to access it remotely, or to add a layer of security.

```
interface Image {
  void display();
}

class RealImage implements Image {
  private String filename;

  public RealImage(String filename) {
    this.filename = filename;
    loadFromDisk();
  }

  private void loadFromDisk() {
    // Load image from disk
  }

  @Override
  public void display() {
    // Display image
  }
}

class ProxyImage implements Image {
  private RealImage realImage;
  private String filename;

  public ProxyImage(String filename) {
    this.filename = filename;
  }

  @Override
  public void display() {
    if (realImage == null) {
      realImage = new RealImage(filename);
    }
    realImage.display();
  }
}
```

While sharing capabilities to extend or simplify accessing systems and object functionalities, understanding their unique purposes ensures that each pattern is used in optimal contexts. Exploring their specific applications clarifies their effective implementation, minimizing design complexity and enhancing maintainability.

3.10 Use Cases for Structural Patterns

Structural design patterns play an essential role in creating systems that are both flexible and robust. Each pattern provides unique solutions to common design problems, enabling more manageable and adaptable code structures. This section delves into specific use cases for each structural pattern discussed in this chapter. By examining these patterns in real-world contexts, we can better understand their practical applications and the architectural benefits they offer.

The Adapter Pattern

The Adapter Pattern is particularly useful when there is a need to integrate a new class or functionality into an existing system with incompatible interfaces. Consider a scenario where an application must leverage a third-party library that does not conform to the interface expected by the current system. The Adapter Pattern allows the new class to seamlessly interact with the existing system without modifying its source code.

```
public interface Target {
    void request();
}

public class Adaptee {
    public void specificRequest() {
        // Implementation code
    }
}

public class Adapter implements Target {
    private Adaptee adaptee;

    public Adapter(Adaptee adaptee) {
        this.adaptee = adaptee;
    }

    @Override
    public void request() {
        adaptee.specificRequest();
    }
}
```

In this example, Adapter makes Adaptee's specificRequest() method compatible with the Target interface, facilitating integration without altering the existing Adaptee class.

The Bridge Pattern

The Bridge Pattern decouples an abstraction from its implementation, making both independently variable. This is valuable in scenarios where both abstraction and implementation may frequently change. An example use case is developing a graphics rendering system where different graphics APIs (e.g., OpenGL, DirectX) can be utilized interchangeably.

```
public abstract class Shape {
    protected DrawAPI drawAPI;

    protected Shape(DrawAPI drawAPI){
        this.drawAPI = drawAPI;
    }
    public abstract void draw();
}

public interface DrawAPI {
    void drawCircle(int radius, int x, int y);
}

public class RedCircle implements DrawAPI {
    @Override
    public void drawCircle(int radius, int x, int y) {
        System.out.println("Drawing Circle[ color: red, radius: " + radius + ", x: " + x
                + ", y: " + y + "]");
    }
}

public class Circle extends Shape {
    private int x, y, radius;

    public Circle(int x, int y, int radius, DrawAPI drawAPI) {
        super(drawAPI);
        this.x = x;
        this.y = y;
        this.radius = radius;
    }

    @Override
    public void draw() {
        drawAPI.drawCircle(radius, x, y);
    }
}
```

Here, Circle uses a DrawAPI to delegate the drawing operation, allowing multiple drawing implementations to be interchanged without altering the shape abstraction.

The Composite Pattern

The Composite Pattern allows the creation of tree-like structures, where individual objects can be treated uniformly. This is especially useful in graphic user interface frameworks, where components such as buttons, panels, and windows must be managed uniformly.

```
import java.util.ArrayList;
import java.util.List;

public interface Graphic {
```

```
    void draw();
}

public class CompositeGraphic implements Graphic {
    private List<Graphic> childGraphics = new ArrayList<>();

    public void add(Graphic graphic) {
        childGraphics.add(graphic);
    }

    public void remove(Graphic graphic) {
        childGraphics.remove(graphic);
    }

    public void draw() {
        for (Graphic graphic : childGraphics) {
            graphic.draw();
        }
    }
}

public class Ellipse implements Graphic {
    @Override
    public void draw() {
        System.out.println("Ellipse");
    }
}

public class Line implements Graphic {
    @Override
    public void draw() {
        System.out.println("Line");
    }
}
```

In this example, CompositeGraphic can contain both Ellipse and Line objects, treating them uniformly for drawing operations.

The Decorator Pattern

The Decorator Pattern is ideal for adding responsibilities to objects dynamically and transparently. A real-world use case is enhancing window components in a GUI application, where additional features like borders or scrollbars can be dynamically added.

```
public interface Window {
    void draw();
}

public class SimpleWindow implements Window {
    @Override
    public void draw() {
        System.out.println("Simple Window");
    }
}

public class WindowDecorator implements Window {
    protected Window decoratedWindow;
```

```
    public WindowDecorator(Window decoratedWindow) {
        this.decoratedWindow = decoratedWindow;
    }

    @Override
    public void draw() {
        decoratedWindow.draw();
    }
}

public class ScrollDecorator extends WindowDecorator {
    public ScrollDecorator(Window decoratedWindow) {
        super(decoratedWindow);
    }

    @Override
    public void draw() {
        super.draw();
        System.out.println("Adding scroll bars");
    }
}
```

Here, WindowDecorator extends the functionality of SimpleWindow by adding optional features, allowing for flexible enhancements without modifying the base class.

The Facade Pattern

The Facade Pattern provides a simplified interface to a complex subsystem. This is particularly useful in large systems, where interaction with numerous classes and interfaces can be streamlined. Consider a library management system handling book loans, returns, and user notifications.

```
public class LibraryFacade {
    private BookLoanSystem bookLoanSystem;
    private BookReturnSystem bookReturnSystem;
    private NotificationSystem notificationSystem;

    public LibraryFacade() {
        bookLoanSystem = new BookLoanSystem();
        bookReturnSystem = new BookReturnSystem();
        notificationSystem = new NotificationSystem();
    }

    public void borrowBook(String bookId, String memberId) {
        if (bookLoanSystem.loan(bookId, memberId)) {
            notificationSystem.notify("Book borrowed: " + bookId);
        }
    }

    public void returnBook(String bookId, String memberId) {
        bookReturnSystem.returnBook(bookId, memberId);
        notificationSystem.notify("Book returned: " + bookId);
    }
}
```

In this instance, LibraryFacade simplifies the interaction with the book loan and return systems, hiding the complexity from the client.

The Flyweight Pattern

The Flyweight Pattern benefits systems that require a large number of similar objects by minimizing memory usage. A classic use case is rendering text, where individual character objects can share common state, such as font style, but differ in intrinsic state, like position.

```
import java.util.HashMap;

public class FlyweightFactory {
    private static final HashMap<String, Character> flyweights = new HashMap<>();

    public static Character getCharacter(String key) {
        Character character = flyweights.get(key);
        if (character == null) {
            character = new Character(key);
            flyweights.put(key, character);
        }
        return character;
    }
}

public class Character {
    private final String symbol;

    public Character(String symbol) {
        this.symbol = symbol;
    }

    public void display(int x, int y) {
        System.out.println("Character " + symbol + " at position (" + x + ", " + y +
            ")");
    }
}
```

Using FlyweightFactory to manage character instances minimizes memory overhead, especially efficient for large-scale text rendering applications.

The Proxy Pattern

The Proxy Pattern acts as an intermediary for another object, providing a surrogate or placeholder. This is advantageous in situations requiring additional functionality like access control, lazy initialization, or logging. For instance, a virtual proxy can control access to a resource-intensive object, initializing it only on demand.

```
public interface Image {
    void display();
}

public class RealImage implements Image {
    private String fileName;
```

```
    public RealImage(String fileName){
        this.fileName = fileName;
        loadFromDisk();
    }

    private void loadFromDisk() {
        System.out.println("Loading " + fileName);
    }

    @Override
    public void display() {
        System.out.println("Displaying " + fileName);
    }
}

public class ProxyImage implements Image {
    private RealImage realImage;
    private String fileName;

    public ProxyImage(String fileName) {
        this.fileName = fileName;
    }

    @Override
    public void display() {
        if (realImage == null) {
            realImage = new RealImage(fileName);
        }
        realImage.display();
    }
}
```

In this example, ProxyImage controls access to RealImage, deferring instantiation until the display() method is called.

Through these use cases, we can observe the versatile applications of structural patterns in creating efficient, well-structured systems. Each pattern addresses a unique aspect of software design, providing robust solutions to common and complex problems, enhancing code maintainability and evolution.

3.11 Best Practices in Applying Structural Patterns

When applying structural patterns in software design, adhering to best practices can greatly enhance the flexibility, maintainability, and efficiency of the resulting architecture. This section delineates several critical best practices that can inform the application of structural patterns such as Adapter, Bridge, Composite, Decorator, Facade, Flyweight, and Proxy in Java.

- **Understanding Requirements:** Before selecting any structural pattern, it is essential to have a thorough understanding of the problem at hand. Analyze the system requirements meticulously to determine whether a structural pattern is necessary and, if so, which one would be the most appropriate. For example, if the system requires integrating with a legacy component, the Adapter pattern may be useful.

- **Keeping Interfaces Stable:** When employing structural patterns, such as the Adapter or Bridge patterns, it is crucial to design stable interfaces. This stability ensures that changes in implementation do not affect clients. Make sure the public interfaces are well-designed and encompass all necessary functionalities while keeping future expandability in mind.

- **Promoting Reusability:** Structural patterns should be designed in a way to promote reusability across different parts of the application. For instance, the Composite pattern allows treating individual objects and compositions of objects uniformly, promoting the reuse of component objects across diverse scenarios.

- **Minimizing Dependencies:** Reducing dependencies between different parts of the system can be achieved using patterns like the Facade or Proxy. The Facade pattern offers a simplified interface to a complex subsystem, thereby minimizing coupling between clients and the subsystem. Likewise, the Proxy pattern helps control access to an object, reducing the dependencies and potential impact of changes.

- **Optimizing Performance:** Performance consideration is critical when applying structural patterns. For instance, the Flyweight pattern is particularly beneficial in reducing memory usage when dealing with a large number of similar objects. It shares as much data as possible with other similar objects; when using this pattern, ensure intrinsic state is shared and extrinsic state is passed whenever the object is used.

- **Applying the Single Responsibility Principle:** Ensure that each pattern applied adheres to the single responsibility principle. For example, when using the Decorator pattern, each decorator should focus on a single area of concern, thus enhancing clarity and ease of maintenance.

- **Using Composition Over Inheritance:** Emphasize composition over inheritance to achieve flexible reuse of classes. Patterns like

Decorator, Composite, and Bridge exemplify this principle by enabling behavior to be added to classes dynamically or permitting multiple implementations to be interchanged without altering the client code.

- **Ensuring Clear Documentation:** Maintaining comprehensive documentation when applying structural patterns is vital. Each pattern's role, the problem it solves, and how it integrates into the broader system should be clearly articulated. This practice helps future developers understand and extend the system effectively without unintended consequences.

An exemplary use of the Adapter pattern in Java can be seen in adapting an existing interface to meet the requirements of a new client.

```
public interface Target {
    void request();
}

public class Adaptee {
    public void specificRequest() {
        System.out.println("Called specificRequest()");
    }
}

public class Adapter implements Target {
    private Adaptee adaptee;

    public Adapter(Adaptee adaptee) {
        this.adaptee = adaptee;
    }

    @Override
    public void request() {
        adaptee.specificRequest();
    }
}
```

In this example, Target specifies the domain-specific interface that the client uses. Adaptee contains some useful behavior, but its interface does not conform to Target. The Adapter class bridges this gap by implementing Target and internally calling Adaptee's methods.

Another illustration involves the Composite pattern, demonstrating how it enables uniform treatment of individual and composite objects.

```
import java.util.ArrayList;
import java.util.List;

interface Component {
    void operation();
}

class Leaf implements Component {
```

```
    @Override
    public void operation() {
        System.out.println("Leaf operation");
    }
}

class Composite implements Component {
    private List<Component> children = new ArrayList<>();

    public void add(Component child) {
        children.add(child);
    }

    public void remove(Component child) {
        children.remove(child);
    }

    @Override
    public void operation() {
        for (Component child : children) {
            child.operation();
        }
    }
}
```

In the Composite pattern, Component declares the interface that both Leaf and Composite implement. Leaf represents an individual object, while Composite represents an object that can have children, allowing clients to treat them uniformly and enhancing flexibility and reusability.

Clear, effective implementation and adherence to these best practices not only facilitate the creation of robust and flexible systems but also significantly streamline maintenance and scalability in the long run.

3.12 Common Mistakes and How to Avoid Them

Understanding structural patterns is essential for constructing maintainable and flexible software. However, there are common pitfalls that developers encounter when implementing these patterns. This section identifies these mistakes, explains why they occur, and provides strategies to avoid them.

Misuse of Patterns

A frequent mistake is the misuse of structural patterns, often resulting from a misunderstanding of the problem the pattern aims to solve. For instance, developers might use the Facade pattern to simplify an interface but end up concealing important interactions within the system.

Alternatively, the Adapter pattern might be incorrectly employed in situations where a structural change in the class hierarchy would be more appropriate.

- **Solution:** Prior to selecting a pattern, thoroughly analyze the problem domain to ensure the pattern aligns with the intended use case. Document the rationale for choosing a specific pattern and consider alternative solutions to confirm its suitability.

Overgeneralization

In attempts to make systems highly flexible, developers often overgeneralize structures. This is a common error with the Composite pattern, where developers might create overly abstract hierarchies leading to unwieldy and hard-to-understand code.

- **Solution:** Apply the KISS (Keep It Simple, Stupid) principle. Start with the simplest version that solves the problem and derive more general solutions only when clear requirements arise. Use concrete examples to validate the necessity of abstraction layers.

Inefficient Use of Memory

The Flyweight pattern is designed to minimize memory usage by sharing objects. A common mistake is to misuse this pattern, leading to increased memory consumption or degraded performance due to excessive object sharing.

- **Solution:** Profile the application to ensure appropriate use of the Flyweight pattern. Avoid premature optimization; implement the pattern only after confirming significant memory benefits. Ensure that the overhead of managing shared objects does not outweigh their memory benefits.

Circular Dependencies

Circular dependencies can occur when applying structural patterns such as Decorator or Proxy, leading to tight coupling and increased difficulty in maintaining the code.

- **Solution:** Conduct dependency checks and use dependency inversion principles to break cycles. Consider dependency injection and other design principles that promote loose coupling. Review and refactor code periodically to identify and resolve any circular dependencies.

Overuse of Patterns

Patterns should solve specific problems, but there is a tendency to overuse them, leading to over-engineered solutions that are complex and difficult to maintain. For example, employing the Bridge pattern where a simple inheritance hierarchy would suffice can introduce unnecessary complexity.

- **Solution:** Focus on simplicity and clarity. Evaluate patterns based on actual requirements and avoid ingraining patterns into the code merely because they are available. Discuss with peers and review architectural decisions to align on the necessity and appropriateness of patterns.

Neglect of Pattern Composition

When multiple patterns are used together, developers might overlook how these patterns compose and interact. Poor pattern composition can lead to unintended behaviors and maintenance challenges.

- **Solution:** Carefully document and review interactions between patterns. Create sequence diagrams and flow charts to visualize interactions. Conduct code reviews with a focus on pattern composition and synergy.

Rigid Structures

While structural patterns aim for flexibility, their incorrect application can result in rigid structures. Misimplementing the Adapter or Facade patterns can lead to systems that are hard to change and adapt.

- **Solution:** Regularly revisit and refactor implementations to maintain flexibility. Use automated tests to ensure that changes do not break the system, thus retaining adaptability. Encourage a culture of continuous improvement and revisitation of design choices.

Understanding these common mistakes and how to avoid them is crucial for leveraging structural patterns effectively. By recognizing and mitigating these errors, a developer can create software that is robust, flexible, and easier to maintain.

Chapter 4

Behavioral Patterns: Managing Algorithms and Responsibilities

This chapter focuses on Behavioral Patterns, which are essential for defining the communication and responsibilities among objects. It examines patterns such as Chain of Responsibility, Command, Interpreter, Iterator, Mediator, Memento, Observer, State, Strategy, Template Method, and Visitor. For each pattern, the chapter provides a detailed look at implementation strategies in Java, the specific problems they address, and their benefits and drawbacks. Additionally, it includes best practices, common mistakes to avoid, and real-world examples to enhance understanding and practical application.

4.1 Introduction to Behavioral Patterns

Behavioral patterns define the ways in which classes or objects interact and communicate with each other. Unlike creational patterns, which concern themselves with object creation mechanisms, or structural patterns, which deal with object composition, behavioral patterns delineate the protocols for object cooperation. This often leads to realizing a particular flow of control within a system, thereby ensuring system responsibility distribution and enhanced manageability.

The intent behind behavioral patterns is to encapsulate, decouple, or manage complex flows within software applications by integrating a systematic approach to handle responsibilities. With behavioral patterns, software developers can simplify complex control flows by breaking them into smaller, reusable, and well-defined interactions among objects.

Key Behavioral Patterns Overview

- **Chain of Responsibility**: This pattern allows an object to pass a request along a chain of potential handlers until the request is processed.
- **Command**: Encapsulates a request as an object, thereby allowing for parameterization of clients.
- **Interpreter**: Defines a grammatical representation for a language and provides an interpreter to deal with this representation.
- **Iterator**: Provides a way to access the elements of an aggregate object sequentially without exposing its underlying representation.
- **Mediator**: Defines an object that encapsulates how a set of objects interact, promoting loose coupling by preventing objects from referring to each other explicitly.
- **Memento**: Captures and externalizes an object's internal state without violating encapsulation, allowing the object to be restored to this state later.
- **Observer**: Defines a one-to-many dependency between objects so that when one object changes state, all its dependents are notified and updated automatically.
- **State**: Allows an object to alter its behavior when its internal state changes. The object will appear to change its class.
- **Strategy**: Defines a family of algorithms, encapsulates each one, and makes them interchangeable.
- **Template Method**: Defines the skeleton of an algorithm in a method, deferring some steps to subclasses.

- **Visitor**: Represents an operation to be performed on the elements of an object structure.

Each pattern addresses specific challenges and scenarios, lending themselves to a wide array of design situations. Let us look at how these patterns can be effectively implemented and utilized within Java, focusing on their structure and applicability.

Example: Chain of Responsibility Pattern

The Chain of Responsibility pattern is particularly useful for dealing with scenarios where multiple objects can handle a request, but the exact object that will service the request isn't known until runtime. It's a way of passing a request between a chain of objects, where each object in the chain can either handle the request or pass it along.

Consider an example in which we need to process various types of log messages, such as INFO, DEBUG, and ERROR, each potentially handled by a different logger. The Logger class abstracts a single handler:

```
abstract class Logger {
    public static int INFO = 1;
    public static int DEBUG = 2;
    public static int ERROR = 3;

    protected int level;
    protected Logger nextLogger;

    public void setNextLogger(Logger nextLogger) {
        this.nextLogger = nextLogger;
    }

    public void logMessage(int level, String message) {
        if (this.level <= level) {
            write(message);
        }
        if (nextLogger != null) {
            nextLogger.logMessage(level, message);
        }
    }

    abstract protected void write(String message);
}
```

Concrete logger implementations then extend this abstract class:

```
class ConsoleLogger extends Logger {
    public ConsoleLogger(int level) {
        this.level = level;
    }

    @Override
    protected void write(String message) {
        System.out.println("Standard Console::Logger: " + message);
    }
}
```

```
class ErrorLogger extends Logger {
    public ErrorLogger(int level) {
        this.level = level;
    }

    @Override
    protected void write(String message) {
        System.err.println("Error Console::Logger: " + message);
    }
}

class FileLogger extends Logger {
    public FileLogger(int level) {
        this.level = level;
    }

    @Override
    protected void write(String message) {
        System.out.println("File::Logger: " + message);
    }
}
```

To set up the chain of responsibility, we instantiate and link the handlers:

```
public class ChainPatternDemo {
    private static Logger getChainOfLoggers() {
        Logger errorLogger = new ErrorLogger(Logger.ERROR);
        Logger fileLogger = new FileLogger(Logger.DEBUG);
        Logger consoleLogger = new ConsoleLogger(Logger.INFO);

        errorLogger.setNextLogger(fileLogger);
        fileLogger.setNextLogger(consoleLogger);

        return errorLogger;
    }

    public static void main(String[] args) {
        Logger loggerChain = getChainOfLoggers();

        loggerChain.logMessage(Logger.INFO, "This is an informational message.");
        loggerChain.logMessage(Logger.DEBUG, "This is a debug level message.");
        loggerChain.logMessage(Logger.ERROR, "This is an error message.");
    }
}
```

```
Standard Console::Logger: This is an informational message.
File::Logger: This is a debug level message.
Standard Console::Logger: This is a debug level message.
Error Console::Logger: This is an error message.
File::Logger: This is an error message.
Standard Console::Logger: This is an error message.
```

By decoupling the sender of a request from its receiver, the Chain of Responsibility pattern promotes loose coupling between objects. This modular approach can greatly improve code maintainability and flexibility, especially in complex systems where handling responsibilities dynamically is crucial.

The introduction provides a high-level understanding of how behavioral patterns operate and their benefits in managing object communication and responsibilities within a system. Subsequent sections will delve into the specific implementation, advantages, and challenges associated with each pattern in detail, reinforcing the key concepts introduced here.

4.2 The Chain of Responsibility Pattern

The Chain of Responsibility pattern aims to decouple the sender of a request from its receiver, giving multiple objects a chance to handle the request. This pattern is defined by creating a chain of receiver objects, where each object contains a reference to the next handler in the sequence. When a request is received, it is passed along the chain until an object capable of processing it handles it.

This pattern is beneficial when multiple handlers could potentially fulfill a request, but only one should ultimately do so. It enhances flexibility in assigning responsibilities to objects and promotes loose coupling between the objects.

Concepts and Structure

A typical Chain of Responsibility pattern contains the following components:

- Handler: An interface or abstract class defining an operation for handling requests, as well as a method for setting the next handler in the chain.
- Concrete Handler: Specific subclasses or implementations of Handler that either handle the request or pass it to the next handler.
- Client: The client object that initiates the request to be processed.

Consider the following example implementation in Java that applies these components to process a chain of logging requests, each request being handled by different levels of logging severity.

```
abstract class Logger {
    public static int INFO = 1;
    public static int DEBUG = 2;
    public static int ERROR = 3;
```

```
    protected int level;

    // next element in chain of responsibility
    protected Logger nextLogger;

    public void setNextLogger(Logger nextLogger) {
        this.nextLogger = nextLogger;
    }

    public void logMessage(int level, String message) {
        if (this.level <= level) {
            write(message);
        }
        if (nextLogger != null) {
            nextLogger.logMessage(level, message);
        }
    }

    abstract protected void write(String message);
}

class ConsoleLogger extends Logger {
    public ConsoleLogger(int level) {
        this.level = level;
    }

    @Override
    protected void write(String message) {
        System.out.println("Standard Console::Logger: " + message);
    }
}

class ErrorLogger extends Logger {
    public ErrorLogger(int level) {
        this.level = level;
    }

    @Override
    protected void write(String message) {
        System.out.println("Error Console::Logger: " + message);
    }
}

class FileLogger extends Logger {
    public FileLogger(int level) {
        this.level = level;
    }

    @Override
    protected void write(String message) {
        System.out.println("File::Logger: " + message);
    }
}
```

Client Code

The client is responsible for building the chain and making requests. Each logger in the chain is set with a specific severity level. The client constructs the chain by setting the next logger for each handler as demonstrated below:

```
public class ChainPatternDemo {

    private static Logger getChainOfLoggers() {
        Logger errorLogger = new ErrorLogger(Logger.ERROR);
        Logger fileLogger = new FileLogger(Logger.DEBUG);
        Logger consoleLogger = new ConsoleLogger(Logger.INFO);

        errorLogger.setNextLogger(fileLogger);
        fileLogger.setNextLogger(consoleLogger);

        return errorLogger;
    }

    public static void main(String[] args) {
        Logger loggerChain = getChainOfLoggers();

        loggerChain.logMessage(Logger.INFO, "This is an information.");
        loggerChain.logMessage(Logger.DEBUG, "This is a debug level information.");
        loggerChain.logMessage(Logger.ERROR, "This is an error information.");
    }
}
```

When executed, the client code will produce the following output:

```
Standard Console::Logger: This is an information.
File::Logger: This is a debug level information.
Standard Console::Logger: This is a debug level information.
Error Console::Logger: This is an error information.
File::Logger: This is an error information.
Standard Console::Logger: This is an error information.
```

Benefits

- Reduces coupling: The sender of a request is decoupled from its receiver since the chain can be modified independently of the client that sends requests to these handlers.
- Flexibility in assigning responsibility: Responsibility for handling a request is determined at runtime based on the chains composition.
- Enhances system robustness: Adding or removing handlers in the chain can be done dynamically without affecting the client code.

Drawbacks

- Uncertain outcomes: There is no automatic guarantee that a request will be handled. If the chain is not properly configured, requests could go unhandled.

- Debugging complexity: Tracing the flow of a request through a chain can be challenging, especially when chains are long or involve many handlers with potential loops.

Best practices when implementing the Chain of Responsibility pattern include ensuring that the chain has at least one concrete handler capable of handling a request. Additionally, avoid long chains to minimize performance overhead and complexity. Properly document the chain configuration and the scenarios under which each handler should be activated to maintain clarity in the system.

4.3 The Command Pattern

The Command Pattern is an essential behavioral design pattern used to encapsulate a request as an object, thereby allowing users to parameterize clients with queues, requests, and operations. It also enables the storage of requests in a sequence to support operations such as undoable actions.

The Command Pattern involves several key participants:

- Command: An interface for executing an operation.
- ConcreteCommand: A class that implements the Command interface to perform actions on the receiver objects.
- Client: The initiator of the command object.
- Invoker: The object that invokes the command.
- Receiver: The object that performs the actual operation.

Command Interface

The command interface declares a method for executing a command. In Java, it may look as follows:

```
public interface Command {
    void execute();
}
```

ConcreteCommand Class

The ConcreteCommand class implements the Command interface, defining the binding between the action and the receiver. It calls the appropriate operations on the receiver.

```
public class LightOnCommand implements Command {
    private Light light;

    public LightOnCommand(Light light) {
        this.light = light;
    }

    @Override
    public void execute() {
        light.on();
    }
}
```

In the example above, LightOnCommand is a concrete implementation of the Command interface. It executes the on() method of the Light receiver.

Client Class

The client class creates Command objects and sets their receivers. It might be responsible for creating the ConcreteCommand objects.

```
public class RemoteControlTest {
    public static void main(String[] args) {
        RemoteControl remote = new RemoteControl();
        Light livingRoomLight = new Light("Living Room");

        LightOnCommand livingRoomLightOn = new LightOnCommand(
                livingRoomLight);

        remote.setCommand(livingRoomLightOn);
        remote.buttonWasPressed();
    }
}
```

Invoker Class

The invoker class knows how to execute a command but does not know how the command operates upon the receiver.

```
public class RemoteControl {
    private Command command;

    public void setCommand(Command command) {
        this.command = command;
    }

    public void buttonWasPressed() {
        command.execute();
    }
}
```

Receiver Class

The receiver contains some business logic. Almost any object can act as a receiver.

```
public class Light {
    private String location;

    // Constructor
    public Light(String location) {
        this.location = location;
    }

    public void on() {
        System.out.println(location + " light is on");
    }

    public void off() {
        System.out.println(location + " light is off");
    }
}
```

The above implementation allows the invocation of commands without knowing the exact details of the operation, adhering to the Command Pattern's core principle. This pattern offers several advantages, including:

- Decoupling the objects that send requests from the objects that execute these requests.
- Allowing for easy addition of new commands without changing existing code.
- Providing support for undoable operations.

Undo Operation

To implement an undo operation, the Command interface can define an undo() method:

```
public interface Command {
    void execute();
    void undo();
}
```

The concrete commands need to implement the undo() method. For example:

```
public class LightOffCommand implements Command {
    private Light light;

    public LightOffCommand(Light light) {
        this.light = light;
    }

    @Override
    public void execute() {
        light.off();
```

```
    }

    @Override
    public void undo() {
        light.on();
    }
}
```

The Invoker class can then maintain a history of executed commands and invoke the undo() method to reverse actions.

```
import java.util.Stack;

public class RemoteControlWithUndo {
    private Command command;
    private Stack<Command> commandHistory = new Stack<>();

    public void setCommand(Command command) {
        this.command = command;
    }

    public void buttonWasPressed() {
        command.execute();
        commandHistory.push(command);
    }

    public void undoButtonWasPressed() {
        if (!commandHistory.isEmpty()) {
            Command undoCommand = commandHistory.pop();
            undoCommand.undo();
        }
    }
}
```

This implementation ensures that each command can be undone by maintaining a history stack, thus supporting the undo functionality seamlessly.

Macro Commands

Macro commands allow grouping multiple commands into a single command, which can be executed in one go. This is achieved by creating a MacroCommand class:

```
public class MacroCommand implements Command {
    private Command[] commands;

    public MacroCommand(Command[] commands) {
        this.commands = commands;
    }

    @Override
    public void execute() {
        for (Command command : commands) {
            command.execute();
        }
    }
```

```
    @Override
    public void undo() {
        for (Command command : commands) {
            command.undo();
        }
    }
}
```

Application of Command Pattern

The Command Pattern is widely used in designing frameworks that utilize operations such as transaction management systems, request handling queues, and GUI-based applications. Systems requiring an audit log of actions, or the ability to support undo operations, benefit greatly from the Command Pattern.

This section builds a comprehensive understanding of the Command Pattern through a detailed yet straightforward illustration of its components, implementation, and practical applications.

4.4 The Interpreter Pattern

The Interpreter Pattern is a design pattern that specifies how to evaluate sentences in a language. This pattern is primarily used to define a grammatical representation for a language and provide an interpreter to deal with this grammar. It is particularly useful in scenarios where domain-specific languages (DSLs) are required to interpret user input or execute certain tasks defined dynamically during runtime.

The structure of the Interpreter Pattern involves defining a hierarchy of language elements (usually, this means tokens or other atomic components) that can be interpreted by executing their methods. These elements are typically represented as classes in Object-Oriented Programming (OOP).

Java, with its strong typing and object-oriented features, provides an excellent environment for implementing the Interpreter Pattern. Below, we delve into the essential components of this pattern and demonstrate their implementation in Java.

Components of the Interpreter Pattern:

- $\mathrm{AbstractExpression}$: Declares an abstract $\mathrm{interpret(Context)}$ method.
- $\mathrm{TerminalExpression}$: Implements the interpretation operation as-

sociated with terminal symbols in the grammar.

- NonTerminalExpression: Implements the interpretation operation associated with non-terminal symbols in the grammar.
- Context: Contains information that is global to the interpreter.
- Client: Constructs the abstract syntax tree representing a particular sentence in the language that the interpreter can interpret.

Example Implementation in Java:

Consider a simple language for interpreting mathematical expressions consisting of addition and subtraction.

```
import java.util.Stack;

abstract class Expression {
    public abstract int interpret();
}

class Number extends Expression {
    private int number;

    public Number(int number) {
        this.number = number;
    }

    public int interpret() {
        return this.number;
    }
}

class Plus extends Expression {
    private Expression leftExpression;
    private Expression rightExpression;

    public Plus(Expression left, Expression right) {
        this.leftExpression = left;
        this.rightExpression = right;
    }

    public int interpret() {
        return leftExpression.interpret() + rightExpression.interpret();
    }
}

class Minus extends Expression {
    private Expression leftExpression;
    private Expression rightExpression;

    public Minus(Expression left, Expression right) {
        this.leftExpression = left;
        this.rightExpression = right;
    }

    public int interpret() {
        return leftExpression.interpret() - rightExpression.interpret();
    }
```

```
}

class InterpreterEngine {
    public int interpret(String expression) {
        Stack<Expression> stack = new Stack<>();

        for (String token: expression.split(" ")) {
            if (token.equals("+")) {
                Expression right = stack.pop();
                Expression left = stack.pop();
                Expression operator = new Plus(left, right);
                int result = operator.interpret();
                stack.push(new Number(result));
            } else if (token.equals("-")) {
                Expression right = stack.pop();
                Expression left = stack.pop();
                Expression operator = new Minus(left, right);
                int result = operator.interpret();
                stack.push(new Number(result));
            } else {
                Expression number = new Number(Integer.parseInt(token));
                stack.push(number);
            }
        }
        return stack.pop().interpret();
    }
}
```

```
Output for "7 3 - 2 1 + +"
Result: 7 - 3 + (2 + 1) = 7
```

In the above implementation, the 'Expression' class serves as the AbstractExpression. The Number, Plus, and Minus classes act as the TerminalExpression and NonTerminalExpression components by implementing the interpret() method. The InterpreterEngine class functions as the Context, containing the parsing logic and managing the evaluation of the expression.

Advantages:

- Easy to change and extend the grammar.
- Simple implementation for small grammars.

Drawbacks:

- Complex grammars are hard to maintain.
- Performance can be an issue for complex grammars due to depth of recursion.

Use Cases:

- Simple DSLs.

- Configuration languages.
- Parsing and interpreting expressions in mathematical applications.

Building upon these concepts, you can handle more complex scenarios by introducing a more sophisticated parsing mechanism or supporting additional operations within the language. The Interpreter Pattern brings a robust way to evaluate custom and domain-specific languages within Java, ensuring that extensions and modifications in the language can be managed with minimal disruption to existing code.

4.5 The Iterator Pattern

The Iterator Pattern is a fundamental behavioral design pattern in Java that provides a way to access the elements of a collection object sequentially without exposing its underlying representation. This pattern is particularly useful when you need to traverse a collection, such as a list or a set, without needing to understand the intricacies of the collection's internal structure.

The key components of the Iterator Pattern include the Iterator interface, which defines methods for traversing elements, and the ConcreteIterator classes, which implement this interface for specific collection types. Java provides a built-in iterator mechanism through the java.util.Iterator interface, which includes the following primary methods:

- hasNext(): Returns true if the iteration has more elements.
- next(): Returns the next element in the iteration.
- remove(): Removes from the underlying collection the last element that was returned by the iterator (optional operation).

Below is an example implementation of an iterator for a custom collection in Java:

```
import java.util.Iterator;
import java.util.NoSuchElementException;

public class CustomCollection<T> implements Iterable<T> {
    private T[] elements;
    private int size = 0;
```

```
    public CustomCollection(int capacity) {
        elements = (T[]) new Object[capacity];
    }

    public void add(T element) {
        if (size == elements.length) {
            throw new IllegalStateException("Collection is full");
        }
        elements[size++] = element;
    }

    @Override
    public Iterator<T> iterator() {
        return new CustomIterator();
    }

    private class CustomIterator implements Iterator<T> {
        private int cursor = 0;

        @Override
        public boolean hasNext() {
            return cursor < size;
        }

        @Override
        public T next() {
            if (!hasNext()) {
                throw new NoSuchElementException();
            }
            return elements[cursor++];
        }

        @Override
        public void remove() {
            throw new UnsupportedOperationException("Remove not supported");
        }
    }
}
```

In this example, CustomCollection implements the Iterable<T> interface, which requires an iterator() method that returns an Iterator<T>. The inner class CustomIterator implements the Iterator<T> interface, encapsulating the traversal logic.

The hasNext() method checks if there are more elements to iterate over by comparing the current position, cursor, to the size of the collection. The next() method returns the next element in the iterator, and advances the cursor.

When using the iterator, the client code can traverse the collection without needing to know the specific details of how the collection stores its elements. Here's an example of how to use the CustomCollection and its iterator:

```
public class IteratorPatternDemo {
    public static void main(String[] args) {
```

```
        CustomCollection<String> collection = new CustomCollection<>(10);
        collection.add("Element1");
        collection.add("Element2");
        collection.add("Element3");

        Iterator<String> iterator = collection.iterator();
        while (iterator.hasNext()) {
            String element = iterator.next();
            System.out.println(element);
        }
    }
}
```

```
Element1
Element2
Element3
```

The output demonstrates the traversal of the CustomCollection using the iterator, by printing each element in the collection.

Advantages of the Iterator Pattern

1. **Decouples algorithms from the container structure**: The iterator exposes a way to traverse a collection without revealing the underlying representation. This offers flexibility in the collection's implementation details.

2. **Simplifies traverse logic**: Clients can use the iterator without needing to handle internal bookkeeping of element positions, which simplifies the code and reduces the potential for errors.

3. **Supports various traversal strategies**: Iterators can be implemented to support different ways of traversing collections, such as forward, backward, or even in a sorted order.

Built-in Java Collections and Iterators

Java's java.util package includes several collection classes which provide iterators. For example, ArrayList, HashSet, and LinkedList all implement Iterable, and their iterator() methods return iterators specific to these collections.

Here is how you can iterate over an ArrayList:

```
import java.util.ArrayList;
import java.util.Iterator;

public class ArrayListIteratorDemo {
    public static void main(String[] args) {
        ArrayList<String> arrayList = new ArrayList<>();
        arrayList.add("ElementA");
        arrayList.add("ElementB");
        arrayList.add("ElementC");

        Iterator<String> iterator = arrayList.iterator();
```

```
        while (iterator.hasNext()) {
            String element = iterator.next();
            System.out.println(element);
        }
    }
}
```

ElementA
ElementB
ElementC

Limitations and Considerations

When using iterators, it is important to be aware of potential limitations:

1. **Concurrent Modification**: If the underlying collection is modified while iterating (other than via the iterator's own remove() method), the iterator may throw a ConcurrentModificationException. This ensures the integrity of the traversal but requires careful handling in multi-threaded environments.

2. **Unsupported Operations**: Some collection types may not support certain iterator operations, such as remove() or specific traversal orders. As shown in the CustomCollection example above, attempting to call an unsupported operation may result in an UnsupportedOperationException.

Understanding and effectively implementing the Iterator Pattern is crucial for handling collections in a maintainable and scalable way, improving the clarity of traversal logic while promoting encapsulation and separation of concerns. This pattern's versatility and integration into the Java Standard Library make it an indispensable tool for Java developers working with collections.

4.6 The Mediator Pattern

The Mediator Pattern is a behavioral design pattern that defines an object that encapsulates how a set of objects interact. This pattern is applicable when the set of objects communicate in complex but well-defined ways. It allows for loose coupling by preventing objects from referring to each other explicitly, and it lets their interaction vary independently.

Intent: The primary intent of the Mediator Pattern is to centralize complex communications and control between related objects. This promotes collaboration by ensuring that objects do not need to be aware of each other's presence, promoting decoupling.

Problem Addressed: When multiple objects interact in a tightly coupled manner, it becomes challenging to change or understand how an object works independently. Adding or changing the interaction logic involves altering multiple classes. This pattern addresses this issue by making objects communicate through a central mediator object.

Structure: The UML class diagram for the Mediator Pattern consists of the following components:

- Mediator: An interface defining methods for communicating with Colleague objects.
- ConcreteMediator: Implements the Mediator interface and coordinates communication between Colleague objects.
- Colleague: Each Colleague communicates with its mediator whenever it would have otherwise communicated with another Colleague.

Implementation in Java: To demonstrate the Mediator Pattern in Java, consider an example where a ChatRoom acts as the mediator between User objects.

```
public interface ChatRoom {
    void showMessage(User user, String message);
}
```

The ChatRoomImpl class implements the ChatRoom interface:

```
import java.time.LocalDateTime;
import java.time.format.DateTimeFormatter;

public class ChatRoomImpl implements ChatRoom {
    @Override
    public void showMessage(User user, String message) {
        String timeStamp = LocalDateTime.now().format(DateTimeFormatter.ofPattern
            ("yyyy-MM-dd HH:mm:ss"));
        System.out.println(timeStamp + " [" + user.getName() + "]: " + message);
    }
}
```

The User class represents the Colleague objects:

```
public class User {
    private String name;
    private ChatRoom chatRoom;

    public User(String name, ChatRoom chatRoom) {
        this.name = name;
        this.chatRoom = chatRoom;
```

```
    }

    public String getName() {
        return name;
    }

    public void sendMessage(String message) {
        chatRoom.showMessage(this, message);
    }
}
```

Here's how we can use these components to enable communication through the mediator:

```
public class MediatorPatternDemo {
    public static void main(String[] args) {
        ChatRoom chatRoom = new ChatRoomImpl();

        User user1 = new User("John", chatRoom);
        User user2 = new User("Doe", chatRoom);

        user1.sendMessage("Hello, Doe!");
        user2.sendMessage("Hi, John!");
    }
}
```

```
2023-03-14 15:30:00 [John]: Hello, Doe!
2023-03-14 15:30:01 [Doe]: Hi, John!
```

This example illustrates how the mediator (ChatRoomImpl) facilitates communication between User objects, thus decoupling them from directly referencing each other.

Benefits:

- Decoupling of Colleagues: Each Colleague is isolated from the others, only communicating through the Mediator.
- Simplified Object Protocols: The interaction between objects is simplified by centralizing the communication logic.
- Enhanced Code Legibility: With the interaction logic centralized, understanding and maintaining the code becomes more manageable.

Drawbacks:

- Mediator Complexity: As the Mediator bears the interaction logic, it can become complex if the interaction between Colleagues is sophisticated.

- Performance Overhead: An intermediary mediator may introduce additional layers of communication, potentially degrading performance.

Best Practices: Ensure that the responsibilities assigned to the mediator do not overlap with other patterns such as the observer. This maintains clear boundaries and avoids ambiguities in code roles. If mediator complexity grows, assess whether certain responsibilities should be delegated to dedicated mediator classes or other structural patterns.

Understanding the Mediator Pattern and properly implementing it can substantially improve the modularity and inter-object communication logistics within an application. By decoupling classes and simplifying interaction logic, this pattern significantly enhances software maintainability and flexibility.

4.7 The Memento Pattern

The Memento Pattern is a behavioral design pattern that provides the capability to restore an object to its previous state. It is particularly useful in situations where you need to implement undo mechanisms or maintain snapshots of an object's state at different points in time. This pattern encapsulates the state of an object, ensuring that the internal state is not exposed or modified unintentionally.

The fundamental components of the Memento Pattern are:

- The Originator class, which creates a memento containing a snapshot of its current internal state and uses mementos to revert to previous states.
- The Memento class, which stores the internal state of the Originator. The Memento class is typically immutable to prevent accidental changes.
- The Caretaker class, which requests a Memento from the Originator, and keeps track of the memento, but does not modify or inspect its contents.

The following Java implementation demonstrates the Memento Pattern by modeling a simple text editor with undo functionality.

```
class TextEditor {
```

```
    private StringBuilder text;

    public TextEditor() {
        text = new StringBuilder();
    }

    public void write(String str) {
        text.append(str);
    }

    public String read() {
        return text.toString();
    }

    public Memento save() {
        return new Memento(text.toString());
    }

    public void undoToLastSave(Object obj) {
        Memento memento = (Memento) obj;
        text = new StringBuilder(memento.getSavedState());
    }

    private static class Memento {
        private final String state;

        public Memento(String stateToSave) {
            state = stateToSave;
        }

        public String getSavedState() {
            return state;
        }
    }
}

class Caretaker {
    private Object obj;

    public void saveState(TextEditor editor) {
        this.obj = editor.save();
    }

    public void restoreState(TextEditor editor) {
        editor.undoToLastSave(this.obj);
    }
}
```

In this example, TextEditor is the Originator that can create and restore mementos. The inner Memento class encapsulates the state to be saved. The Caretaker class is responsible for maintaining the memento and providing it back to the TextEditor for restoring its previous state. Below is a simple demonstration of how to use these classes.

```
public static void main(String[] args) {
    TextEditor editor = new TextEditor();
    Caretaker caretaker = new Caretaker();

    editor.write("Hello, ");
    caretaker.saveState(editor);
```

```
    editor.write("world!");
    System.out.println(editor.read()); // Output: Hello, world!

    caretaker.restoreState(editor);
    System.out.println(editor.read()); // Output: Hello,
}
```

The output of the above main method would be:

```
Hello, world!
Hello,
```

Using this approach, the current state of the TextEditor can be saved, and it can revert to a prior state on demand.

A key benefit of the Memento Pattern is the ease of implementing undo operations. It separates the state-saving logic from the main business logic, ensuring that states are encapsulated within mementos. Another advantage is that multiple states of an object can be managed without directly exposing the object's internals, which preserves the integrity and encapsulation.

It is essential to consider that mementos can consume significant memory when dealing with objects having large states or high-frequency state changes. In such cases, an optimization strategy or a different pattern may be more appropriate to mitigate memory overhead.

Leveraging the Memento Pattern can simplify the complexity of state management, creating a more maintainable and understandable codebase in scenarios requiring duration or historic state management.

4.8 The Observer Pattern

The Observer Pattern is a behavioral design pattern that enables an object, referred to as the Subject, to maintain a list of its dependents, known as Observers, and notify them automatically of any state changes, typically by calling one of their methods. This pattern is pivotal in scenarios where a change in one piece of data necessitates updates to multiple related objects, fostering low coupling between the subject and its observers.

Intent: Define a one-to-many dependency between objects so that when one object changes state, all its dependents are notified and updated automatically.

Motivation: Consider a real-time data display, such as a stock market data feed. The stock data stream can be seen as the Subject, while various display components, such as charts and tables, are Observers. Any change in the stock data should automatically update all display components to reflect the new information.

- **Subject:** The object that holds the state and sends notifications.
- **Observer:** The object that needs to be notified of changes in the subject.

Structure:

- Subject interface or abstract class:

```
public interface Subject {
    void registerObserver(Observer o);
    void removeObserver(Observer o);
    void notifyObservers();
}
```

- Observer interface:

```
public interface Observer {
    void update(float temp, float humidity, float pressure);
}
```

- ConcreteSubject class:

```
import java.util.ArrayList;

public class WeatherData implements Subject {
    private ArrayList<Observer> observers;
    private float temperature;
    private float humidity;
    private float pressure;

    public WeatherData() {
        observers = new ArrayList<Observer>();
    }

    public void registerObserver(Observer o) {
        observers.add(o);
    }

    public void removeObserver(Observer o) {
        int i = observers.indexOf(o);
        if (i >= 0) {
            observers.remove(i);
        }
    }

    public void notifyObservers() {
        for (int i = 0; i < observers.size(); i++) {
            Observer observer = (Observer)observers.get(i);
```

```
            observer.update(temperature, humidity, pressure);
        }
    }

    public void measurementsChanged() {
        notifyObservers();
    }

    public void setMeasurements(float temperature, float humidity, float pressure
        ) {
        this.temperature = temperature;
        this.humidity = humidity;
        this.pressure = pressure;
        measurementsChanged();
    }

    // Other WeatherData methods here
}
```

- ConcreteObserver class:

```
public class CurrentConditionsDisplay implements Observer {
    private float temperature;
    private float humidity;
    private Subject weatherData;

    public CurrentConditionsDisplay(Subject weatherData) {
        this.weatherData = weatherData;
        weatherData.registerObserver(this);
    }

    public void update(float temperature, float humidity, float pressure) {
        this.temperature = temperature;
        this.humidity = humidity;
        display();
    }

    public void display() {
        System.out.println("Current conditions: " + temperature + "F degrees
            and "
        + humidity + "% humidity");
    }
}
```

Implementation Steps:

- Define a Subject interface with methods to register, remove, and notify observers.
- Create a ConcreteSubject class that implements the Subject interface and maintains a list of observers.
- Define an Observer interface with an update method for receiving updates from the subject.

- Develop ConcreteObserver classes that implement the Observer interface and handle state changes appropriately.

Advantages:

- Helps promote loose coupling between the subject and its observers.
- Provides a mechanism for multiple objects to stay updated in response to changes in another object.

Disadvantages:

- Can lead to memory leaks if observers are not correctly deregistered.
- Dynamic dependencies can result in unexpected updates, making debugging more complex.

Real-World Examples:

- Model-View-Controller (MVC) architectural pattern: The view components act as observers to the model component, which is the subject.
- Event handling systems in GUI frameworks such as Java's Swing or JavaFX, where UI components listen for events from a subject like a button or a text field.

The Observer Pattern significantly enhances the capability of software components to communicate and synchronize with each other in a coherent and organized manner. By using this pattern, developers can build adaptable and responsive systems that react promptly to changes in state, improving the overall usability and maintainability of the software.

4.9 The State Pattern

The State Pattern is particularly useful in object-oriented design for situations where an object's behavior is dependent on its state. This pattern allows an object to change its behavior when its internal state changes, as if the object were to change its class. By implementing the State Pattern, the state-specific behavior is encapsulated within state objects, and the context object delegates its behavior to the current state object.

Intent: The intent of the State Pattern is to allow an object to alter its behavior when its internal state changes, making it appear as if the object changes its class.

Applicability:

- Use the State Pattern when an object's behavior depends on its state, and it must change its behavior at runtime depending on that state.
- This pattern is useful when various states involve significant, distinct, and complex behaviors that might clutter and complicate a single class with many conditional statements.

Participants:

- Context: This class maintains an instance of a ConcreteState subclass that defines the current state.
- State: This interface defines the behavior that is specific to various states.
- ConcreteState: These are classes that implement the State interface and encapsulate the behavior associated with a particular state of the Context.

Structure:

```
+---------------+     +-------------------+      +------------------+
|  Context      |<------|ConcreteStateA    | . . . |ConcreteStateZ      |
+---------------+     +-------------------+      +------------------+
|+ request()    |      | + handle()        |       | + handle()        |
|               |    +-------------------+     +------------------+
| - state:State |--------------+
+---------------+              |
                              |
              +-------------//
             //+------------------+
              |State              |
              +------------------+
              | + handle()         |
              +------------------+
```

Implementation:

Let's consider a simple example in Java, using a context of a Document that can be in different states: Draft, Moderation, and Published. We'll define these states and the behaviors associated with being in each state.

```
interface State {
    void handleRequest();
}

class Draft implements State {
    public void handleRequest() {
        System.out.println("The document is in Draft state.");
    }
}

class Moderation implements State {
    public void handleRequest() {
        System.out.println("The document is in Moderation state.");
    }
}

class Published implements State {
    public void handleRequest() {
        System.out.println("The document is Published.");
    }
}

class Document {
    private State state;

    public Document() {
        this.state = new Draft(); // Default state is Draft
    }

    public void setState(State state) {
        this.state = state;
    }

    public void applyState() {
        this.state.handleRequest();
    }
}
```

In this example, a Document object can change its state, and the behaviors for each state are encapsulated within the state classes. The Document class maintains a reference to the current state object and delegates the applyState behavior to the state object.

Client Code:

```
public class StatePatternExample {
    public static void main(String[] args) {
        Document doc = new Document();

        doc.applyState();
        doc.setState(new Moderation());
        doc.applyState();
        doc.setState(new Published());
        doc.applyState();
```

```
    }
}
```

```
The document is in Draft state.
The document is in Moderation state.
The document is Published.
```

The Context class Document transitions through various states, demonstrates how the behavior changes accordingly when invoking the applyState method.

Benefits:

- **Single Responsibility Principle (SRP)**: By localizing state-specific behavior within dedicated classes, the State Pattern adheres to the Single Responsibility Principle.
- **Open/Closed Principle (OCP)**: The State Pattern supports the Open/Closed Principle by allowing the addition of new states without altering existing state classes or the context.
- **Simplified Maintenance**: Complexity is reduced as code related to specific state behaviors is encapsulated within dedicated state classes, making the system easier to maintain.

Drawbacks:

- **Increased Number of Classes**: The State Pattern can lead to an increase in the number of classes, as each state and state-specific behavior requires a separate class.
- **Overhead in Transitions**: The frequent changing of state objects might introduce a performance overhead, depending on the implementation.

By applying the State Pattern appropriately, you can achieve a more modular design that is easy to extend and maintain, particularly in scenarios with complex state-dependent behaviors. This pattern is a powerful tool for managing state changes and behaviors in an object-oriented system.

4.10 The Strategy Pattern

The Strategy Pattern defines a family of algorithms, encapsulates each algorithm, and makes them interchangeable. This pattern allows the algorithm to vary independently from clients that utilize it. The primary intent of the Strategy Pattern is to enable a class behavior or its algorithm to be selected at runtime.

Context and Problem: In many software systems, a class defines multiple behaviors, and these behaviors often appear as conditional statements within the class's methods. One approach to cope with this situation is to use the traditional inheritance; however, this often leads to a large number of subclasses and maintenance challenges. The Strategy Pattern offers a cleaner alternative by delegating the algorithm's logic to a set of interchangeable objects called strategies.

Structure: The Strategy Pattern consists of three main components:

- Strategy: An interface common to all supported algorithms. The Context uses this interface to call the algorithm defined by a ConcreteStrategy.
- ConcreteStrategy: A class that implements the Strategy interface and provides an actual implementation for the algorithm.
- Context: A class that is configured with a Strategy object and maintains a reference to a Strategy object. The Context forwards requests to the Strategy object.

Implementation:

Let's illustrate the Strategy Pattern with a Java example. Suppose we have a context where we need different sorting algorithms. We'll define a family of sorting algorithms using the Strategy Pattern.

Firstly, we define the Strategy interface:

```
public interface SortStrategy {
    void sort(int[] numbers);
}
```

Next, we create concrete implementations of the Strategy interface. These are the specific sorting algorithms:

```
public class BubbleSortStrategy implements SortStrategy {
    @Override
    public void sort(int[] numbers) {
        int n = numbers.length;
        for (int i = 0; i < n - 1; i++) {
            for (int j = 0; j < n - i - 1; j++) {
                if (numbers[j] > numbers[j + 1]) {
                    // Swap numbers[j] and numbers[j + 1]
                    int temp = numbers[j];
                    numbers[j] = numbers[j + 1];
```

```
                    numbers[j + 1] = temp;
                }
            }
        }
    }
}

public class QuickSortStrategy implements SortStrategy {
    @Override
    public void sort(int[] numbers) {
        quickSort(numbers, 0, numbers.length - 1);
    }

    private void quickSort(int[] array, int low, int high) {
        if (low < high) {
            int pi = partition(array, low, high);
            quickSort(array, low, pi - 1);
            quickSort(array, pi + 1, high);
        }
    }

    private int partition(int[] array, int low, int high) {
        int pivot = array[high];
        int i = (low - 1);
        for (int j = low; j < high; j++) {
            if (array[j] < pivot) {
                i++;
                int temp = array[i];
                array[i] = array[j];
                array[j] = temp;
            }
        }
        int temp = array[i + 1];
        array[i + 1] = array[high];
        array[high] = temp;
        return i + 1;
    }
}
```

Now, we define the Context class that will use the SortStrategy:

```
public class SortContext {
    private SortStrategy strategy;

    public SortContext(SortStrategy strategy) {
        this.strategy = strategy;
    }

    public void setStrategy(SortStrategy strategy) {
        this.strategy = strategy;
    }

    public void sortArray(int[] numbers) {
        strategy.sort(numbers);
    }
}
```

Client Code Example:

```
public class StrategyPatternDemo {
    public static void main(String[] args) {
```

```
        int[] data = {34, 7, 23, 32, 5, 62};

        SortContext context = new SortContext(new BubbleSortStrategy());
        System.out.println("Using Bubble Sort Strategy:");
        context.sortArray(data);
        System.out.println(Arrays.toString(data));

        // changing strategy to QuickSort
        context.setStrategy(new QuickSortStrategy());
        int[] data2 = {34, 7, 23, 32, 5, 62};
        System.out.println("Using Quick Sort Strategy:");
        context.sortArray(data2);
        System.out.println(Arrays.toString(data2));
    }
}
```

```
Using Bubble Sort Strategy:
[5, 7, 23, 32, 34, 62]
Using Quick Sort Strategy:
[5, 7, 23, 32, 34, 62]
```

Benefits and Drawbacks:

- **Benefits**:
  - Provides a way to configure a class with one of many behaviors dynamically.
  - Eliminates conditional statements in the context.
  - Promotes the Open/Closed Principle, allowing new algorithms to be introduced without modifying existing code.
- **Drawbacks**:
  - Strategy Pattern increases the number of objects.
  - Clients must be aware of different strategies.
  - Communication overhead between context and strategy.

Best Practices:

- Define strategies as interfaces, and each algorithm as a class implementing the interface.
- Context classes should maintain a reference to the Strategy interface, promoting loose coupling.
- Strategies should be reusable and not change their state; use them as stateless classes.

Understanding when to apply the Strategy Pattern requires recognizing situations where various algorithms can be interchanged independently of the clients that use them. By doing so, the system adheres more closely to SOLID principles, namely the Open/Closed Principle and Single Responsibility Principle. This strategic flexibility is particularly beneficial in financial systems, sorting algorithms, and other domains where multiple algorithms can offer distinct benefits and trade-offs.

4.11 The Template Method Pattern

The Template Method Pattern is a fundamental behavioral design pattern that encapsulates the skeleton of an algorithm within a template method in a base class. This pattern allows subclasses to redefine specific steps of the algorithm without altering its structure. By defining the invariant parts of the algorithm at a high level, the Template Method promotes reuse and extension.

To illustrate the Template Method Pattern, consider a scenario where different kinds of data need to be processed. Each type of data may require a specific preprocessing and postprocessing step, but the core processing algorithm remains consistent across all data types. The Template Method ensures that these steps are executed in a defined order, while subclasses implement the variable parts.

```
abstract class DataProcessor {

    // Template method defining the skeleton of the algorithm
    public final void process() {
        preprocess();
        processData();
        postprocess();
    }

    // Abstract methods to be implemented by subclasses
    protected abstract void preprocess();
    protected abstract void processData();
    protected abstract void postprocess();
}
```

In this example, the DataProcessor class defines the template method process, which outlines the steps of the algorithm. The steps include preprocess, processData, and postprocess, which are abstract and need to be implemented by concrete subclasses.

```
class CSVDataProcessor extends DataProcessor {

    @Override
    protected void preprocess() {
```

```
        // Specific preprocessing for CSV Data
        System.out.println("Preprocessing CSV Data");
    }

    @Override
    protected void processData() {
        // Core processing algorithm for CSV Data
        System.out.println("Processing CSV Data");
    }

    @Override
    protected void postprocess() {
        // Specific postprocessing for CSV Data
        System.out.println("Postprocessing CSV Data");
    }
}
```

```
class XMLDataProcessor extends DataProcessor {

    @Override
    protected void preprocess() {
        // Specific preprocessing for XML Data
        System.out.println("Preprocessing XML Data");
    }

    @Override
    protected void processData() {
        // Core processing algorithm for XML Data
        System.out.println("Processing XML Data");
    }

    @Override
    protected void postprocess() {
        // Specific postprocessing for XML Data
        System.out.println("Postprocessing XML Data");
    }
}
```

Both CSVDataProcessor and XMLDataProcessor provide concrete implementations for the steps defined in DataProcessor. The template method process in the base class ensures that the steps are executed in the defined order, regardless of whether the data is in CSV or XML format.

The Template Method Pattern provides several advantages:

- **Code Reuse:** Common code resides in the base class, reducing duplication in subclasses.
- **Consistency:** Enforces a consistent algorithm structure across different implementations.
- **Extensibility:** Allows subclasses to extend or modify specific steps without changing the overall algorithm.

However, there are also some potential drawbacks:

- **Inheritance Constraints:** Subclasses are tightly coupled to the base class, which can limit flexibility.
- **Complexity:** For algorithms with many steps, managing and understanding the interplay between base and subclass methods can become complex.

For a practical understanding, consider a scenario with a more complex algorithm. Suppose we are developing a framework for reading different document formats - such as PDF, DOCX, and TXT - which involves steps for opening the document, reading content, and closing the document.

```
abstract class DocumentReader {

    // Template method defining the algorithm skeleton
    public final void readDocument() {
        openDocument();
        readContent();
        closeDocument();
    }

    // Abstract methods to be implemented by subclasses
    protected abstract void openDocument();
    protected abstract void readContent();
    protected abstract void closeDocument();
}
```

```
class PDFDocumentReader extends DocumentReader {

    @Override
    protected void openDocument() {
        // Specific steps to open a PDF document
        System.out.println("Opening PDF Document");
    }

    @Override
    protected void readContent() {
        // Specific steps to read content from a PDF document
        System.out.println("Reading PDF Content");
    }

    @Override
    protected void closeDocument() {
        // Specific steps to close a PDF document
        System.out.println("Closing PDF Document");
    }
}
```

Similarly, we can implement readers for DOCX and TXT formats by extending the DocumentReader class:

```
class DOCXDocumentReader extends DocumentReader {
```

```
    @Override
    protected void openDocument() {
        // Specific steps to open a DOCX document
        System.out.println("Opening DOCX Document");
    }

    @Override
    protected void readContent() {
        // Specific steps to read content from a DOCX document
        System.out.println("Reading DOCX Content");
    }

    @Override
    protected void closeDocument() {
        // Specific steps to close a DOCX document
        System.out.println("Closing DOCX Document");
    }
}
```

```
class TXTDocumentReader extends DocumentReader {

    @Override
    protected void openDocument() {
        // Specific steps to open a TXT document
        System.out.println("Opening TXT Document");
    }

    @Override
    protected void readContent() {
        // Specific steps to read content from a TXT document
        System.out.println("Reading TXT Content");
    }

    @Override
    protected void closeDocument() {
        // Specific steps to close a TXT document
        System.out.println("Closing TXT Document");
    }
}
```

When the readDocument() method is called on any of these concrete classes, the algorithm's steps will be executed in the predefined order, ensuring consistency and reliability.

The Template Method Pattern is instrumental in providing a structured approach to defining algorithms. It allows developers to capture the invariant part of an algorithm and delegate the variable behavior to subclasses. This not only promotes code reuse and maintainability but also enhances the clarity of the algorithm's structure. Applying this pattern effectively requires a clear understanding of the common and variable aspects of the algorithm, which increases adaptability to evolving requirements while maintaining a consistent behavior across different contexts.

4.12 The Visitor Pattern

The Visitor Pattern is a design pattern that allows you to add further operations to objects without modifying them. It follows the principle of separating an algorithm from the object structure upon which it operates. This is particularly beneficial in a system where the object structure is stable, but operations on those objects need to be extended frequently. The Visitor Pattern consists of two key components: the Visitor interface and the Element interface, which the objects to be visited must implement.

Visitor Interface: The Visitor interface declares a visit method for each type of concrete element in the object structure. Here is a simplified example in Java:

```
public interface Visitor {
    void visit(ConcreteElementA element);
    void visit(ConcreteElementB element);
    // add methods for other concrete elements
}
```

Element Interface: The Element interface declares an accept method that takes a visitor as an argument. This method will call the visitor's visit method.

```
public interface Element {
    void accept(Visitor visitor);
}
```

Concrete elements implement the Element interface and define how they accept a visitor. Below is an example of concrete element classes:

```
public class ConcreteElementA implements Element {
    @Override
    public void accept(Visitor visitor) {
        visitor.visit(this);
    }

    public void operationA() {
        // Implementation of operationA
    }
}

public class ConcreteElementB implements Element {
    @Override
    public void accept(Visitor visitor) {
        visitor.visit(this);
    }

    public void operationB() {
        // Implementation of operationB
    }
}
```

ConcreteVisitor: Concrete visitors implement the Visitor interface and define specialized behaviors for each element type.

```
public class ConcreteVisitor implements Visitor {
    @Override
    public void visit(ConcreteElementA element) {
        element.operationA();
        // Additional behavior for ConcreteElementA
    }

    @Override
    public void visit(ConcreteElementB element) {
        element.operationB();
        // Additional behavior for ConcreteElementB
    }
}
```

Client Code: The client is responsible for creating visitor instances and passing them to elements through the accept method. The client can have multiple visitor implementations and choose the appropriate one at runtime, thus dynamically applying different operations to the object structure.

```
public class Client {
    public static void main(String[] args) {
        List<Element> elements = Arrays.asList(new ConcreteElementA(), new
                ConcreteElementB());
        Visitor visitor = new ConcreteVisitor();

        for (Element element : elements) {
            element.accept(visitor);
        }
    }
}
```

Advantages:

- **Single Responsibility Principle**: Adding new operations is facilitated by visitor classes, adhering to the single responsibility principle.
- **Open/Closed Principle**: The pattern adheres to the open/closed principle by allowing classes to remain open for extension but closed for modification.
- **Separate Algorithms**: Encapsulating the operations in visitor objects separates concerns and enhances maintainability.

Drawbacks:

- **Circular Dependency**: Visitor classes need to be aware of all concrete element types, causing a circular dependency.
- **Implementation Complexity**: Adding new element types requires modifying all visitor classes, leading to increased complexity.
- **Less Flexibility in Extending Element Hierarchies**: If new element types are frequently added, the visitor pattern can become less manageable.

The Visitor Pattern is particularly useful in scenarios where operations on a set of objects are frequently changing and need to be extended without modifying each object's code. This separation of concerns makes the Visitor Pattern a powerful tool in a developer's toolbox.

Lastly, correct implementation of the Visitor Pattern demands meticulous planning and a deep understanding of the interactions between elements and visitors. Developers should also balance the benefits against potential drawbacks like increased complexity and circular dependencies. The proper application of this pattern can lead to enhanced flexibility and maintainability, especially in complex systems with a stable object structure and a dynamic set of operations.

4.13 Comparing Behavioral Patterns

Behavioral patterns facilitate the interaction between various objects, aiding in efficient communication and delegation of responsibilities. While each pattern has a distinct purpose and method of implementation, understanding their nuanced differences and practical applicability is fundamental for adept system design.

Behavioral patterns can be compared across several dimensions: intent, implementation, relationships between objects, flexibility, and real-world use cases. This section elucidates these aspects, supporting the reader's ability to select and apply the most appropriate pattern for a given scenario.

Intent: Each behavioral pattern addresses a specific problem by defining how objects communicate to complete tasks.

- **Chain of Responsibility:** Delegates requests to a chain of handlers until one processes the request.

- **Command:** Encapsulates a request as an object, allowing for parameterization of clients.
- **Interpreter:** Defines the grammar and behavior for interpreting a particular language.
- **Iterator:** Provides a standardized way to traverse elements of a collection without exposing the underlying representation.
- **Mediator:** Centralizes communication between various objects to avoid direct interaction and dependencies.
- **Memento:** Allows the capture and restoration of an object's state without violating encapsulation.
- **Observer:** Establishes a one-to-many dependency between objects where a state change in one object notifies all dependents.
- **State:** Allows an object to alter its behavior when its internal state changes.
- **Strategy:** Defines a family of algorithms, encapsulating each as an object, and making them interchangeable.
- **Template Method:** Defines the skeleton of an algorithm in a method, deferring some steps to subclasses.
- **Visitor:** Encapsulates operations to be performed on elements of an object structure, allowing the addition of new operations without changing the elements.

Implementation:

The structural differences in implementation significantly influence the behavior and flexibility of each pattern. The following Java code snippets provide clear examples:

```
abstract class Handler {
    protected Handler successor;

    public void setSuccessor(Handler successor) {
        this.successor = successor;
    }

    public abstract void handleRequest(String request);
}

class ConcreteHandler1 extends Handler {
    public void handleRequest(String request) {
        if (request.equals("request1")) {
            System.out.println("ConcreteHandler1 handling request1");
```

```
        } else if (successor != null) {
            successor.handleRequest(request);
        }
    }
}
```

```
public interface Command {
    void execute();
}

class ConcreteCommand implements Command {
    private Receiver receiver;

    public ConcreteCommand(Receiver receiver) {
        this.receiver = receiver;
    }

    public void execute() {
        receiver.action();
    }
}

class Invoker {
    private Command command;

    public void setCommand(Command command) {
        this.command = command;
    }

    public void executeCommand() {
        command.execute();
    }
}
```

Relationships between Objects:

Patterns differ in how objects interrelate and manage dependencies.

- **Chain of Responsibility:** Objects are linked in a chain, each holding a reference to its successor.
- **Mediator:** Objects interact solely through the mediator, reducing direct communication and dependencies.
- **Observer:** Subjects maintain a list of observers, which are notified of changes in the subject's state.

Flexibility:

Flexibility varies across patterns; some are more adaptable to changes, while others are more rigid but simpler.

- **Strategy:** Very flexible, allowing algorithms to be swapped out at runtime.

- **Template Method:** Less flexible due to its reliance on subclassing to modify behavior.
- **State:** Adds flexibility by allowing objects to change behavior dynamically.

Real-World Use Cases:

Examining real-world applications helps appreciate the practical utility of each pattern.

- **Command:** Useful in implementing undo functionality in applications.
- **Interpreter:** Suitable for designing configurations systems and domain-specific languages.
- **Observer:** Widely used in implementing event-driven systems like GUI frameworks.

```
import java.util.ArrayList;
import java.util.List;

interface Observer {
    void update(String message);
}

class ConcreteObserver implements Observer {
    private String name;

    public ConcreteObserver(String name) {
        this.name = name;
    }

    public void update(String message) {
        System.out.println(name + " received: " + message);
    }
}

class Subject {
    private List<Observer> observers = new ArrayList<>();

    public void addObserver(Observer observer) {
        observers.add(observer);
    }

    public void notifyObservers(String message) {
        for (Observer observer : observers) {
            observer.update(message);
        }
    }
}
```

To wrap up, recognizing the differences in intent, implementation, and flexibility enhances the ability to select and implement the appropriate pattern efficiently. Each pattern serves unique purposes and implementing them correctly ensures responsive and maintainable system architecture.

4.14 Use Cases for Behavioral Patterns

Behavioral design patterns are integral in ensuring that objects in a system interact in a flexible and extensible manner. They focus on how objects communicate with each other and are concerned with the assignment of responsibilities between objects. Here, we will delve into practical scenarios where each of the behavioral patterns discussed in this chapter can be effectively utilized.

Chain of Responsibility Pattern: This pattern is particularly useful in scenarios where multiple objects can handle a request, but the exact handler is not known in advance. It allows the request to be passed along a chain of potential handlers until it is processed.

- Use Case: Implementing a logging system where different levels of logs (info, debug, error) are handled by different logging mechanisms. For instance:

```
abstract class Logger {
    protected Logger nextLogger;
    public void setNextLogger(Logger nextLogger) {
        this.nextLogger = nextLogger;
    }
    public void logMessage(String message) {
        if(nextLogger != null) {
            nextLogger.logMessage(message);
        }
    }
}

class ConsoleLogger extends Logger {
    public void logMessage(String message) {
        System.out.println("Console Logger: " + message);
        super.logMessage(message);
    }
}

class FileLogger extends Logger {
    public void logMessage(String message) {
        System.out.println("File Logger: " + message);
        super.logMessage(message);
    }
}
```

```
public class Client {
    public static void main(String[] args) {
        Logger consoleLogger = new ConsoleLogger();
        Logger fileLogger = new FileLogger();
        consoleLogger.setNextLogger(fileLogger);
        consoleLogger.logMessage("An error has occurred.");
    }
}
```

Command Pattern: This pattern is useful in scenarios where you need to decouple the sender of the request from its receiver. It encapsulates a request as an object, thereby allowing for parameterization of clients with different requests, queuing of requests, and logging the requests.

- Use Case: Designing an undo mechanism in a text editor where each action (like type, delete) is encapsulated as a command object. For example:

```
interface Command {
    void execute();
    void undo();
}

class TextEditor {
    private String text = "";
    public void addText(String newText) {
        text += newText;
    }
    public void deleteLast() {
        text = text.substring(0, text.length() - 1);
    }
    public String getText() {
        return text;
    }
}

class AddTextCommand implements Command {
    private TextEditor textEditor;
    private String textToAdd;
    public AddTextCommand(TextEditor textEditor, String textToAdd) {
        this.textEditor = textEditor;
        this.textToAdd = textToAdd;
    }
    public void execute() {
        textEditor.addText(textToAdd);
    }
    public void undo() {
        for (int i = 0; i < textToAdd.length(); i++) {
            textEditor.deleteLast();
        }
    }
}

public class Client {
    public static void main(String[] args) {
        TextEditor textEditor = new TextEditor();
        Command addTextCommand = new AddTextCommand(textEditor, "
            Hello World");
```

```
        addTextCommand.execute();
        System.out.println(textEditor.getText()); // Output: Hello World
        addTextCommand.undo();
        System.out.println(textEditor.getText()); // Output:
    }
}
```

Interpreter Pattern: This pattern is suitable for defining a language's grammar and provides an interpreter to deal with this grammar. It is used when there is a need to interpret expressions in a language.

- Use Case: Designing a mathematical expression evaluator where each type of operation is encapsulated in a class. For example:

```
interface Expression {
    int interpret();
}

class NumberExpression implements Expression {
    private int number;
    public NumberExpression(int number) {
        this.number = number;
    }
    public int interpret() {
        return number;
    }
}

class AddExpression implements Expression {
    private Expression leftExpression;
    private Expression rightExpression;
    public AddExpression(Expression leftExpression, Expression rightExpression)
            {
        this.leftExpression = leftExpression;
        this.rightExpression = rightExpression;
    }
    public int interpret() {
        return leftExpression.interpret() + rightExpression.interpret();
    }
}

public class Client {
    public static void main(String[] args) {
        Expression expr = new AddExpression(new NumberExpression(3), new
                NumberExpression(7));
        System.out.println(expr.interpret()); // Output: 10
    }
}
```

Iterator Pattern: This pattern is used to provide a way to access the elements of an aggregate object sequentially without exposing its underlying representation.

- Use Case: Implementing a custom collection class and its iterator for traversing through the collection. For example:

```
interface Iterator<E> {
    boolean hasNext();
    E next();
}

class CustomCollection<E> {
    private List<E> items = new ArrayList<>();
    public void addItem(E item) {
        items.add(item);
    }
    public Iterator<E> iterator() {
        return new Iterator<E>() {
            private int index = 0;
            public boolean hasNext() {
                return index < items.size();
            }
            public E next() {
                if(hasNext()) {
                    return items.get(index++);
                }
                return null;
            }
        };
    }
}

public class Client {
    public static void main(String[] args) {
        CustomCollection<String> collection = new CustomCollection<>();
        collection.addItem("Item1");
        collection.addItem("Item2");
        Iterator<String> iterator = collection.iterator();
        while(iterator.hasNext()) {
            System.out.println(iterator.next());
        }
    }
}
```

Mediator Pattern: This pattern is appropriate when you need to reduce complex communication and dependencies between a group of objects. It promotes loose coupling by preventing objects from referring to each other explicitly.

- Use Case: Designing a chat room application where the mediator manages the interaction between users. For example:

```
interface Mediator {
    void sendMessage(String msg, User user);
}

class ChatMediator implements Mediator {
    private List<User> users;
    public ChatMediator() {
        this.users = new ArrayList<>();
    }
    public void addUser(User user) {
        users.add(user);
```

```
    }
    public void sendMessage(String msg, User user) {
        for(User u : users) {
            if(u != user) {
                u.receive(msg);
            }
        }
    }
}

class User {
    private String name;
    private Mediator mediator;
    public User(String name, Mediator mediator) {
        this.name = name;
        this.mediator = mediator;
    }
    public void send(String msg) {
        System.out.println(name + ": Sending Message=" + msg);
        mediator.sendMessage(msg, this);
    }
    public void receive(String msg) {
        System.out.println(name + ": Received Message=" + msg);
    }
}

public class Client {
    public static void main(String[] args) {
        Mediator mediator = new ChatMediator();
        User user1 = new User("User1", mediator);
        User user2 = new User("User2", mediator);
        mediator.addUser(user1);
        mediator.addUser(user2);
        user1.send("Hello, User2");
    }
}
```

Memento Pattern: This pattern is useful for capturing and externalizing an object's internal state, so that the object can be restored to this state later without violating encapsulation.

- Use Case: Implementing a mechanism to create checkpoints in a game so that the game state can be saved and restored. For example:

```
class GameState {
    private String level;
    private int score;

    public GameState(String level, int score) {
        this.level = level;
        this.score = score;
    }
    public String getLevel() {
        return level;
    }
    public int getScore() {
        return score;
```

```
    }
}

class Game {
    private String level;
    private int score;
    public void set(String level, int score) {
        this.level = level;
        this.score = score;
    }
    public GameState save() {
        return new GameState(level, score);
    }
    public void load(GameState gameState) {
        this.level = gameState.getLevel();
        this.score = gameState.getScore();
    }
}

public class Client {
    public static void main(String[] args) {
        Game game = new Game();
        game.set("Level1", 3000);
        GameState savedState = game.save();
        game.set("Level2", 4000);
        game.load(savedState);
        System.out.println("Restored to " + savedState.getLevel() + " with score
              " + savedState.getScore());
    }
}
```

Observer Pattern: This pattern is suitable for scenarios where an object (subject) has one-to-many dependencies with other objects (observers). When the state of the subject changes, all its observers are notified and updated automatically.

- Use Case: Implementing a notification system where different observers (email, SMS) are notified of a change in user account status. For example:

```
interface Observer {
    void update(String status);
}

class UserAccount implements Subject {
    private List<Observer> observers = new ArrayList<>();
    private String status;

    public void registerObserver(Observer observer) {
        observers.add(observer);
    }
    public void removeObserver(Observer observer) {
        observers.remove(observer);
    }
    public void notifyObservers() {
        for (Observer observer : observers) {
            observer.update(status);
```

```
            }
        }
        public void setStatus(String status) {
            this.status = status;
            notifyObservers();
        }
        public String getStatus() {
            return status;
        }
}

class EmailNotification implements Observer {
        public void update(String status) {
            System.out.println("Email Notification: User account status changed to "
                    + status);
        }
}

class SMSNotification implements Observer {
        public void update(String status) {
            System.out.println("SMS Notification: User account status changed to "
                    + status);
        }
}

public class Client {
        public static void main(String[] args) {
            UserAccount userAccount = new UserAccount();
            Observer emailObserver = new EmailNotification();
            Observer smsObserver = new SMSNotification();
            userAccount.registerObserver(emailObserver);
            userAccount.registerObserver(smsObserver);
            userAccount.setStatus("Active");
        }
}
```

State Pattern: This pattern is apt for scenarios where an object changes its behavior based on its internal state. It allows the object to change its behavior when its state changes.

- Use Case: Designing a vending machine that changes states from waiting for coin to dispensing item and back based on user actions. For example:

```
interface State {
    void insertCoin();
    void dispenseItem();
}

class WaitingForCoinState implements State {
    public void insertCoin() {
        System.out.println("Coin inserted.");
    }
    public void dispenseItem() {
        System.out.println("Insert coin first.");
    }
}
```

```
class DispensingState implements State {
    public void insertCoin() {
        System.out.println("Wait for current item to be dispensed.");
    }
    public void dispenseItem() {
        System.out.println("Item dispensed.");
    }
}

class VendingMachine {
    private State state;
    public VendingMachine() {
        state = new WaitingForCoinState();
    }
    public void setState(State state) {
        this.state = state;
    }
    public void insertCoin() {
        state.insertCoin();
        setState(new DispensingState());
    }
    public void dispenseItem() {
        state.dispenseItem();
        setState(new WaitingForCoinState());
    }
}

public class Client {
    public static void main(String[] args) {
        VendingMachine vm = new VendingMachine();
        vm.insertCoin();
        vm.dispenseItem();
    }
}
```

Strategy Pattern: This pattern is beneficial when you have multiple algorithms for a specific task and you want to choose the algorithm at runtime. It defines a family of algorithms, encapsulates each one, and makes them interchangeable.

- Use Case: Implementing a sorting application that can switch between different sorting algorithms (bubble sort, quick sort). For example:

```
interface SortingStrategy {
    void sort(int[] array);
}

class BubbleSortStrategy implements SortingStrategy {
    public void sort(int[] array) {
        int n = array.length;
        for (int i = 0; i < n-1; i++) {
            for (int j = 0; j < n-i-1; j++) {
                if (array[j] > array[j+1]) {
                    int temp = array[j];
                    array[j] = array[j+1];
                    array[j+1] = temp;
```

```
                }
            }
        }
    }
}

class QuickSortStrategy implements SortingStrategy {
    public void sort(int[] array) {
        quickSort(array, 0, array.length - 1);
    }
    private void quickSort(int[] array, int low, int high) {
        if (low < high) {
            int pi = partition(array, low, high);
            quickSort(array, low, pi-1);
            quickSort(array, pi+1, high);
        }
    }
    private int partition(int[] array, int low, int high) {
        int pivot = array[high];
        int i = (low-1);
        for (int j = low; j < high; j++) {
            if (array[j] < pivot) {
                i++;
                int temp = array[i];
                array[i] = array[j];
                array[j] = temp;
            }
        }
        int temp = array[i+1];
        array[i+1] = array[high];
        array[high] = temp;
        return i+1;
    }
}

class SortingContext {
    private SortingStrategy strategy;
    public void setStrategy(SortingStrategy strategy) {
        this.strategy = strategy;
    }
    public void sortArray(int[] array) {
        if(strategy != null) {
            strategy.sort(array);
        }
    }
}

public class Client {
    public static void main(String[] args) {
        SortingContext context = new SortingContext();
        int[] array = {5, 2, 9, 1, 5, 6};
        context.setStrategy(new BubbleSortStrategy());
        context.sortArray(array); // bubble sort is used
        System.out.println(Arrays.toString(array));
        context.setStrategy(new QuickSortStrategy());
        context.sortArray(array); // quick sort is used
        System.out.println(Arrays.toString(array));
    }
}
```

Template Method Pattern: This pattern is useful when you have an algorithm with some invariant parts and you want to encapsulate these invariant parts in a method, deferring the variable parts to subclasses. It defines the skeleton of an algorithm in a method, deferring some steps to subclasses.

- Use Case: Designing a data mining framework where the process of reading data, processing it, and saving results can be reused with specific steps varying. For example:

```
abstract class DataMiner {
    public void mine() {
        readData();
        processData();
        saveResults();
    }
    protected abstract void readData();
    protected abstract void processData();
    protected abstract void saveResults();
}

class CSVDataMiner extends DataMiner {
    protected void readData() {
        System.out.println("Reading data from CSV file.");
    }
    protected void processData() {
        System.out.println("Processing CSV data.");
    }
    protected void saveResults() {
        System.out.println("Saving results to CSV file.");
    }
}

class XMLDataMiner extends DataMiner {
    protected void readData() {
        System.out.println("Reading data from XML file.");
    }
    protected void processData() {
        System.out.println("Processing XML data.");
    }
    protected void saveResults() {
        System.out.println("Saving results to XML file.");
    }
}

public class Client {
    public static void main(String[] args) {
        DataMiner csvMiner = new CSVDataMiner();
        csvMiner.mine();
        DataMiner xmlMiner = new XMLDataMiner();
        xmlMiner.mine();
    }
}
```

Visitor Pattern: This pattern is suitable when you want to add further operations on elements of an object structure without modifying the objects themselves. It allows you to define new operations without changing the classes of the elements on which it operates.

- Use Case: Implementing a document structure where various types of content elements (paragraph, image) need to be processed by different operations (rendering, spell-checking). For example:

```
interface DocumentVisitor {
    void visit(Paragraph paragraph);
    void visit(Image image);
}

class Paragraph {
    public void accept(DocumentVisitor visitor) {
        visitor.visit(this);
    }
}

class Image {
    public void accept(DocumentVisitor visitor) {
        visitor.visit(this);
    }
}

class RenderVisitor implements DocumentVisitor {
    public void visit(Paragraph paragraph) {
        System.out.println("Rendering paragraph.");
    }
    public void visit(Image image) {
        System.out.println("Rendering image.");
    }
}

class SpellCheckVisitor implements DocumentVisitor {
    public void visit(Paragraph paragraph) {
        System.out.println("Checking spelling in paragraph.");
    }
    public void visit(Image image) {
        // No spell check for images
    }
}

public class Client {
    public static void main(String[] args) {
        Paragraph paragraph = new Paragraph();
        Image image = new Image();
        RenderVisitor renderVisitor = new RenderVisitor();
        SpellCheckVisitor spellCheckVisitor = new SpellCheckVisitor();
        paragraph.accept(renderVisitor);
        image.accept(renderVisitor);
        paragraph.accept(spellCheckVisitor);
    }
}
```

Behavioral design patterns effectively address various software design problems by focusing on the interaction between objects and the delegation of responsibilities. Their application leads to more maintainable, flexible, and robust systems significantly simplifying complex interactions.

4.15 Best Practices in Applying Behavioral Patterns

When applying behavioral patterns in Java, adhering to best practices ensures the development of robust, maintainable, and efficient software systems. The following guidelines are comprehensive and provide a nuanced understanding of how to effectively employ these patterns.

- **Understand the Problem Domain:** Begin by thoroughly understanding the domain-specific problem that you aim to solve. Behavioral patterns should address specific communication and responsibility-sharing issues among objects. Recognize scenarios where a pattern can simplify or enhance interactions.
- **Choose the Right Pattern:** Selecting the appropriate pattern is crucial. Each behavioral pattern addresses different types of problems. For instance, use the Observer pattern when an object change needs to automatically notify dependent objects, and the Strategy pattern when interchangeable algorithms need to be selected at runtime.
- **Foster Loose Coupling:** Behavioral patterns often enable loose coupling between objects. Use interfaces and abstract classes to decouple components, allowing them to vary independently. Properly applied, patterns like Command and Mediator can significantly reduce dependencies within your codebase.

Implementation Details:

Correct implementation of behavioral patterns requires careful consideration of design principles. Take the Command pattern as an example. This pattern encapsulates a request as an object, thereby allowing parameterization and queuing of requests. Below is a practical implementation in Java.

```
interface Command {
    void execute();
}
```

```
class Light {
    void on() {
        System.out.println("Light is ON");
    }
    void off() {
        System.out.println("Light is OFF");
    }
}

class LightOnCommand implements Command {
    private Light light;

    LightOnCommand(Light light) {
        this.light = light;
    }
    public void execute() {
        light.on();
    }
}

class LightOffCommand implements Command {
    private Light light;

    LightOffCommand(Light light) {
        this.light = light;
    }
    public void execute() {
        light.off();
    }
}

class RemoteControl {
    private Command command;

    void setCommand(Command command) {
        this.command = command;
    }

    void pressButton() {
        command.execute();
    }
}

public class CommandPatternDemo {
    public static void main(String[] args) {
        Light livingRoomLight = new Light();

        Command lightOn = new LightOnCommand(livingRoomLight);
        Command lightOff = new LightOffCommand(livingRoomLight);

        RemoteControl remote = new RemoteControl();

        remote.setCommand(lightOn);
        remote.pressButton();

        remote.setCommand(lightOff);
        remote.pressButton();
    }
}
```

The following output illustrates how the Command pattern

decouples the invoker (RemoteControl) from the action executors (LightOnCommand and LightOffCommand).

```
Light is ON
Light is OFF
```

- **Leverage Polymorphism and Inheritance:** Behavioral patterns often exploit polymorphism and inheritance to manage object interactions effectively. Ensure that your implementations adhere to the Liskov Substitution Principle (LSP), which promotes substitutability of base class objects with derived class objects without altering the desirable properties of the program.

- **Utilize Standard Libraries and Frameworks:** Make use of existing libraries and frameworks that provide implementations of behavioral patterns. For instance, Java's java.util.Observer and java.util.Observable classes can simplify the application of the Observer pattern. Similarly, take advantage of the Java Collections Framework for iterator patterns rather than implementing custom iterations.

- **Promote Code Reusability:** Structure your code to maximize reusability. Encapsulate pattern-specific logic within reusable components to facilitate application across different projects. For example, generic command objects can be reused for various invocations, thereby enhancing modularity.

- **Document Your Pattern Usage:** Comprehensive documentation aids future maintenance and knowledge transfer. Clearly annotate your code to elucidate where and why a particular behavioral pattern is used. Include class diagrams and sequence diagrams to visually represent the interaction and collaboration among classes and objects.

- **Conduct Code Reviews and Refactoring:** Regular code reviews and refactoring are vital to identify and eliminate antipatterns or redundant implementations. Collaborate with peers to ensure adherence to best practices and to gain insights into potential improvements.

- **Ensure Scalability and Performance:** Evaluate the scalability and performance of your pattern implementations. Patterns like Chain of Responsibility can introduce latency if not carefully managed. Employ performance profiling and optimization techniques to ensure efficient execution.

- **Test Extensively:** Comprehensive unit and integration tests are essential for verifying correct behavior. Utilize testing frameworks such as JUnit to automate tests for various use cases and edge scenarios. For behavioral patterns particularly, mock objects and stubs can help simulate object interactions and verify expected outcomes.

Design Patterns Through Example:

Consider an implementation of the Observer pattern, which B demonstrates best practices in documenting pattern usage. This pattern is useful when you have a one-to-many dependency between objects, such that when one object changes state, all its dependents are notified and updated automatically.

```
import java.util.ArrayList;
import java.util.List;

interface Observer {
    void update(String message);
}

class Subject {
    private List<Observer> observers = new ArrayList<>();

    void attach(Observer observer) {
        observers.add(observer);
    }

    void detach(Observer observer) {
        observers.remove(observer);
    }

    void notifyObservers(String message) {
        for (Observer observer : observers) {
            observer.update(message);
        }
    }
}

class ConcreteObserver implements Observer {
    private String name;

    ConcreteObserver(String name) {
        this.name = name;
    }

    public void update(String message) {
        System.out.println(name + " received: " + message);
    }
}

public class ObserverPatternDemo {
    public static void main(String[] args) {
        Subject subject = new Subject();

        Observer observer1 = new ConcreteObserver("Observer 1");
```

```
        Observer observer2 = new ConcreteObserver("Observer 2");

        subject.attach(observer1);
        subject.attach(observer2);

        subject.notifyObservers("Hello Observers");

        subject.detach(observer1);

        subject.notifyObservers("Hello again");
    }
}
```

The output from the Observer pattern implementation will be as follows:

```
Observer 1 received: Hello Observers
Observer 2 received: Hello Observers
Observer 2 received: Hello again
```

The provided code effectively illustrates the pattern, with minimal coupling between Subject and Observer classes. Comments and clear naming conventions further enhance understandability and facilitate maintenance.

Applying these best practices in behavioral patterns strengthens the overall quality of the software design, making it more adaptable, efficient, and easier to maintain.

4.16 Common Mistakes and How to Avoid Them

When implementing behavioral patterns in Java, several common mistakes can impede the effectiveness and efficiency of the code. Recognizing these mistakes and understanding how to avoid them is crucial for leveraging the benefits of design patterns fully.

- **Overuse of Patterns:** One frequent error is the over-application of design patterns. Developers sometimes apply patterns without fully understanding the problem domain, leading to unnecessary complexity. It is essential to assess whether a design pattern is genuinely beneficial for solving the specific issue at hand. Consider the following example:

```
// Unnecessary use of the Strategy pattern

interface PaymentStrategy {
    void pay(int amount);
}
```

```
class CreditCardPayment implements PaymentStrategy {
    @Override
    public void pay(int amount) {
        // Implementation
    }
}

class PaypalPayment implements PaymentStrategy {
    @Override
    public void pay(int amount) {
        // Implementation
    }
}

class PaymentProcessor {
    private PaymentStrategy strategy;

    public PaymentProcessor(PaymentStrategy strategy) {
        this.strategy = strategy;
    }

    public void processPayment(int amount) {
        strategy.pay(amount);
    }
}

// Use in main class
PaymentProcessor processor = new PaymentProcessor(new
      CreditCardPayment());
processor.processPayment(100);
```

In this scenario, if only one payment method is required, applying the Strategy pattern is unnecessary. Instead, a simpler solution would be more straightforward and maintainable.

- **Insufficient Encapsulation:** Another common mistake is inadequate encapsulation of internal details. Objects must manage their state and behavior, exposing only necessary interfaces while hiding implementation specifics. For instance:

```
// Poor encapsulation example
class BankAccount {
    public double balance;

    public void deposit(double amount) {
        balance += amount;
    }

    public void withdraw(double amount) {
        if (amount <= balance) {
            balance -= amount;
        }
    }
}

BankAccount account = new BankAccount();
account.balance = 500; // Direct access to balance
```

Proper encapsulation improves maintainability and reduces the risk of errors caused by external entities modifying internal state directly:

```
// Proper encapsulation example
class BankAccount {
    private double balance;

    public void deposit(double amount) {
        balance += amount;
    }

    public void withdraw(double amount) {
        if (amount <= balance) {
            balance -= amount;
        }
    }

    public double getBalance() {
        return balance;
    }
}

BankAccount account = new BankAccount();
account.deposit(500);
```

- **Tight Coupling:** Tight coupling between classes diminishes extensibility and reusability. Behavioral patterns aim to reduce coupling by promoting loose connections between objects. However, improper implementations can still result in interdependent classes. For example:

```
// Tight coupling example
class Button {
    private Lamp lamp;

    public Button(Lamp lamp) {
        this.lamp = lamp;
    }

    public void press() {
        lamp.turnOn();
    }
}

class Lamp {
    public void turnOn() {
        // Turn on the lamp
    }
}
```

To reduce coupling, interfaces or abstract classes can be introduced:

```
// Reduced coupling example
interface Switchable {
    void turnOn();
```

```
}

class Button {
    private Switchable device;

    public Button(Switchable device) {
        this.device = device;
    }

    public void press() {
        device.turnOn();
    }
}

class Lamp implements Switchable {
    @Override
    public void turnOn() {
        // Turn on the lamp
    }
}
```

- **Ignoring Future Requirements:** Implementing patterns without considering future requirements can lead to additional refactoring. Designing with flexibility in mind is crucial for accommodating potential changes. For instance, the Observer pattern allows for dynamic subscription of observers but might be initially implemented with a fixed set of observers:

```
// Fixed observer implementation
class Subject {
    private Observer observer1;
    private Observer observer2;

    public void addObserver1(Observer observer) {
        this.observer1 = observer;
    }

    public void addObserver2(Observer observer) {
        this.observer2 = observer;
    }

    public void notifyObservers() {
        if (observer1 != null) observer1.update();
        if (observer2 != null) observer2.update();
    }
}

interface Observer {
    void update();
}
```

A more flexible implementation involves a list of observers:

```
// Flexible observer implementation
class Subject {
    private List<Observer> observers = new ArrayList<>();

    public void addObserver(Observer observer) {
```

```
        observers.add(observer);
    }

    public void notifyObservers() {
        for (Observer observer : observers) {
            observer.update();
        }
    }
}

interface Observer {
    void update();
}
```

- **Misunderstanding Pattern Intent:** Misinterpreting the purpose of a design pattern can lead to inappropriate applications. Each pattern has a specific problem domain it addresses, and misapplying a pattern can introduce more issues than it resolves. For instance, using the Singleton pattern to maintain global state might solve short-term problems but can reduce testability and complicate concurrency management.

```
// Potential misuse of Singleton for global state
class Configuration {
    private static Configuration instance;

    private Configuration() {
        // Load configuration
    }

    public static Configuration getInstance() {
        if (instance == null) {
            instance = new Configuration();
        }
        return instance;
    }
}

// Accessing configuration globally
Configuration config = Configuration.getInstance();
```

Instead, using dependency injection to manage state promotes better encapsulation and testability:

```
// Better approach with dependency injection
class Configuration {
    // Load configuration
}

class Application {
    private Configuration config;

    public Application(Configuration config) {
        this.config = config;
    }
}
```

```
// Inject configuration
Configuration config = new Configuration();
Application app = new Application(config);
```

- **Neglecting Readability:** Prioritizing design patterns over code readability can create convoluted and hard-to-maintain codebases. Patterns should improve, not hinder, the comprehensibility of the system. Naming conventions, clear documentation, and adhering to the Single Responsibility Principle are essential for maintaining readability.

Understanding and avoiding these common mistakes ensure that design patterns are used effectively to enhance the software's architecture, maintainability, and scalability.

Chapter 5

Factory Pattern: Creating Objects Creatively

This chapter explains the Factory Pattern, which is crucial for managing object creation in a flexible and reusable manner. It covers both the Factory Method and Abstract Factory patterns, detailing their implementation in Java, key differences, and appropriate use cases. The chapter discusses the benefits and drawbacks of each approach, highlights best practices, and outlines common mistakes to avoid. Real-world examples and comparisons with other patterns provide a comprehensive understanding of their practical applications in software design.

5.1 Introduction to the Factory Pattern

The Factory Pattern is a core structural pattern in object-oriented programming that focuses on the creation of objects in a way that enhances flexibility and reusability. This pattern is essential for handling object creation and encapsulating the instantiation logic within a method or class, rather than allowing direct construction or instantiation with the new keyword. By doing so, it promotes loose coupling and adheres to the design principle of "programming to an interface, not an implementation."

The Factory Pattern primarily covers two design patterns: the Factory

Method Pattern and the Abstract Factory Pattern. Both patterns share the objective of deferring the instantiation process to subclasses or helper classes, which in turn, determines the actual class of the objects being instantiated. Let us delve deeper into the foundational principles and motivations behind using these patterns.

The Factory Pattern addresses several key aspects:

- **Encapsulation of object creation**: By encapsulating the creation logic in a separate method or class, the code adhering to the Factory Pattern promotes better separation of concerns. This ensures that the client code remains agnostic of the specifics involved in creating object instances.
- **Flexible code**: The Factory Pattern makes it easier to introduce new classes under an existing hierarchy without altering the client code. This flexibility is crucial for applications requiring extensibility.
- **Promoting reuse**: By centralizing the instantiation process, the Factory Pattern encourages reusability of the object creation code, reducing redundancy.
- **Decoupling code dependencies**: By relying on factory methods or classes to create objects, changes in the object creation logic do not ripple through the system, thereby reducing the impact and scope of changes.

Let us consider a simple example to illustrate the Factory Pattern concept. Suppose we have a base class Shape and several derived classes such as Circle, Square, and Triangle. Rather than instantiating these objects directly in client code, we can use a factory to encapsulate the object creation process.

Here's a straightforward implementation in Java:

```
public abstract class Shape {
    public abstract void draw();
}

public class Circle extends Shape {
    @Override
    public void draw() {
        System.out.println("Drawing a Circle");
    }
}

public class Square extends Shape {
    @Override
```

```
    public void draw() {
        System.out.println("Drawing a Square");
    }
}

public class Triangle extends Shape {
    @Override
    public void draw() {
        System.out.println("Drawing a Triangle");
    }
}

public class ShapeFactory {
    public Shape createShape(String type) {
        if (type.equalsIgnoreCase("Circle")) {
            return new Circle();
        } else if (type.equalsIgnoreCase("Square")) {
            return new Square();
        } else if (type.equalsIgnoreCase("Triangle")) {
            return new Triangle();
        }
        return null;
    }
}
```

In this example, the ShapeFactory class is responsible for creating instances of different Shape subclasses based on the provided input string. The client code can utilize this factory without needing to know the specifics of each shape's instantiation:

```
public class Client {
    public static void main(String[] args) {
        ShapeFactory factory = new ShapeFactory();

        Shape shape1 = factory.createShape("Circle");
        shape1.draw();

        Shape shape2 = factory.createShape("Square");
        shape2.draw();

        Shape shape3 = factory.createShape("Triangle");
        shape3.draw();
    }
}
```

Output:

```
Drawing a Circle
Drawing a Square
Drawing a Triangle
```

This approach offers several advantages over direct instantiation:

- **Centralized creation logic**: All instantiation logic is centralized in ShapeFactory, making it easier to modify or extend the creation process.

- **Ease of maintenance**: Changes to the creation logic or addition of new Shape types can be done in the factory class without impacting the client code.
- **Reduction of client code complexity**: Client code is simplified as it does not need to deal with the specifics of object creation.

The Factory Method Pattern extends this concept by defining an interface for creating objects, but allowing subclasses to alter the type of objects that will be created. This pattern is used to deal with the problem of creating objects without specifying the exact class of object that will be created.

An essential consideration is to ensure that the Factory Pattern does not become overly complex or bloated. Careful analysis of the use case and design goals is necessary to determine the appropriateness of using a factory, and to decide between a simple factory, Factory Method Pattern, or the more complex Abstract Factory Pattern.

5.2 Understanding Factory Method Pattern

The Factory Method Pattern is a creational design pattern that provides an interface for creating objects in a superclass while allowing subclasses to alter the type of objects that will be created. This pattern introduces flexibility in the instantiation process, enabling a class to defer instantiation to its subclasses. This characteristic is beneficial in scenarios where polymorphism is required without coupling the code to specific classes.

The Factory Method Pattern is particularly useful when a class cannot anticipate the types of objects it must create beforehand. By encapsulating the object instantiation process, code becomes more modular, reusable, and easier to maintain.

The central components of the Factory Method Pattern are the Creator and Product interfaces, along with their corresponding concrete implementations. The Creator class declares the factory method that returns an object of type Product. Subclasses of Creator override this factory method to instantiate different concrete products.

To clarify this concept, consider the following Java implementation of the Factory Method Pattern. We start by defining the Product interface and its concrete implementations.

```
public interface Product {
    void use();
}

public class ConcreteProductA implements Product {
    @Override
    public void use() {
        System.out.println("Using ConcreteProductA");
    }
}

public class ConcreteProductB implements Product {
    @Override
    public void use() {
        System.out.println("Using ConcreteProductB");
    }
}
```

In this example, Product is the common interface for all products, and ConcreteProductA and ConcreteProductB are concrete implementations of this interface. Next, we define the Creator class that declares a factory method, createProduct, and its subclasses that override this method.

```
public abstract class Creator {
    public abstract Product createProduct();

    public void someOperation() {
        Product product = createProduct();
        product.use();
    }
}

public class ConcreteCreatorA extends Creator {
    @Override
    public Product createProduct() {
        return new ConcreteProductA();
    }
}

public class ConcreteCreatorB extends Creator {
    @Override
    public Product createProduct() {
        return new ConcreteProductB();
    }
}
```

In this code snippet, Creator is an abstract class that declares the createProduct factory method, and ConcreteCreatorA and ConcreteCreatorB are concrete subclasses that implement the factory method to create specific products. The someOperation method in the Creator class uses the factory method to get a product and then invokes its use method.

By following this pattern, client code can use the Creator classes without knowing the exact type of product that will be created. This decouples the product's creation process from its usage, promoting greater flexibility and maintainability in the codebase.

```
public class Client {
    public static void main(String[] args) {
        Creator creatorA = new ConcreteCreatorA();
        creatorA.someOperation();

        Creator creatorB = new ConcreteCreatorB();
        creatorB.someOperation();
    }
}
```

The client code demonstrates the use of the Factory Method Pattern. Here, a ConcreteCreatorA and a ConcreteCreatorB are instantiated, and their someOperation method is called, which in turn uses the specific product created by each concrete creator.

The Factory Method Pattern offers several benefits:

- **Flexibility**: It allows a class to be independent of how its objects are created.
- **Single Responsibility Principle**: It separates the responsibility of creating a product from the product's usage.
- **Extensibility**: New product types can be introduced without modifying the creator class.

However, it is important to consider potential drawbacks:

- **Code Complexity**: Introducing factory methods can complicate the codebase, especially for simple applications.
- **Additional Subclasses**: Every new product requires a new subclass for its creation, which can lead to an increase in the number of classes.

Understanding the Factory Method Pattern's core principles and implementation is essential for effectively employing it in software design. By encapsulating the creation process, it provides robust flexibility and promotes adherence to design principles.

5.3 Implementing the Factory Method in Java

Implementing the Factory Method involves creating an interface for creating an object, but allows subclasses to alter the type of objects that will be created. This section elaborates on the process of implementing the Factory Method pattern in Java, demonstrating its flexibility and reusability.

To start, consider an example where different types of notifications (e.g., EmailNotification, SMSNotification) need to be sent. The Factory Method will provide a way to encapsulate the creation logic and delegate it to subclasses. The following outlines the steps to implement the Factory Method pattern in Java.

- Define a Notification interface and its concrete implementations.
- Create an abstract NotificationFactory class with a factory method to return Notification objects.
- Implement concrete factories extending NotificationFactory to instantiate specific Notification objects.

First, define the Notification interface and its concrete implementations:

```
public interface Notification {
    void notifyUser();
}

public class EmailNotification implements Notification {
    @Override
    public void notifyUser() {
        System.out.println("Sending an email notification");
    }
}

public class SMSNotification implements Notification {
    @Override
    public void notifyUser() {
        System.out.println("Sending an SMS notification");
    }
}
```

In the above code, Notification is an interface with the method notifyUser, which will be implemented by different notification types: EmailNotification and SMSNotification.

Next, create an abstract class NotificationFactory with a method createNotification that subclasses will override.

```
public abstract class NotificationFactory {
    public abstract Notification createNotification();

    public void notify() {
        Notification notification = createNotification();
        notification.notifyUser();
    }
}
```

The NotificationFactory abstract class provides a template method notify that uses the factory method createNotification to delegate object creation to its concrete subclasses. The method notify then calls notifyUser on the created object.

Implement concrete factories that extend NotificationFactory:

```
public class EmailNotificationFactory extends NotificationFactory {
    @Override
    public Notification createNotification() {
        return new EmailNotification();
    }
}

public class SMSNotificationFactory extends NotificationFactory {
    @Override
    public Notification createNotification() {
        return new SMSNotification();
    }
}
```

The concrete factory classes, EmailNotificationFactory and SMSNotificationFactory, override the createNotification method to instantiate the appropriate Notification objects.

A client program uses these factories to create and send notifications without needing to know which specific Notification class is being instantiated:

```
public class NotificationService {
    public static void main(String[] args) {
        NotificationFactory emailFactory = new EmailNotificationFactory();
        emailFactory.notify();

        NotificationFactory smsFactory = new SMSNotificationFactory();
        smsFactory.notify();
    }
}
```

Output:

```
Sending an email notification
Sending an SMS notification
```

In the client code NotificationService, instances of NotificationFactory are used to send notifications. This design allows easy extension for new notification types. If a new type such as PushNotification is needed, it requires creating a new PushNotification class and a corresponding PushNotificationFactory without altering the client code.

The Factory Method pattern promotes loose coupling by delegating instantiation logic to subclasses, ensuring that the client code depends only on the abstract factory and its interface. This design also adheres to the Open/Closed Principle, allowing the introduction of new classes without modifying existing code, thereby enhancing flexibility and maintainability.

5.4 When to Use the Factory Method Pattern

The Factory Method Pattern provides a systematic approach to instantiating objects. It encapsulates the creation logic in a separate method, avoiding tight coupling between the client and the concrete classes. Understanding when to apply this pattern is essential to leverage its full potential.

The Factory Method Pattern is particularly useful when:

- **Class Instantiation Needs to Be Deferred**: In cases where the exact class of objects to be created is not known until runtime, the Factory Method pattern is effective. It defers instantiation to subclasses, thereby facilitating late binding.

- **Promoting Reusability**: It enables the reuse of existing code. By delegating object creation to factory methods, the client code remains unaltered while new object types can easily be integrated, promoting the Open-Closed Principle.

- **Encapsulating Knowledge of Concrete Classes**: If instantiation details are complex and should not be exposed to the client, the Factory Method encapsulates this complexity. The client merely interacts with a common interface, enhancing maintainability.

- **Decoupling Clients from Particular Implementations**: When there is a need to insulate the client from knowing which specific implementation it is using, defining an interface or abstract class for the factory method provides this decoupling.

- **Class Instances Controlled by Centralized Code**: In scenarios where the lifecycle of classes and their instances need to be centrally controlled (e.g., implementing singletons or managing connections), using a factory method ensures that creation logic remains centrally managed.
- **Needing Varied Representations of Objects**: When a system must create various representations of complex objects and these representations share a common interface, the factory method manages the creation logic robustly.

Example Scenario:

Consider a logging framework that writes logs to different destinations such as files, databases, or remote servers. Since the specific logging destination may not be known until deployment, and may change over time, the Factory Method Pattern is exceedingly appropriate.

```
public abstract class Logger {
    public abstract LogWriter createLogWriter();

    public void log(String message) {
        LogWriter logWriter = createLogWriter();
        logWriter.writeLog(message);
    }
}

public class FileLogger extends Logger {
    @Override
    public LogWriter createLogWriter() {
        return new FileLogWriter();
    }
}

public class DatabaseLogger extends Logger {
    @Override
    public LogWriter createLogWriter() {
        return new DatabaseLogWriter();
    }
}

public interface LogWriter {
    void writeLog(String message);
}

public class FileLogWriter implements LogWriter {
    @Override
    public void writeLog(String message) {
        // Write log to a file
    }
}

public class DatabaseLogWriter implements LogWriter {
    @Override
    public void writeLog(String message) {
        // Write log to a database
```

```
    }
}
```

The Logger class is an abstract class that declares the factory method createLogWriter. The concrete classes FileLogger and DatabaseLogger implement this method, returning instances of FileLogWriter and DatabaseLogWriter, respectively. This structure allows the client code to remain unchanged when new types of loggers are introduced.

Behavioral Flexibility:

By employing the Factory Method Pattern, we achieve several forms of flexibility:

- **Runtime Decisions**: The pattern allows for runtime decisions regarding which class to instantiate, based on application configuration or user preferences. This provides dynamic adaptability in the system.
- **Extensibility**: Adding new log writers (e.g., SocketLogWriter) entails creating a new subclass without modifying existing library code.
- **Substitution Principle**: Clients interact with abstract interfaces, promoting adherence to the Liskov Substitution Principle (LSP). This ensures that objects of a superclass shall be replaceable with objects of a subclass without altering the correctness of the program.

The Factory Method Pattern is also beneficial in concurrent programming. When objects are created and thread safety is a concern, the factory method can include logic to manage this, ensuring robust multithreaded applications.

```
public abstract class Logger {
    protected abstract LogWriter createLogWriter();

    public void log(String message) {
        LogWriter logWriter = createLogWriter();
        synchronized (logWriter) {
            logWriter.writeLog(message);
        }
    }
}

public class SynchFileLogger extends Logger {
    @Override
    protected LogWriter createLogWriter() {
        return new SynchFileLogWriter();
    }
```

```
}
// Similar changes follow for SynchFileLogWriter and other classes
```

In this example, the logging operations execute within a synchronized block to maintain thread safety by ensuring only one thread writes a log at a time.

The Factory Method Pattern's application is not without its limitations. An over-reliance on subclassing can lead to an increase in the number of classes, complicating the system design. It is crucial to balance the benefits of flexibility with maintainability and complexity. When used judiciously, this pattern significantly enhances code reusability, readability, and testability, fostering better software design.

5.5 Advantages and Disadvantages of the Factory Method

The Factory Method pattern provides numerous advantages and disadvantages that developers should carefully consider during design and implementation. Understanding these facets helps in leveraging the pattern effectively to solve specific problems while avoiding potential pitfalls.

Advantages:

- **Encapsulation of Object Creation:** The Factory Method pattern encapsulates the code required to instantiate an object, promoting separation of concerns. This makes the system more modular and easier to maintain.
- **Enhanced Flexibility:** By defining an interface for creating an object but allowing subclasses to alter the type of objects that will be created, the pattern introduces flexibility into the system. This flexibility can be utilized to construct objects in different contexts without modifying the code that uses these objects.
- **Decoupling Client Code:** Client code is decoupled from the instantiation process, adhering to the Open/Closed Principle. This means that existing client code does not need to be altered to instantiate new types of objects, thus preventing potential bugs and reducing the risk of introducing errors during updates.

- **Promotion of Code Reuse:** By localizing the instantiation code within a factory, the Factory Method pattern encourages code reuse. New concrete classes can be created and used without extensive modifications to the existing codebase.
- **Better Handling of Complex Object Creation:** Ideal for creating complex objects where the process might involve multiple steps or configurations. This keeps the client code clean and clear, focusing on higher-level functionalities rather than the intricacies of object creation.

Disadvantages:

- **Increased Complexity:** The Factory Method pattern can introduce increased complexity into the codebase. The necessity to create new classes for each new type of product can result in a proliferation of classes, sometimes making the system harder to understand and maintain.
- **Substantial Boilerplate Code:** Implementing the Factory Method pattern often requires a significant amount of boilerplate code. This can lead to seemingly redundant code, which can be off-putting and require extra development effort.
- **Challenges in Refactoring Existing Code:** Refactoring existing code to use a Factory Method pattern can be non-trivial. The transition requires careful decoupling of object creation logic and could involve substantial refactoring efforts, potentially introducing new bugs.
- **Potential Performance Overhead:** In some scenarios, the additional layer of abstraction introduced by the Factory Method might bring performance overhead. This can be particularly noticeable in performance-critical applications where the frequency of object creation is high.
- **Unnecessary Indirection:**** For simple applications or scenarios where object instantiation logic is straightforward, the use of the Factory Method pattern may introduce unnecessary indirection. This could make the code harder to read and understand, adding little real benefit.

The decision to use the Factory Method pattern should weigh these advantages and disadvantages concerning the specific requirements and constraints of the project. Implementing the pattern effectively allows developers to harness its benefits while mitigating its inherent drawbacks. The key lies in applying it judiciously in contexts where its advantages outweigh its potential downsides. This facilitates creating a modular, maintainable, and extensible system.

5.6 Abstract Factory Pattern Overview

The Abstract Factory Pattern is a creational design pattern that provides an interface for creating families of related or dependent objects without specifying their concrete classes. This pattern is essential when a system must be independent of the way its objects are created, composed, and represented, offering a framework for object creation that adheres to the open/closed principle.

The Abstract Factory Pattern enhances groupings of factories that share a common theme. Each concrete factory in this context is responsible for producing various types of related objects. This design is particularly useful when the client needs to be decoupled from the specifics of the actual creation process. Rather than instantiating objects directly, the client utilizes an abstract factory and relies on polymorphism to instantiate the appropriate objects.

Consideration of the Abstract Factory Pattern centers on its components and structure. The primary participants in this pattern include:

- **AbstractFactory**: Declares an interface for operations that create abstract product objects.
- **ConcreteFactory**: Implements the operations to create concrete product objects.
- **AbstractProduct**: Declares an interface for a type of product object.
- **Product**: Defines a product object to be created by the corresponding concrete factory, implementing the AbstractProduct interface.
- Client: Uses only interfaces declared by AbstractFactory and AbstractProduct classes.

Here is a detailed example illustrating the Abstract Factory Pattern in Java:

```
interface Chair {
    void create();
}

class VictorianChair implements Chair {
    public void create() {
        System.out.println("Victorian Chair created.");
    }
}

class ModernChair implements Chair {
    public void create() {
        System.out.println("Modern Chair created.");
    }
}

interface Sofa {
    void create();
}

class VictorianSofa implements Sofa {
    public void create() {
        System.out.println("Victorian Sofa created.");
    }
}

class ModernSofa implements Sofa {
    public void create() {
        System.out.println("Modern Sofa created.");
    }
}

interface FurnitureFactory {
    Chair createChair();
    Sofa createSofa();
}

class VictorianFurnitureFactory implements FurnitureFactory {
    public Chair createChair() {
        return new VictorianChair();
    }

    public Sofa createSofa() {
        return new VictorianSofa();
    }
}

class ModernFurnitureFactory implements FurnitureFactory {
    public Chair createChair() {
        return new ModernChair();
    }

    public Sofa createSofa() {
        return new ModernSofa();
    }
}

public class Client {
    private Chair chair;
    private Sofa sofa;

    public Client(FurnitureFactory factory) {
```

```
        chair = factory.createChair();
        sofa = factory.createSofa();
    }

    public void createFurniture() {
        chair.create();
        sofa.create();
    }

    public static void main(String[] args) {
        FurnitureFactory victorianFactory = new VictorianFurnitureFactory();
        Client victorianClient = new Client(victorianFactory);
        victorianClient.createFurniture();

        FurnitureFactory modernFactory = new ModernFurnitureFactory();
        Client modernClient = new Client(modernFactory);
        modernClient.createFurniture();
    }
}
```

```
Victorian Chair created.
Victorian Sofa created.
Modern Chair created.
Modern Sofa created.
```

The example demonstrates various aspects of the Abstract Factory Pattern. The interfaces Chair and Sofa represent the abstract products. VictorianChair, ModernChair, VictorianSofa, and ModernSofa are concrete implementations of these products. FurnitureFactory is the abstract factory, with VictorianFurnitureFactory and ModernFurnitureFactory acting as concrete factories creating the respective types of furniture.

The Client class shows how a client interacts with the abstract factory without any knowledge of the actual product classes being instantiated. The client remains agnostic to the concrete implementations, adhering to the principle of dependency inversion by depending on abstractions rather than concretions.

The separation of concerns provided by the Abstract Factory Pattern fosters code that is easier to maintain and extend. When new product families need to be introduced, new concrete factories can be implemented without altering the existing client code, thus maintaining the robustness and flexibility in object-oriented design.

5.7 Implementing the Abstract Factory in Java

The Abstract Factory Pattern is an advanced form of the Factory Pattern that allows the creation of families of related objects without specifying their concrete classes. This pattern provides interfaces for creating families of related or dependent objects without detailing their concrete implementations. It is particularly useful when you have multiple families of products that need to be created together and you want to ensure that the product family is used consistently.

We will consider an example where we need to create different types of GUI components (e.g., Button, TextField, and Label) for different operating systems (e.g., Windows and Mac). The Abstract Factory Pattern helps us achieve this by defining interfaces for each product and an abstract factory interface for creating these products. Then, concrete factories implement these interfaces to create specific products for each operating system.

First, let us define the product interfaces. These interfaces outline the methods available for each product type.

```
public interface Button {
    void render();
}

public interface TextField {
    void render();
}

public interface Label {
    void render();
}
```

Next, we create an abstract factory interface that declares methods for creating each type of product.

```
public interface GUIFactory {
    Button createButton();
    TextField createTextField();
    Label createLabel();
}
```

With the interfaces defined, we can proceed to create concrete products for each operating system. Below are the concrete implementations of the product interfaces for Windows.

```
public class WindowsButton implements Button {
    @Override
```

```
    public void render() {
        System.out.println("Rendering Windows Button");
    }
}

public class WindowsTextField implements TextField {
    @Override
    public void render() {
        System.out.println("Rendering Windows TextField");
    }
}

public class WindowsLabel implements Label {
    @Override
    public void render() {
        System.out.println("Rendering Windows Label");
    }
}
```

Similarly, we create the concrete products for Mac.

```
public class MacButton implements Button {
    @Override
    public void render() {
        System.out.println("Rendering Mac Button");
    }
}

public class MacTextField implements TextField {
    @Override
    public void render() {
        System.out.println("Rendering Mac TextField");
    }
}

public class MacLabel implements Label {
    @Override
    public void render() {
        System.out.println("Rendering Mac Label");
    }
}
```

Now that we have concrete product classes for both Windows and Mac, we need to create the concrete factories that will produce these products. Below is the concrete factory for Windows.

```
public class WindowsFactory implements GUIFactory {
    @Override
    public Button createButton() {
        return new WindowsButton();
    }

    @Override
    public TextField createTextField() {
        return new WindowsTextField();
    }

    @Override
    public Label createLabel() {
        return new WindowsLabel();
```

```
    }
}
```

And the concrete factory for Mac.

```
public class MacFactory implements GUIFactory {
    @Override
    public Button createButton() {
        return new MacButton();
    }

    @Override
    public TextField createTextField() {
        return new MacTextField();
    }

    @Override
    public Label createLabel() {
        return new MacLabel();
    }
}
```

These concrete factories ensure the consistent creation of product families. Finally, we can demonstrate the usage of the Abstract Factory Pattern by creating a simple client application that depends on the abstract factory interface but is independent of the concrete product implementations.

```
public class Application {
    private Button button;
    private TextField textField;
    private Label label;

    public Application(GUIFactory factory) {
        button = factory.createButton();
        textField = factory.createTextField();
        label = factory.createLabel();
    }

    public void render() {
        button.render();
        textField.render();
        label.render();
    }
}
```

The client code can then instantiate the appropriate factory based on the configuration or user input and use it to create the application.

```
public class Main {
    public static void main(String[] args) {
        GUIFactory factory;
        String osType = System.getProperty("os.name").toLowerCase();

        if (osType.contains("win")) {
            factory = new WindowsFactory();
        } else if (osType.contains("mac")) {
```

```
            factory = new MacFactory();
        } else {
            throw new UnsupportedOperationException("Unsupported operating system
                ");
        }

        Application app = new Application(factory);
        app.render();
    }
}
```

Sample Output:
Rendering Windows Button
Rendering Windows TextField
Rendering Windows Label

The Abstract Factory Pattern enhances the flexibility and scalability of your code by isolating the client from concrete product classes and promoting a consistent use of product families. This pattern is particularly advantageous in systems that need to create interdependent products across various families without coupling the client code to specific implementations.

5.8 Comparing Factory Method and Abstract Factory

The Factory Method and Abstract Factory patterns are both creational patterns that deal with object creation. While they share some similarities, they serve different purposes and possess distinct characteristics. This section elucidates the differences and similarities between the Factory Method and Abstract Factory patterns, focusing on their structure, purpose, and practical applications.

The Factory Method pattern defines an interface for creating an object but allows subclasses to alter the type of objects that will be created. It uses inheritance and relies on a subclass to handle the desired object instantiation. This results in a more flexible and reusable code that can be easily extended with new types of objects without modifying the existing codebase.

The Abstract Factory pattern, on the other hand, provides an interface for creating families of related or dependent objects without specifying their concrete classes. This pattern relies on object composition, encapsulating a set of factory methods within a higher-level interface. This approach is especially useful when the system needs to support multiple families of products and ensure that products from different families are not mixed.

To better understand the nuances between these two patterns, we will examine their structure, implementation, and use cases comprehensively.

- **Structure:** - The Factory Method pattern typically involves an abstract creator class that declares the factory method, and concrete creator classes that implement the factory method. The product object created is usually defined by an interface or abstract class. - The Abstract Factory pattern involves an abstract factory class that declares a set of factory methods for creating abstract products. Concrete factory classes implement these factory methods to produce concrete products. The products are often related and form a family of objects.
- **Implementation:** - The Factory Method pattern uses inheritance to change the product instantiation logic. A common approach involves defining a base class with a factory method, and derived classes providing different implementations of the factory method. - In the Abstract Factory pattern, composition is utilized to encapsulate the creation of related products. An abstract factory interface with multiple factory methods is implemented by concrete factory classes, which produce instances of related products.

  The following Java code examples illustrate the implementation of both patterns.

```
abstract class Product {
    abstract void use();
}

class ConcreteProductA extends Product {
    @Override
    void use() {
        System.out.println("Using ConcreteProductA");
    }
}

class ConcreteProductB extends Product {
    @Override
    void use() {
        System.out.println("Using ConcreteProductB");
    }
}

abstract class Creator {
    abstract Product factoryMethod();

    void someOperation() {
        Product product = factoryMethod();
        product.use();
```

```
    }
}
class ConcreteCreatorA extends Creator {
    @Override
    Product factoryMethod() {
        return new ConcreteProductA();
    }
}

class ConcreteCreatorB extends Creator {
    @Override
    Product factoryMethod() {
        return new ConcreteProductB();
    }
}
```

```
interface AbstractProductA {
    void performAction();
}

interface AbstractProductB {
    void performTask();
}

class ConcreteProductA1 implements AbstractProductA {
    @Override
    public void performAction() {
        System.out.println("Action by ConcreteProductA1");
    }
}

class ConcreteProductA2 implements AbstractProductA {
    @Override
    public void performAction() {
        System.out.println("Action by ConcreteProductA2");
    }
}

class ConcreteProductB1 implements AbstractProductB {
    @Override
    public void performTask() {
        System.out.println("Task by ConcreteProductB1");
    }
}

class ConcreteProductB2 implements AbstractProductB {
    @Override
    public void performTask() {
        System.out.println("Task by ConcreteProductB2");
    }
}

interface AbstractFactory {
    AbstractProductA createProductA();
    AbstractProductB createProductB();
}

class ConcreteFactory1 implements AbstractFactory {
    @Override
    public AbstractProductA createProductA() {
        return new ConcreteProductA1();
```

```
    }

    @Override
    public AbstractProductB createProductB() {
        return new ConcreteProductB1();
    }
}

class ConcreteFactory2 implements AbstractFactory {
    @Override
    public AbstractProductA createProductA() {
        return new ConcreteProductA2();
    }

    @Override
    public AbstractProductB createProductB() {
        return new ConcreteProductB2();
    }
}
```

- **Purpose:** - The Factory Method pattern aims to defer the instantiation of objects to subclasses, enabling polymorphic creation of objects and ensuring that the client code is decoupled from the specifics of object creation. - The Abstract Factory pattern addresses the requirement of creating families of related objects without specifying their concrete classes. This ensures that only compatible products are used together and facilitates the exchange of entire product families easily.

- **Use cases:** - The Factory Method pattern is beneficial when a class cannot anticipate the type of objects it must create, when a class wants its subclasses to specify the object types, or to localize the creation of objects. - The Abstract Factory pattern is useful when a system should be independent of how its products are created, when a system needs to use multiple families of products, or to ensure consistency among products within a family.

By understanding the distinct characteristics and purposes of the Factory Method and Abstract Factory patterns, developers can make informed decisions about which pattern to use based on their specific design requirements. Both patterns provide flexible and elegant solutions to various creational problems in software design, enhancing the reusability and maintainability of the codebase.

5.9 Use Cases for Factory Patterns

The Factory Pattern, encompassing both Factory Method and Abstract Factory variants, is instrumental in software design due to its flexibility and ability to decouple object creation from the main code logic. This section delves into specific scenarios that benefit from the application of these patterns, illustrating their significance in real-world software development.

1. When the Exact Class of Objects to be Created is Unknown Until Runtime

In many applications, the type of object required is determined dynamically during execution. The Factory Method pattern is particularly useful in such cases as it allows the instantiation process to be deferred to subclasses. Consider a graphic editor program that supports multiple shape types (e.g., circles, rectangles, triangles) that users can draw. The exact shape type is selected by the user at runtime, necessitating a flexible creation mechanism.

```
abstract class Shape {
    abstract void draw();
}

class Circle extends Shape {
    void draw() {
        System.out.println("Drawing Circle");
    }
}

class Rectangle extends Shape {
    void draw() {
        System.out.println("Drawing Rectangle");
    }
}

abstract class ShapeFactory {
    abstract Shape createShape();
}

class CircleFactory extends ShapeFactory {
    Shape createShape() {
        return new Circle();
    }
}

class RectangleFactory extends ShapeFactory {
    Shape createShape() {
        return new Rectangle();
    }
}

public class GraphicEditor {
    public static void main(String[] args) {
```

```
        ShapeFactory factory = getFactory(args[0]); // dynamically decided
        Shape shape = factory.createShape();
        shape.draw();
    }

    private static ShapeFactory getFactory(String shapeType) {
        if (shapeType.equalsIgnoreCase("Circle")) {
            return new CircleFactory();
        } else if (shapeType.equalsIgnoreCase("Rectangle")) {
            return new RectangleFactory();
        }
        throw new IllegalArgumentException("Unknown shape type");
    }
}
```

2. When Object Creation Involves Complex Processes

If the instantiation of objects involves complex processes, configuration, or dependencies, Factory Patterns provide a structured approach to manage this complexity. For example, consider a system that needs to configure objects with various services or dependencies (e.g., database connections, logging services) before they can be used.

```
interface Service {
    void execute();
}

class DatabaseService implements Service {
    public void execute() {
        System.out.println("Executing Database Query");
    }
}

class LoggingService implements Service {
    public void execute() {
        System.out.println("Logging Application Info");
    }
}

abstract class ServiceFactory {
    abstract Service createService();
}

class DatabaseServiceFactory extends ServiceFactory {
    Service createService() {
        // Complex initialization logic for DatabaseService
        return new DatabaseService();
    }
}

class LoggingServiceFactory extends ServiceFactory {
    Service createService() {
        // Complex initialization logic for LoggingService
        return new LoggingService();
    }
}

public class Application {
    public static void main(String[] args) {
```

```
        ServiceFactory factory = getServiceFactory(args[0]); // dynamically decided
        Service service = factory.createService();
        service.execute();
    }

    private static ServiceFactory getServiceFactory(String serviceType) {
        if (serviceType.equalsIgnoreCase("Database")) {
            return new DatabaseServiceFactory();
        } else if (serviceType.equalsIgnoreCase("Logging")) {
            return new LoggingServiceFactory();
        }
        throw new IllegalArgumentException("Unknown service type");
    }
}
```

3. When You Need to Adhere to the Open/Closed Principle

Adhering to the Open/Closed Principle (OCP) is fundamental in object-oriented design. It dictates that software entities should be open for extension but closed for modification. The Factory Pattern facilitates this by allowing new types to be introduced without altering existing code. For example, adding a new type of shape or service in the previous examples doesn't require changes to the code that uses these objects, only the introduction of new factory subclasses.

4. When Families of Related or Dependent Objects Need to be Created

The Abstract Factory Pattern is particularly adept at situations where a family of interconnected objects is needed, such as in GUI toolkits where different sets of components (like windows, buttons, and dialogs) might be required for different operating systems (Windows, macOS, Linux).

```
interface GUIFactory {
    Button createButton();
    Checkbox createCheckbox();
}

class WinFactory implements GUIFactory {
    public Button createButton() {
        return new WinButton();
    }
    public Checkbox createCheckbox() {
        return new WinCheckbox();
    }
}

class MacFactory implements GUIFactory {
    public Button createButton() {
        return new MacButton();
    }
    public Checkbox createCheckbox() {
        return new MacCheckbox();
    }
}
```

```
interface Button {
    void paint();
}

class WinButton implements Button {
    public void paint() {
        System.out.println("Windows Button");
    }
}

class MacButton implements Button {
    public void paint() {
        System.out.println("Mac Button");
    }
}

interface Checkbox {
    void paint();
}

class WinCheckbox implements Checkbox {
    public void paint() {
        System.out.println("Windows Checkbox");
    }
}

class MacCheckbox implements Checkbox {
    public void paint() {
        System.out.println("Mac Checkbox");
    }
}

public class Application {
    private GUIFactory factory;
    private Button button;
    private Checkbox checkbox;

    public Application(GUIFactory factory) {
        this.factory = factory;
    }

    public void createUI() {
        this.button = factory.createButton();
        this.checkbox = factory.createCheckbox();
    }

    public void paint() {
        button.paint();
        checkbox.paint();
    }

    public static void main(String[] args) {
        GUIFactory factory;
        String os = System.getProperty("os.name").toLowerCase();
        if (os.contains("win")) {
            factory = new WinFactory();
        } else {
            factory = new MacFactory();
        }
        Application app = new Application(factory);
        app.createUI();
```

```
        app.paint();
    }
}
```

In these examples, the use of the Factory Pattern allows each family of related components to be created consistently, ensuring that the application maintains compatibility with the operating system it's running on without requiring extensive conditionals or modifications in the primary application logic.

5. When the System Needs to Allow Plugins or Configurable Components

Plugins and configurable components are common in large-scale software applications. Using Factory Patterns enables a system to dynamically include and configure these plugins while keeping the core system closed for modification. For instance, a web server might allow different authentication mechanisms (e.g., OAuth, JWT, BasicAuth) to be plugged in via factories.

```
interface Authenticator {
    void authenticate();
}

class OAuthAuthenticator implements Authenticator {
    public void authenticate() {
        System.out.println("Authenticating via OAuth");
    }
}

class JWTAuthenticator implements Authenticator {
    public void authenticate() {
        System.out.println("Authenticating via JWT");
    }
}

abstract class AuthenticatorFactory {
    abstract Authenticator createAuthenticator();
}

class OAuthAuthenticatorFactory extends AuthenticatorFactory {
    Authenticator createAuthenticator() {
        return new OAuthAuthenticator();
    }
}

class JWTAuthenticatorFactory extends AuthenticatorFactory {
    Authenticator createAuthenticator() {
        return new JWTAuthenticator();
    }
}

public class WebServer {
    private Authenticator authenticator;

    public void setAuthenticatorFactory(AuthenticatorFactory factory) {
```

```
        this.authenticator = factory.createAuthenticator();
    }

    public void authenticateRequest() {
        authenticator.authenticate();
    }

    public static void main(String[] args) {
        WebServer server = new WebServer();
        AuthenticatorFactory factory = getAuthenticatorFactory(args[0]); //
            dynamically decided
        server.setAuthenticatorFactory(factory);
        server.authenticateRequest();
    }

    private static AuthenticatorFactory getAuthenticatorFactory(String authType) {
        if (authType.equalsIgnoreCase("OAuth")) {
            return new OAuthAuthenticatorFactory();
        } else if (authType.equalsIgnoreCase("JWT")) {
            return new JWTAuthenticatorFactory();
        }
        throw new IllegalArgumentException("Unknown authenticator type");
    }
}
```

These use cases showcase the versatility and robustness of Factory Patterns in handling complex object creation scenarios, maintaining adherence to design principles, and facilitating extensibility.

5.10 Best Practices in Applying Factory Patterns

When implementing Factory patterns, several best practices should be observed to ensure the design remains robust, maintainable, and flexible. This section details these practices, providing guidance for leveraging the full potential of Factory patterns in Java.

To begin with, always strive for clear separation of concerns. The factory classes should be solely responsible for the creation of objects. Any additional logic related to the use of these objects should be contained within other classes. This principle maintains clean and manageable code, isolating the construction logic from business logic.

It's imperative to use interfaces or abstract classes to define the common types that will be instantiated by the factory. This abstraction decouples client code from specific implementations, augmenting code reusability and flexibility. Consider the following example where the Shape interface defines the type for different shape objects created by the factory:

```
public interface Shape {
    void draw();
}
```

Ensure that the factory classes adhere to the Single Responsibility Principle, meaning each factory should only have one reason to change. For instance, a ShapeFactory should only be concerned with creating different types of Shape instances and not with their behaviour or how they are used.

Applying the Open/Closed Principle is also critical. The factory should be open for extension but closed for modification. New products should be introducible without modifying the existing code. Using the Factory Method pattern, this principle can be illustrated as:

```
public abstract class ShapeFactory {
    public abstract Shape createShape();
}
class CircleFactory extends ShapeFactory {
    @Override
    public Shape createShape() {
        return new Circle();
    }
}
class SquareFactory extends ShapeFactory {
    @Override
    public Shape createShape() {
        return new Square();
    }
}
```

Favor composition over inheritance to reduce the risk of tight coupling and to promote greater flexibility and reuse. A factory might internally use other helper classes or smaller factories to handle the creation of complex objects.

If the factory requires configuration or depends on particular parameters, consider using a configuration class or method injection to pass these parameters. This approach promotes a cleaner and more maintainable codebase. For instance:

```
public class ConfigurableShapeFactory {
    private String shapeType;

    public ConfigurableShapeFactory(String shapeType) {
        this.shapeType = shapeType;
    }

    public Shape createShape() {
        if ("circle".equalsIgnoreCase(shapeType)) {
            return new Circle();
        } else if ("square".equalsIgnoreCase(shapeType)) {
            return new Square();
```

```
        }
        throw new IllegalArgumentException("Unknown shape type");
    }
}
```

In the context of the Abstract Factory pattern, ensure that related factories are grouped together to maintain coherency and consistency. Each factory within the abstract factory should follow the same interface or abstract class, enabling easy substitution and maintainability.

Document the factory classes thoroughly. Annotate what specific paradigms each factory implements, and what each class is responsible for. Good documentation fosters better understanding and ease of use for other developers who might manipulate or extend the factory classes.

Testing factory implementations is crucial. Rigorous unit testing should be performed to ensure that the correct objects are instantiated and that the expected behaviours are executed. Employ mock objects where direct instantiation is required for testing purposes. For example:

```
@Test
public void testCircleFactory() {
    ShapeFactory factory = new CircleFactory();
    Shape shape = factory.createShape();
    assertTrue(shape instanceof Circle);
}
```

Incorporate logging within factory classes when dealing with complex object creation procedures. This practice helps in tracing issues during runtime and provides insight into the object creation process. Use the following example employing a Logging Framework:

```
import org.slf4j.Logger;
import org.slf4j.LoggerFactory;

public class LoggingShapeFactory implements ShapeFactory {
    private static final Logger logger = LoggerFactory.getLogger(LoggingShapeFactory.
        class);

    @Override
    public Shape createShape() {
        logger.info("Creating a circle instance");
        return new Circle();
    }
}
```

When dealing with multithreaded environments, ensure that factory classes are thread-safe. This might include employing synchronization techniques or using thread-safe collections and utilities provided by the Java concurrency utilities, as shown below:

```
public class ThreadSafeShapeFactory {
    private final Map<String, Shape> shapeCache = Collections.synchronizedMap(new
          HashMap<>());

    public Shape getShape(String shapeType) {
        synchronized (shapeCache) {
            if (!shapeCache.containsKey(shapeType)) {
                shapeCache.put(shapeType, createShape(shapeType));
            }
        }
        return shapeCache.get(shapeType);
    }

    private Shape createShape(String shapeType) {
        if ("circle".equalsIgnoreCase(shapeType)) {
            return new Circle();
        } else if ("square".equalsIgnoreCase(shapeType)) {
            return new Square();
        }
        throw new IllegalArgumentException("Unknown shape type");
    }
}
```

Finally, monitor the performance of the factories, especially if the creation process is resource-intensive. Lazy loading and caching strategies can be employed to optimize performance by delaying object creation until necessary and reusing already created objects.

By adhering to these best practices, developers can ensure that their application of the Factory patterns is both effective and efficient, resulting in scalable and maintainable code.

5.11 Common Mistakes and How to Avoid Them

There are several common pitfalls that developers may encounter when working with the Factory Pattern. Awareness and proactive management of these mistakes can greatly improve the efficacy and maintainability of your design.

One typical mistake is failing to adhere to the Open/Closed Principle. When a Factory class is responsible for creating instances of many different product classes, adding new types often requires modifying the Factory class. This introduces rigidity and makes the code less maintainable.

Consider the following example:

```
public class ShapeFactory {
```

```
    public Shape createShape(String shapeType) {
        if (shapeType == null) {
            return null;
        }
        if (shapeType.equalsIgnoreCase("CIRCLE")) {
            return new Circle();
        } else if (shapeType.equalsIgnoreCase("RECTANGLE")) {
            return new Rectangle();
        }
        return null;
    }
}
```

This ShapeFactory class violates the Open/Closed Principle as it must be modified to introduce any new shape type.

A better approach is to use a more flexible design. Refactor the factory to follow the principle by employing a registry of creators:

```
import java.util.HashMap;
import java.util.Map;

public class ShapeFactory {
    private static final Map<String, Supplier<Shape>> registry = new HashMap<>();

    static {
        registry.put("CIRCLE", Circle::new);
        registry.put("RECTANGLE", Rectangle::new);
    }

    public static void registerShape(String shapeId, Supplier<Shape> supplier) {
        registry.put(shapeId, supplier);
    }

    public static Shape createShape(String shapeId) {
        Supplier<Shape> shapeSupplier = registry.get(shapeId);
        if (shapeSupplier != null) {
            return shapeSupplier.get();
        }
        throw new IllegalArgumentException("Unknown shape type: " + shapeId);
    }
}
```

This approach allows new shapes to be added without modifying the existing code, adhering to the Open/Closed Principle.

Another common mistake is intertwining object creation logic directly within business logic. This can be demonstrated as follows:

```
public class DrawingService {
    public void drawShape(String shapeType) {
        Shape shape;
        if (shapeType.equalsIgnoreCase("CIRCLE")) {
            shape = new Circle();
        } else if (shapeType.equalsIgnoreCase("RECTANGLE")) {
            shape = new Rectangle();
        } else {
            throw new IllegalArgumentException("Unknown shape type: " + shapeType)
```

```
                ;
        }
        shape.draw();
    }
}
```

This code mixes creation and usage, making the DrawingService class less flexible and testing more difficult. Instead, we should delegate the creation of objects to a factory class:

```
public class DrawingService {
    private final ShapeFactory shapeFactory;

    public DrawingService(ShapeFactory shapeFactory) {
        this.shapeFactory = shapeFactory;
    }

    public void drawShape(String shapeType) {
        Shape shape = shapeFactory.createShape(shapeType);
        shape.draw();
    }
}
```

Here, DrawingService delegates the responsibility of shape creation to the ShapeFactory, leading to a cleaner separation of concerns.

Another common error is neglecting to handle exceptions and edge cases properly within factory methods. Factories should be robust against unexpected inputs and must fail gracefully. Consider improving exception handling as follows:

```
public Shape createShape(String shapeType) {
    if (shapeType == null || shapeType.trim().isEmpty()) {
        throw new IllegalArgumentException("Shape type must not be null or empty.");
    }
    shapeType = shapeType.toUpperCase();
    Supplier<Shape> shapeSupplier = registry.get(shapeType);
    if (shapeSupplier != null) {
        return shapeSupplier.get();
    }
    throw new IllegalArgumentException("Unknown shape type: " + shapeType);
}
```

Proper exception handling ensures that the factory method is reliable and easier to debug when errors occur.

Lastly, overlooking the importance of clear and comprehensive documentation can lead to significant misunderstandings and misuse of the factory method. Always document the factory methods, explaining parameters, return types, and possible exceptions.

By avoiding these common mistakes, you can leverage the full benefits of the Factory Pattern, creating more flexible, maintainable, and robust code.

5.12 Real-World Examples of Factory Patterns in Java

The practical implementation of the Factory Patterns offers significant benefits in real-world applications. This section presents detailed examples highlighting the usage of both Factory Method and Abstract Factory patterns in Java, demonstrating their relevance in creating maintainable and scalable code solutions.

The Factory Method pattern can be found in various Java platform libraries. For instance, the java.util.Calendar class uses the Factory Method pattern to create instances of Calendar. The following is an illustrative example:

```
import java.util.Calendar;

public class FactoryMethodExample {
    public static void main(String[] args) {
        Calendar calendar = Calendar.getInstance();
        System.out.println("Current Date and Time: " + calendar.getTime());
    }
}
```

The Calendar.getInstance() method encapsulates the instantiation logic, allowing for flexibility in the type of Calendar instance being returned based on the locale and time zone, decoupling the client code from the specific implementations.

A more comprehensive example can be seen in the context of a graphics rendering system where different shapes need to be created dynamically:

```
interface Shape {
    void draw();
}

class Circle implements Shape {
    @Override
    public void draw() {
        System.out.println("Drawing a Circle");
    }
}

class Rectangle implements Shape {
    @Override
    public void draw() {
        System.out.println("Drawing a Rectangle");
    }
```

```
}

abstract class ShapeFactory {
    abstract Shape createShape(String type);
}
class ConcreteShapeFactory extends ShapeFactory {
    @Override
    Shape createShape(String type) {
        switch (type.toLowerCase()) {
            case "circle":
                return new Circle();
            case "rectangle":
                return new Rectangle();
            default:
                throw new IllegalArgumentException("Unknown shape type.");
        }
    }
}

public class FactoryMethodExample {
    public static void main(String[] args) {
        ShapeFactory factory = new ConcreteShapeFactory();
        Shape shape1 = factory.createShape("circle");
        shape1.draw();

        Shape shape2 = factory.createShape("rectangle");
        shape2.draw();
    }
}
```

This implementation of the Factory Method pattern allows for the creation of different shape objects, adhering to the Open/Closed Principle by extending the range of shapes without modifying the existing code.

For the Abstract Factory pattern, a real-world example is evident in widget toolkits for graphical user interfaces (GUIs). Creating families of related or dependent objects without specifying their concrete classes can be beneficial. Consider a scenario where GUI components vary between different operating systems:

```
interface Button {
    void paint();
}

interface Checkbox {
    void paint();
}

class WinButton implements Button {
    @Override
    public void paint() {
        System.out.println("Rendering a Windows button.");
    }
}

class MacButton implements Button {
    @Override
```

```
    public void paint() {
        System.out.println("Rendering a Mac button.");
    }
}

class WinCheckbox implements Checkbox {
    @Override
    public void paint() {
        System.out.println("Rendering a Windows checkbox.");
    }
}

class MacCheckbox implements Checkbox {
    @Override
    public void paint() {
        System.out.println("Rendering a Mac checkbox.");
    }
}

interface GUIFactory {
    Button createButton();
    Checkbox createCheckbox();
}

class WinFactory implements GUIFactory {
    @Override
    public Button createButton() {
        return new WinButton();
    }

    @Override
    public Checkbox createCheckbox() {
        return new WinCheckbox();
    }
}

class MacFactory implements GUIFactory {
    @Override
    public Button createButton() {
        return new MacButton();
    }

    @Override
    public Checkbox createCheckbox() {
        return new MacCheckbox();
    }
}

class Application {
    private Button button;
    private Checkbox checkbox;

    public Application(GUIFactory factory) {
        button = factory.createButton();
        checkbox = factory.createCheckbox();
    }

    public void paint() {
        button.paint();
        checkbox.paint();
    }
}
```

```
public class AbstractFactoryExample {
    public static void main(String[] args) {
        Application app;
        GUIFactory factory;
        String osName = System.getProperty("os.name").toLowerCase();

        if (osName.contains("win")) {
            factory = new WinFactory();
        } else if (osName.contains("mac")) {
            factory = new MacFactory();
        } else {
            throw new IllegalArgumentException("Unsupported OS.");
        }

        app = new Application(factory);
        app.paint();
    }
}
```

The Abstract Factory pattern gives a systematic way to encapsulate a group of individual factories that share a common theme. The preceding example demonstrates the versatility of the Abstract Factory pattern, allowing an application to remain adaptable to different operating environments without altering the client code.

Implementing the Factory patterns in real-world applications simplifies object creation, enhances scalability, maintains code cohesion, and adheres to SOLID principles. This section has provided explicit examples to embody these advantages in Java, showcasing their practical usage and benefits in software design.

Chapter 6

Singleton Pattern: Ensuring a Single Instance

This chapter covers the Singleton Pattern, which ensures that a class has only one instance while providing a global point of access to it. The chapter details various implementation methods in Java, including basic, thread-safe, lazy initialization, Bill Pugh, and enum approaches. It explores the benefits and potential drawbacks of using the Singleton pattern, alongside best practices and common pitfalls to avoid. Real-world examples illustrate the pattern's application, highlighting scenarios where it is most effective.

6.1 Introduction to the Singleton Pattern

The Singleton pattern is a design pattern that restricts the instantiation of a class to exactly one instance for the duration of a program's execution. This pattern provides a controlled mechanism to ensure that there is only one instance while also granting global access to this instance. The Singleton pattern is particularly useful when managing shared resources such as database connections, configuration settings, and logging mechanisms.

A succinct definition by the "Gang of Four" who first documented this pattern in *Design Patterns: Elements of Reusable Object-Oriented Software* is: "Ensure a class has only one instance and provide a global point of access to it."

To understand the practicality and necessity of employing the Singleton pattern, consider the scenarios where a unique instance might be required:

- **Resource Management:** When an application needs a coordinated and controlled access to a limited resource such as filesystem handles, database connections, or networking sockets.
- **Configuration Settings:** When an application's configuration parameters need to be consistent and globally accessible.
- **Logging:** Centralized logging where logs need to be aggregated into a single log file or system, ensuring that all parts of the application write logs consistently.
- **Caching:** When managing caches to store reusable data across various parts of the application, ensuring that there's only one cache instance.

The Singleton pattern implementation revolves around three crucial elements:

- **Private Constructor:** Ensures that no other code can instantiate the class directly.
- **Static Method:** Provides a way to instantiate the class and to return the one and only instance.
- **Static Variable:** Holds the one instance of the class.

Let us consider a simplistic implementation of the Singleton pattern in Java to illustrate these principles:

```
public class Singleton {
    private static Singleton instance;

    // Private constructor prevents instantiation from other classes
    private Singleton() {}

    // Static method to provide global access point
    public static Singleton getInstance() {
        if (instance == null) {
```

```
            instance = new Singleton();
        }
        return instance;
    }
}
```

In this implementation, the Singleton class has a private constructor, which prevents instantiation from outside the class. The getInstance method checks if the instance variable is null. If it is, it creates a new object of the Singleton class; otherwise, it returns the existing object.

This basic implementation ensures that the Singleton class can only have one instance at any given time. However, it comes with a significant limitation: it is not thread-safe. In a multithreaded environment, multiple threads could enter the getInstance method simultaneously when instance is null and create multiple instances of the Singleton class.

To address this limitation, more advanced techniques such as synchronized methods, double-checked locking, the Bill Pugh Singleton design, and enumeration-based Singleton which is inherently thread-safe, can be employed. These methods provide enhanced thread safety and are discussed further in the subsequent sections of this chapter.

The benefits of using the Singleton pattern are clear:

- **Controlled Access:** The Singleton pattern controls the point of access to the instance, ensuring that proper initialization and cleanup can be performed.
- **Reduced Namespace Pollution:** By having a single instance accessed globally, we avoid the proliferation of global variables for common resources.
- **Consistency:** As there is only one instance, the state of this instance remains consistent across the whole application.

Despite its many advantages, the Singleton pattern can also present certain pitfalls if not carefully implemented:

- **Single Point of Failure:** If the Singleton instance becomes corrupted or misconfigured, it can affect the entire application.
- **Global State Management:** Improper handling can lead to hidden dependencies across the system, making the code harder to understand and maintain.

- **Testing Challengers:** Singletons can complicate unit testing since they introduce hidden dependencies which can affect test isolation.

Understanding when and how to use the Singleton pattern effectively is crucial for leveraging its benefits while mitigating the associated risks. This chapter aims to delve deeper into various implementations, use cases, and best practices to guide developers in making informed decisions about integrating Singletons into their design.

6.2 Understanding Singleton Pattern

The Singleton Pattern is a design pattern that restricts the instantiation of a class to one single instance. This ensures controlled access to the instance and consistency throughout the application. The pattern is employed in scenarios where exactly one instance of a class is sufficient, often to coordinate actions across the system.

The Singleton Pattern is characterized by the following principles:

- **Single Instance:** Ensures only one instance of a class exists.
- **Global Access:** Provides a global access point to the single instance.

A typical Singleton class includes a private constructor, a static method to provide access to the instance, and a private static variable to hold the single instance.

Basic Structure

The structure of a basic Singleton class in Java is as follows:

```
public class Singleton {
    private static Singleton uniqueInstance;

    private Singleton() {
        // Private constructor to prevent instantiation
    }

    public static Singleton getInstance() {
        if (uniqueInstance == null) {
            uniqueInstance = new Singleton();
        }
        return uniqueInstance;
```

```
    }
}
```

In the above implementation:

- uniqueInstance is a private static variable that holds the single instance of the Singleton class.
- The Singleton() constructor is private, preventing any other class from instantiating it.
- The getInstance() method checks if the instance already exists. If not, it creates the instance and then returns it.

Preventing Multiple Instantiations

Despite the basic structure's simplicity, it is crucial to consider scenarios such as multiple threads attempting to access the getInstance() method simultaneously. Without proper handling, multiple instances could be created, violating the Singleton Pattern.

To make the Singleton class thread-safe, different approaches can be applied. One common method involves synchronizing the getInstance() method:

```
public class Singleton {
    private static Singleton uniqueInstance;

    private Singleton() {
        // Private constructor to prevent instantiation
    }

    public static synchronized Singleton getInstance() {
        if (uniqueInstance == null) {
            uniqueInstance = new Singleton();
        }
        return uniqueInstance;
    }
}
```

Using the synchronized keyword ensures that only one thread can execute the getInstance() method at a time. However, this method has a performance cost due to the synchronization overhead each time the method is invoked.

Lazy Initialization

In some cases, it is beneficial to delay the initialization of the Singleton instance until the first request. The lazy initialization approach helps improve performance by ensuring that the Singleton instance is created only when it is needed:

```
public class Singleton {
    private static Singleton uniqueInstance;

    private Singleton() {
        // Private constructor to prevent instantiation
    }

    public static Singleton getInstance() {
        if (uniqueInstance == null) {
            uniqueInstance = new Singleton();
        }
        return uniqueInstance;
    }
}
```

If thread safety is a concern and synchronization is too costly, the "Double-Checked Locking" principle can be used. This combines lazy initialization and synchronization efficiently:

```
public class Singleton {
    private static volatile Singleton uniqueInstance;

    private Singleton() {
        // Private constructor to prevent instantiation
    }

    public static Singleton getInstance() {
        if (uniqueInstance == null) {
            synchronized (Singleton.class) {
                if (uniqueInstance == null) {
                    uniqueInstance = new Singleton();
                }
            }
        }
        return uniqueInstance;
    }
}
```

In this implementation:

- volatile ensures visibility of uniqueInstance across threads.
- The first check if (uniqueInstance == null) is not synchronized to avoid performance overhead.
- The second check inside the synchronized block ensures that no other thread has initialized uniqueInstance before the current

thread acquires the lock.

Bill Pugh Singleton Design

Another effective method to implement the Singleton Pattern is the Bill Pugh Singleton Design, which leverages the Java memory model and class loading mechanism:

```
public class Singleton {
    private Singleton() {
        // Private constructor to prevent instantiation
    }

    private static class SingletonHolder {
        private static final Singleton INSTANCE = new Singleton();
    }

    public static Singleton getInstance() {
        return SingletonHolder.INSTANCE;
    }
}
```

This approach:

- Utilizes a private static inner class, SingletonHolder, responsible for instantiating the Singleton instance.
- Ensures INSTANCE is only created when the getInstance() method is called, following the lazy initialization principle.
- Avoids synchronization issues by relying on the class loader mechanism, which guarantees that the instance is created only when the class is accessed.

Understanding the Singleton Pattern and its various implementations is vital for ensuring correctness and performance in Java applications. While each method has its trade-offs, selecting the appropriate implementation depends on the specific requirements and constraints of the application.

6.3 Implementing Singleton in Java - Basic Approach

The Singleton Pattern is one of the simplest design patterns in object-oriented programming. It ensures that a class has only a single instance and provides a global access point to this instance. The basic approach to implementing the Singleton Pattern in Java involves creating a class where:

- The constructor is made private to prevent the direct instantiation of the class from outside.
- A static variable holds the single instance of the class.
- A public static method provides the global access point to the instance.

Let us consider a class called BasicSingleton. Here is how we can implement the Singleton Pattern using the basic approach:

```
public class BasicSingleton {
    // The static variable to hold the single instance.
    private static BasicSingleton instance;

    // Private constructor to prevent instantiation from other classes.
    private BasicSingleton() {
        // Initialization code here
    }

    // Public static method to provide the global access point.
    public static BasicSingleton getInstance() {
        if (instance == null) {
            instance = new BasicSingleton();
        }
        return instance;
    }
}
```

In this implementation, BasicSingleton class has a private static variable instance which holds the single instance of the class. The constructor is private, preventing any external instantiation of the class. The getInstance() method is public and static, which means it can be called without creating an object of the class. If instance is null, a new BasicSingleton instance is created; otherwise, the existing instance is returned.

Consider the following example of using the BasicSingleton class:

```
public class Main {
    public static void main(String[] args) {
        BasicSingleton singleton1 = BasicSingleton.getInstance();
        BasicSingleton singleton2 = BasicSingleton.getInstance();

        // Verify that both variables hold the same instance.
        System.out.println(singleton1 == singleton2); // Outputs: true
    }
}
```

In this example, both singleton1 and singleton2 reference the same instance of BasicSingleton. The expression singleton1 == singleton2 evaluates to true because the Singleton Pattern ensures only one instance is created.

It is important to note that while the basic implementation is straightforward, it is not thread-safe. If multiple threads call getInstance() simultaneously when instance is null, multiple instances of BasicSingleton could be created. Here is an example demonstrating this issue:

```
public class MultiThreadDemo implements Runnable {
    @Override
    public void run() {
        BasicSingleton singleton = BasicSingleton.getInstance();
        System.out.println(singleton);
    }

    public static void main(String[] args) {
        Thread thread1 = new Thread(new MultiThreadDemo());
        Thread thread2 = new Thread(new MultiThreadDemo());

        thread1.start();
        thread2.start();
    }
}
```

When running the above code, it is possible to see different BasicSingleton instances being printed if thread interleaving causes multiple threads to pass the null check simultaneously.

To address thread-safety concerns, more sophisticated implementation techniques—covered in later sections—need to be employed. For instance, synchronized methods or utilizing volatile keywords can ensure that only one instance is created even in multi-threaded environments.

Thus, while implementing the Singleton Pattern using the basic approach offers simplicity and ease of understanding, it is essential to be aware of its limitations, particularly regarding thread safety. More advanced techniques should be considered for applications in concurrent execution contexts, which will be discussed in subsequent sections.

6.4 Thread-safe Singleton Implementation

Ensuring that the Singleton is thread-safe is critical in a multi-threaded environment to prevent multiple instances from being created. If the Singleton pattern is used in applications that handle multiple threads, the implementation must guarantee that only one instance is created, even if multiple threads are attempting to create an instance simultaneously.

A common approach to implementing a thread-safe Singleton pattern in Java involves using synchronized methods. By synchronizing the method that provides access to the Singleton instance, we ensure that only one thread can execute this method at a time. Here is an example of a thread-safe Singleton implementation using the synchronized keyword:

```
public class ThreadSafeSingleton {
    private static ThreadSafeSingleton instance;

    private ThreadSafeSingleton() {
        // Private constructor to prevent instantiation
    }

    public static synchronized ThreadSafeSingleton getInstance() {
        if (instance == null) {
            instance = new ThreadSafeSingleton();
        }
        return instance;
    }
}
```

In this implementation, the getInstance() method is synchronized, ensuring that only one thread can execute this method at a time. If the instance is null, the method creates a new instance of ThreadSafeSingleton. Otherwise, it returns the existing instance.

This approach is straightforward and guarantees thread safety. However, using the synchronized keyword in this manner can lead to performance issues. The synchronization bottleneck can be an overhead since every call to getInstance() requires acquiring and releasing a lock, even after the instance has been created.

An optimization of this approach is to use double-checked locking. Double-checked locking minimizes synchronization overhead by ensuring that synchronization is only used when the Singleton instance is being created. Once the instance is created, subsequent calls to getInstance() will not require synchronization. Here is the implementation of a Singleton using double-checked locking:

```
public class DoubleCheckedLockingSingleton {
    private volatile static DoubleCheckedLockingSingleton instance;

    private DoubleCheckedLockingSingleton() {
        // Private constructor to prevent instantiation
    }

    public static DoubleCheckedLockingSingleton getInstance() {
        if (instance == null) {
```

```
            synchronized (DoubleCheckedLockingSingleton.class) {
                if (instance == null) {
                    instance = new DoubleCheckedLockingSingleton();
                }
            }
        }
        return instance;
    }
}
```

In this example, the instance variable is declared as volatile, which ensures that multiple threads handle the instance variable correctly when it is being initialized. The getInstance() method checks if the instance is null before entering the synchronized block. If it is null, the method proceeds to synchronize on the class object. Inside the synchronized block, the method checks the instance variable again and creates a new instance if it is still null.

The volatile keyword is essential in this context to prevent issues due to instruction reordering by the compiler or processor. Without volatile, it is possible for the instance variable to appear as if it's fully constructed and ready for use by one thread while another thread is still in the process of constructing the instance.

Another efficient way to create a thread-safe Singleton without the drawbacks of the previous two methods is to use the Bill Pugh Singleton design. This approach leverages the Java class loading mechanism, which ensures thread safety without requiring synchronized methods or volatile fields. Here is an example implementation:

```
public class BillPughSingleton {

    private BillPughSingleton() {
        // Private constructor to prevent instantiation
    }

    private static class SingletonHelper {
        private static final BillPughSingleton INSTANCE = new BillPughSingleton();
    }

    public static BillPughSingleton getInstance() {
        return SingletonHelper.INSTANCE;
    }
}
```

In this implementation, the Singleton instance is created in a static inner class, SingletonHelper. The JVM guarantees that the class will be loaded and the static initializer executed only when the class is first accessed. This ensures that the instantiation of BillPughSingleton is thread-safe and only occurs once. The getInstance() method provides access to the Singleton instance by returning SingletonHelper.INSTANCE.

While each thread-safe Singleton implementation has its advantages and potential drawbacks, the choice of approach depends on the specific requirements of the application, including performance concerns and the complexity of the implementation. Ensuring thread safety without compromising performance is crucial when using the Singleton pattern in multi-threaded environments.

6.5 Lazy Initialization in Singleton

Lazy initialization is a design technique employed to delay the creation of an instance of a class until it is required. This technique is particularly useful in resource management, as it defers the cost of resource allocation until the point it is actually needed. In the context of the Singleton pattern, lazy initialization ensures that the Singleton instance is created only when it is accessed for the first time, rather than at the time of class loading.

The primary advantage of lazy initialization in the Singleton pattern is that it can improve the startup time of an application by deferring the instantiation of the Singleton until it is called upon. Another advantage is that it helps manage resources more effectively, especially in scenarios where the Singleton instance is heavy to create.

Lazy initialization can be implemented in various ways. Here, the most straightforward method involves the use of a private static instance variable and a public static method to initialize this variable if it hasn't already been initialized. Below is a basic example illustrating the lazy initialization approach in the Singleton pattern:

```
public class LazySingleton {
    private static LazySingleton instance;

    private LazySingleton() {
        // Private constructor to prevent instantiation
    }

    public static LazySingleton getInstance() {
        if (instance == null) {
            instance = new LazySingleton();
        }
        return instance;
    }
}
```

In this example, the instance variable is declared as private static, ensuring that it belongs to the class and is not accessible from outside the class. The constructor is made private to prevent instantiation from outside the class. The getInstance() method contains a check to see if the instance variable is null; if it is, a new LazySingleton object is created and assigned to instance. This way, the Singleton instance is only created when getInstance() is first called.

While the basic lazy initialization approach is straightforward, it is not thread-safe. If multiple threads simultaneously call getInstance() during the initial access, multiple instances of the LazySingleton class may be created, violating the Singleton principle. To address this, we can use synchronized methods or blocks to ensure thread safety.

The simplest approach to make this thread-safe is to synchronize the getInstance() method:

```
public class ThreadSafeLazySingleton {
    private static ThreadSafeLazySingleton instance;

    private ThreadSafeLazySingleton() {
        // Private constructor to prevent instantiation
    }

    public static synchronized ThreadSafeLazySingleton getInstance() {
        if (instance == null) {
            instance = new ThreadSafeLazySingleton();
        }
        return instance;
    }
}
```

In this implementation, the synchronized keyword ensures that only one thread can execute getInstance() at a time, thus preventing multiple instances creation. However, synchronizing the entire method can be costly in terms of performance due to the overhead associated with synchronization.

To reduce the synchronization overhead, the Double-Checked Locking (DCL) idiom can be employed. This technique involves a double level of checking along with synchronized block to optimize the performance:

```
public class DoubleCheckedLockingSingleton {
    private static volatile DoubleCheckedLockingSingleton instance;

    private DoubleCheckedLockingSingleton() {
        // Private constructor to prevent instantiation
    }

    public static DoubleCheckedLockingSingleton getInstance() {
        if (instance == null) {
            synchronized (DoubleCheckedLockingSingleton.class) {
                if (instance == null) {
                    instance = new DoubleCheckedLockingSingleton();
```

```
                }
            }
        }
        return instance;
    }
}
```

In the DCL implementation, the volatile keyword ensures that multiple threads handle the instance variable correctly when it is being initialized to the DoubleCheckedLockingSingleton instance. The outer if statement checks if the instance is null, and only if it is, the synchronized block is entered. Within the synchronized block, another if statement ensures that no other thread has initialized instance while the current thread was waiting for the lock.

Although DCL fixes the problem of synchronization overhead, it is worth mentioning that the volatile keyword is essential in this context for the DCL pattern to work correctly in Java.

Lastly, the Bill Pugh Singleton Design provides an elegant and thread-safe solution to lazy initialization without the need for synchronization, leveraging Java's class loader mechanism.

```
public class BillPughSingleton {
    private BillPughSingleton() {
        // Private constructor to prevent instantiation
    }

    private static class SingletonHelper {
        private static final BillPughSingleton INSTANCE = new BillPughSingleton();
    }

    public static BillPughSingleton getInstance() {
        return SingletonHelper.INSTANCE;
    }
}
```

In Bill Pugh Singleton Design, the SingletonHelper inner static class contains the instance of the BillPughSingleton class. When the BillPughSingleton class is loaded, the inner class SingletonHelper is not loaded into memory and only when someone calls the getInstance() method, the SingletonHelper class gets loaded and creates the BillPughSingleton instance. This solution is thread-safe and doesn't require explicit synchronization.

Understanding and choosing the right lazy initialization strategy for the Singleton pattern depends on the specific requirements and constraints of the application, emphasizing the critical balance between simplicity, performance, and thread safety. Among the methods discussed, each has its place in software design, catering to varied scenarios and demands.

6.6 Bill Pugh Singleton Design

The Bill Pugh Singleton Design addresses the drawbacks associated with traditional lazy initialization and thread-safety when implementing the Singleton pattern in Java. This method leverages the Java Memory Model's guarantee of class initialization and the use of inner static helper classes to achieve a more robust Singleton implementation.

Bill Pugh's approach uses a concept known as the *Initialization-on-demand Holder Idiom*. This idiom ensures that the Singleton instance is created only when it is actually needed, combining lazy initialization with thread safety. Here is how this approach can be implemented in Java:

```
public class SingletonBillPugh {
    private SingletonBillPugh() {
        // private constructor to prevent instantiation
    }

    // Inner static helper class
    private static class SingletonHelper {
        private static final SingletonBillPugh INSTANCE = new SingletonBillPugh();
    }

    public static SingletonBillPugh getInstance() {
        return SingletonHelper.INSTANCE;
    }
}
```

In this implementation, the private static inner class SingletonHelper contains a static final instance of the SingletonBillPugh class. This instance is only created when the getInstance() method is called for the first time. The class loader mechanism guarantees that the instance is created in a thread-safe manner, ensuring no additional synchronization is required.

To understand this approach in more depth, let's break down its key components:

- **Private Constructor:** The constructor of SingletonBillPugh is made private to prevent any external instantiation.

- **Static Inner Class:** The SingletonHelper inner class is declared as private and static. The static declaration ensures that the class is not loaded into memory until it is referenced, and the private access restricts visibility to only the enclosing class.

- **Static Final Instance:** The static final instance of SingletonBillPugh within SingletonHelper is instantiated when the SingletonHelper class is first loaded into memory. According to the Java Memory Model, the class loader handles this loading in a thread-safe manner, enforcing singleton properties without requiring explicit synchronization.

- **Global Access Point:** The getInstance() method provides a global access point to the SingletonBillPugh instance held by SingletonHelper. When getInstance() is called, the SingletonHelper class is loaded, ensuring that the instance is created only once and in a secure manner.

The advantage of using this pattern lies in the efficient and lazy initialization of the Singleton instance while maintaining thread safety without the need for synchronized blocks or checks, which can cause performance bottlenecks.

Consider the following Java program to demonstrate how the SingletonBillPugh class works in practice:

```
public class SingletonPatternDemo {
    public static void main(String[] args) {
        SingletonBillPugh instance1 = SingletonBillPugh.getInstance();
        SingletonBillPugh instance2 = SingletonBillPugh.getInstance();

        // Compare the two instances to verify that they are the same
        if (instance1 == instance2) {
            System.out.println("Both instances are the same.");
        } else {
            System.out.println("Different instances exist.");
        }
    }
}
```

When this program is executed, the output confirms that both instance1 and instance2 refer to the same Singleton instance, highlighting the successful implementation of the Singleton pattern using Bill Pugh Singleton Design.

```
Both instances are the same.
```

The Bill Pugh Singleton Design is particularly effective because it ensures both lazy initialization and thread safety, which were challenging to achieve simultaneously in previous implementations. By leveraging the inner static helper class, this design provides a simple yet powerful solution aligning with the principles of the Singleton pattern, making it an optimal choice for various real-world applications.

6.7 Enum Singleton in Java

The Enum Singleton approach leverages the inherent properties of the enum type in Java to achieve a robust, thread-safe Singleton design with minimal effort. By utilizing enum, you inherently avoid many pitfalls associated with other Singleton implementation techniques, such as handling serialization and reflection attacks. This section delves into the mechanism and advantages of using enum for the Singleton pattern, alongside a detailed example.

The fundamental premise of using enum is that it provides a natural guarantee against multiple instantiation, supports serialization by default, and ensures thread safety without additional synchronization. The JVM assures that any enum value is instantiated only once in a Java program, making it a perfect candidate for the Singleton pattern.

```
public enum Singleton {
    INSTANCE;

    // Add instance methods you need here
    public void someMethod() {
        // your logic here
    }
}
```

In the provided example, the Singleton is defined as an enum with a single element INSTANCE, representing the singleton instance. Methods specific to the singleton instance can be added to the enum as needed.

```
Singleton.INSTANCE.someMethod();
```

The above line demonstrates the usage of the Singleton instance, invoking someMethod() on the single INSTANCE.

Advantages of Enum Singleton:

- **Thread Safety:** Enums are inherently thread-safe, therefore no need for explicit synchronization.
- **Serialization:** Enums provide a built-in serialization mechanism. The class automatically ensures that deserialization preserves the single instance property.

- **Protection Against Reflection:** Enums cannot be instantiated via reflection, mitigating one of the critical drawbacks of other Singleton implementations.

Enum Singleton and Serialization:

The serialization mechanism in Java can create multiple instances of the Singleton through deserialization unless additional methods like readResolve() are implemented, as shown in other forms of Singleton implementations. Enums elegantly handle this by their inherent properties. When an enum value is deserialized, the JVM ensures that the same instance is returned.

```
import java.io.*;

public enum Singleton {
    INSTANCE;

    // Sample method
    public void display() {
        System.out.println("Singleton using Enum");
    }
}
public class EnumSingletonTest {
    public static void main(String[] args) {
        try {
            Singleton instance1 = Singleton.INSTANCE;
            ObjectOutput out = new ObjectOutputStream(new FileOutputStream("file.
                ser"));
            out.writeObject(instance1);
            out.close();

            // Deserialize from file to object
            ObjectInput in = new ObjectInputStream(new FileInputStream("file.ser"));
            Singleton instance2 = (Singleton) in.readObject();
            in.close();

            System.out.println(instance1.hashCode());
            System.out.println(instance2.hashCode());
            System.out.println(instance1 == instance2);
        } catch (Exception e) {
            e.printStackTrace();
        }
    }
}
```

In the above example, the Singleton is serialized into a file and then deserialized. The hash codes of both the original and the deserialized instance are printed, along with the equality check. You will observe that both hash codes are identical and the equality check returns true, confirming that the same instance is preserved across serialization and deserialization processes.

Limitation:

The primary limitation of using Enum for Singleton is that enums are somewhat inflexible. Enum types are not ordinary classes and thus do not offer the same level of control or customization. This approach might not be suitable for Singletons with elaborate initialization.

Reflection Proof:

Reflective instantiation of enum types is restricted in Java. The use of reflection to instantiate a class bypassing the constructor calls does not apply to enums, further safeguarding the Singleton property.

In cases where the Singleton pattern's simplicity and reliability are paramount, the Enum Singleton approach stands out as an optimal choice, balancing ease of implementation with robust thread safety and serialization guarantees.

6.8 Comparison of Different Singleton Implementations

To comprehend the trade-offs and best scenarios for each Singleton implementation strategy in Java, a thorough comparison is imperative. This comparative analysis will cover six major implementations: Basic, Thread-Safe, Lazy Initialization, Bill Pugh, Enum Singleton, and Double-Checked Locking. Each method offers distinct advantages and constraints concerning thread safety, performance, and complexity.

Basic Singleton Implementation

The basic approach to implementing a Singleton is straightforward but inadequate for multithreaded environments.

```
public class BasicSingleton {
    private static BasicSingleton instance;

    private BasicSingleton() {
        // private constructor
    }

    public static BasicSingleton getInstance() {
        if (instance == null) {
            instance = new BasicSingleton();
        }
        return instance;
    }
}
```

This implementation is not thread-safe, which could lead to multiple instances if called simultaneously by different threads.

Thread-Safe Singleton

A thread-safe Singleton implementation can be achieved using the synchronized keyword to block concurrent access.

```
public class ThreadSafeSingleton {
    private static ThreadSafeSingleton instance;

    private ThreadSafeSingleton() {
        // private constructor
    }

    public static synchronized ThreadSafeSingleton getInstance() {
        if (instance == null) {
            instance = new ThreadSafeSingleton();
        }
        return instance;
    }
}
```

While this approach resolves concurrency issues by ensuring mutual exclusion, the use of synchronized impacts performance due to constant locking.

Lazy Initialization Singleton

Lazy Initialization ensures that the instance is created only when it is first required.

```
public class LazySingleton {
    private static LazySingleton instance;

    private LazySingleton() {
        // private constructor
    }

    public static LazySingleton getInstance() {
        if (instance == null) {
            instance = new LazySingleton();
        }
        return instance;
    }
}
```

This example is essentially identical to the basic non-thread-safe Singleton. Introducing lazy initialization without additional measures does not address concurrency issues.

Bill Pugh Singleton Design

The Bill Pugh Singleton Design employs an inner static helper class for thread safety without synchronization overhead.

```
public class BillPughSingleton {
    private BillPughSingleton() {
        // private constructor
    }

    private static class SingletonHelper {
```

```
        private static final BillPughSingleton INSTANCE = new BillPughSingleton();
    }

    public static BillPughSingleton getInstance() {
        return SingletonHelper.INSTANCE;
    }
}
```

The Bill Pugh approach leverages the Java Memory Model to ensure that the class is loaded and initialized in a thread-safe manner when first accessed.

Enum Singleton

The Enum Singleton pattern is the simplest and most robust Singleton implementation, leveraging Java's enumeration.

```
public enum EnumSingleton {
    INSTANCE;

    public void someMethod() {
        // some method implementation
    }
}
```

Enums in Java are inherently serializable and automatically ensure against multiple instantiation, even in the face of serialization or reflection attacks.

Double-Checked Locking Singleton

Double-Checked Locking aims to improve upon synchronized methods by reducing the overhead but maintaining thread safety.

```
public class DoubleCheckedLockingSingleton {
    private static volatile DoubleCheckedLockingSingleton instance;

    private DoubleCheckedLockingSingleton() {
        // private constructor
    }

    public static DoubleCheckedLockingSingleton getInstance() {
        if (instance == null) {
            synchronized (DoubleCheckedLockingSingleton.class) {
                if (instance == null) {
                    instance = new DoubleCheckedLockingSingleton();
                }
            }
        }
        return instance;
    }
}
```

The use of volatile is crucial to ensure proper publishing of the instance variable across threads. While reducing synchronization overhead, this method introduces additional complexity.

Performance and Thread Safety
Thread-safety and performance implications vary greatly across these methods. The following points summarize this comparison:

- Basic Singleton: Not thread-safe.
- Thread-Safe Singleton: Ensures thread safety using synchronized but suffers from performance degradation due to excessive locking.
- Lazy Initialization Singleton: Not thread-safe without additional synchronization.
- Bill Pugh Singleton: Provides lazy initialization with thread safety and minimal performance impact.
- Enum Singleton: Combines simplicity with inherent thread safety and serialization guarantees.
- Double-Checked Locking Singleton: Balances thread safety and performance, but introduces complexity.

Choosing the appropriate implementation depends on specific requirements such as the need for lazy initialization, potential performance bottlenecks, and the complexity of implementation. Advanced implementations like Bill Pugh and Enum Singleton are typically recommended for their assurity in concurrency control and performance efficiency.

6.9 Use Cases for Singleton Pattern

The Singleton Pattern is particularly useful in scenarios where a single point of control over the class is necessary. This section elaborates on various real-world situations where the Singleton pattern proves to be effective. The pattern's importance stems from its ability to restrict instantiation, offering an efficient and controlled mechanism for managing resources and configurations that should not be replicated. Below are some specific use cases where the Singleton Pattern is especially beneficial.

- **Configuration Management:** Many applications require a centralized configuration manager—an object where settings are defined once and accessed globally. The Singleton pattern ensures that the configuration object is only instantiated once, avoiding inconsistencies and redundant memory usage. For instance, a Java application might utilize a Singleton to maintain settings read from a configuration file.

```
public class ConfigurationManager {
    private static ConfigurationManager instance;

    private Properties properties;

    private ConfigurationManager() {
        properties = new Properties();
        // Load the properties file
        try (InputStream input = getClass().getClassLoader().
                getResourceAsStream("config.properties")) {
            properties.load(input);
        } catch (IOException ex) {
            ex.printStackTrace();
        }
    }

    public static ConfigurationManager getInstance() {
        if (instance == null) {
            synchronized (ConfigurationManager.class) {
                if (instance == null) {
                    instance = new ConfigurationManager();
                }
            }
        }
        return instance;
    }

    public String getProperty(String key) {
        return properties.getProperty(key);
    }
}
```

Output:
config.properties loaded successfully.

- **Logging:** Logging systems usually require a Singleton to manage log files or console outputs to maintain a coherent and organized logging trail. This approach prevents the pitfalls associated with multiple loggers creating disordered entries.

```
public class Logger {
    private static Logger logger;

    private Logger() {
        // private constructor
    }

    public static Logger getInstance() {
        if (logger == null) {
            synchronized (Logger.class) {
                if (logger == null) {
                    logger = new Logger();
                }
            }
```

```
        }
        return logger;
    }

    public void log(String message) {
        System.out.println(message);
    }
}
```

Output:
Log message: Singleton logger instance created.

- **Database Connections:** When managing database connections, a Singleton can be used to ensure that only one connection instance is created, thereby controlling resource usage and ensuring thread safety.

```
public class DatabaseConnection {
    private static DatabaseConnection instance;
    private Connection connection;

    private DatabaseConnection() {
        try {
            Class.forName("com.mysql.jdbc.Driver");
            connection = DriverManager.getConnection("jdbc:mysql://localhost
                :3306/myDB", "user", "password");
        } catch (SQLException | ClassNotFoundException ex) {
            ex.printStackTrace();
        }
    }

    public static DatabaseConnection getInstance() {
        if (instance == null) {
            synchronized (DatabaseConnection.class) {
                if (instance == null) {
                    instance = new DatabaseConnection();
                }
            }
        }
        return instance;
    }

    public Connection getConnection() {
        return connection;
    }
}
```

Output:
Database connection established successfully.

- **Thread Pool:** A thread pool can benefit from being a Singleton, ensuring that the thread management logic and resource allocation are consistently applied across the application.

```
public class ThreadPoolManager {
    private static ThreadPoolManager instance;
    private ExecutorService executorService;
```

```
    private ThreadPoolManager() {
        executorService = Executors.newFixedThreadPool(10);
    }

    public static ThreadPoolManager getInstance() {
        if (instance == null) {
            synchronized (ThreadPoolManager.class) {
                if (instance == null) {
                    instance = new ThreadPoolManager();
                }
            }
        }
        return instance;
    }

    public ExecutorService getExecutorService() {
        return executorService;
    }
}
```

Output:
Thread pool initialized with 10 threads.

- **Cache Management:** Manage in-memory caches through a Singleton to avoid multiple instances maintaining separate caches, thereby ensuring consistency and reducing memory pressure.

```
public class CacheManager {
    private static CacheManager instance;
    private Map<String, Object> cache;

    private CacheManager() {
        cache = new ConcurrentHashMap<>();
    }

    public static CacheManager getInstance() {
        if (instance == null) {
            synchronized (CacheManager.class) {
                if (instance == null) {
                    instance = new CacheManager();
                }
            }
        }
        return instance;
    }

    public void addToCache(String key, Object value) {
        cache.put(key, value);
    }

    public Object getFromCache(String key) {
        return cache.get(key);
    }
}
```

Output:
CacheManager instance is being used to manage the application cache.

- **Global Access Points:** Singletons serve as global access points for service locators, creating a single instance that can be accessed throughout the application.

```
public class ServiceLocator {
    private static ServiceLocator instance;
    private Map<String, Service> services;

    private ServiceLocator() {
        services = new HashMap<>();
    }

    public static ServiceLocator getInstance() {
        if (instance == null) {
            synchronized (ServiceLocator.class) {
                if (instance == null) {
                    instance = new ServiceLocator();
                }
            }
        }
        return instance;
    }

    public void registerService(String key, Service service) {
        services.put(key, service);
    }

    public Service getService(String key) {
        return services.get(key);
    }
}
```

```
Output:
ServiceLocator provides a global access point for services.
```

These are just a few examples to illustrate the many scenarios where the Singleton Pattern can be applied effectively. Its strategic implementation ensures that resource management, consistency, and control are maintained across various application components.

6.10 Singleton Pattern Best Practices

One of the most crucial aspects of utilizing the Singleton pattern effectively lies in adhering to best practices that ensure robustness, maintainability, and efficiency. Herein, we discuss a series of essential practices that should be observed when implementing the Singleton pattern in Java.

Private Constructor: A cornerstone of the Singleton pattern is having a private constructor. This ensures that the class cannot be instantiated from outside the class scope, maintaining the control over instance creation.

```
public class Singleton {
    private static Singleton instance = new Singleton();

    private Singleton() {
        // private constructor
    }

    public static Singleton getInstance() {
        return instance;
    }
}
```

Global Access Point: The getInstance method serves as the global access point to fetch the singleton instance. It can be static because it is called in a static context without requiring an object.

Thread Safety: Ensuring thread-safety is critical when the Singleton pattern is implemented in multi-threaded environments. Without proper synchronization, it's possible for multiple threads to create multiple instances of the Singleton. Below is an example using synchronized keyword to make the method thread-safe:

```
public class Singleton {
    private static Singleton instance;

    private Singleton() {
        // private constructor
    }

    public static synchronized Singleton getInstance() {
        if (instance == null) {
            instance = new Singleton();
        }
        return instance;
    }
}
```

While this approach guarantees thread-safety, it can be inefficient due to the overhead of acquiring and releasing locks every time getInstance is invoked. A more refined approach can be accomplished using the Bill Pugh initialization method that employs an inner static helper class.

```
public class Singleton {
    private Singleton() {
        // private constructor
    }

    private static class SingletonHelper {
        private static final Singleton INSTANCE = new Singleton();
    }

    public static Singleton getInstance() {
        return SingletonHelper.INSTANCE;
    }
}
```

Serialization Protection: When Singletons are serialized and deserialized, it can potentially create a new instance, which violates the Singleton principle. To avoid this, implement readResolve method to ensure that the existing instance is returned upon deserialization.

```
import java.io.Serializable;

public class Singleton implements Serializable {
    private static final long serialVersionUID = -1L;

    private Singleton() {
        // private constructor
    }

    private static class SingletonHelper {
        private static final Singleton INSTANCE = new Singleton();
    }

    public static Singleton getInstance() {
        return SingletonHelper.INSTANCE;
    }

    protected Object readResolve() {
        return getInstance();
    }
}
```

Avoid Reflection Attack: Reflection can be used to invoke constructors; thus, creating multiple instances of the Singleton class. To guard against this, throwing an exception within the constructor if an instance already exists reinforces the Singleton guarantee.

```
public class Singleton {
    private static boolean instanceCreated = false;

    private Singleton() {
        if (instanceCreated) {
            throw new RuntimeException("Use getInstance() method to create");
        }
        instanceCreated = true;
    }

    private static class SingletonHelper {
        private static final Singleton INSTANCE = new Singleton();
    }

    public static Singleton getInstance() {
        return SingletonHelper.INSTANCE;
    }
}
```

Enum Approach: Using an enum is a straightforward and elegant way to implement a Singleton. Java ensures that any enum value is instantiated only once, making it inherently immune to serialization and reflection attacks.

```
public enum Singleton {
    INSTANCE;

    // other methods
}
```

Eager Initialization: Eager initialization creates the instance at the time of class loading, which can be beneficial where the Singleton instance is required throughout the application, ensuring no thread-safety issues. However, this can be resource-intensive if the instance is never used.

```
public class Singleton {
    private static final Singleton instance = new Singleton();

    private Singleton() {
        // private constructor
    }

    public static Singleton getInstance() {
        return instance;
    }
}
```

When selecting an implementation strategy, consider the specific requirements of the application, such as whether lazy initialization or thread safety is needed. A comprehensive understanding of these best practices will empower efficient and reliable use of the Singleton pattern in Java, providing a robust design with controlled instance management.

6.11 Common Mistakes with Singleton Pattern

Implementing the Singleton pattern correctly can be challenging, especially for developers new to design patterns or concurrency. Several common mistakes are frequently made during the implementation of Singleton. Understanding these errors is crucial for avoiding them in your applications.

1. Forgetting to Make the Constructor Private

A common oversight is to declare the constructor of the Singleton class as public instead of private. This oversight allows multiple instances of the class to be created from outside the class, defeating the purpose of the Singleton pattern. The constructor should be defined as follows:

```
public class Singleton {
    private static Singleton instance;

    private Singleton() {
        // private constructor to prevent instantiation
    }
}
```

2. Not Synchronized in Multithreaded Environments

Neglecting synchronization can lead to multiple instances being created in a multithreaded environment. When multiple threads call the getInstance method simultaneously, they might end up creating multiple Singleton instances if the method is not properly synchronized. This issue can be mitigated by synchronizing the getInstance method:

```
public static synchronized Singleton getInstance() {
    if (instance == null) {
        instance = new Singleton();
    }
    return instance;
}
```

Alternatively, the Double-Checked Locking (DCL) mechanism provides an optimized approach:

```
public static Singleton getInstance() {
    if (instance == null) {
        synchronized (Singleton.class) {
            if (instance == null) {
                instance = new Singleton();
            }
        }
    }
    return instance;
}
```

3. Serialization Issues

Another frequent mistake involves the incorrect handling of serialization. Without proper handling, a singleton instance can be violated by the serialization mechanism. To prevent this, implement the readResolve method. This method will ensure that the original singleton instance is returned during deserialization:

```
private Object readResolve() {
    return getInstance();
}
```

4. Cloneable Interface

Implementing the Cloneable interface can inadvertently allow multiple instances of the Singleton class to be created. To prevent this, override the clone method and throw a CloneNotSupportedException:

```
@Override
protected Object clone() throws CloneNotSupportedException {
    throw new CloneNotSupportedException();
}
```

5. Reflection Attack

Reflection can break the Singleton pattern by directly invoking the private constructor. To safeguard against this, you can modify the constructor to throw an exception if an instance already exists:

```
public class Singleton {
    private static Singleton instance;

    private Singleton() {
        if (instance != null) {
            throw new IllegalStateException("Already instantiated");
        }
    }

    public static synchronized Singleton getInstance() {
        if (instance == null) {
            instance = new Singleton();
        }
        return instance;
    }
}
```

6. Enum-Based Singleton

Forgetting to use the enum-based Singleton approach when a simpler implementation suffices can be a missed opportunity for enhanced simplicity and inherent protection against reflection attacks:

```
public enum SingletonEnum {
    INSTANCE;
}
```

Enclosing the singleton instance within an enumeration provides a clean, concise, and efficient solution to the most common problems encountered with Singleton implementations, while inherently providing serialization and reflection protection.

7. Improper Initialization in Multi-Tier Systems

In large-scale applications composed of multiple tiers, improperly handling the initialization of the Singleton can lead to issues specific to context or lifecycle management. Ensure that the Singleton initialization logic is appropriately handled within the correct context, such as using dependency injection frameworks.

Missteps in applying the Singleton pattern can lead to serious consequences, such as resource leaks, performance bottlenecks, or violations of the single-instance constraint. A meticulous understanding and careful implementation are essential to harness the full benefits of the Singleton pattern.

6.12 Real-World Examples of Singleton Pattern in Java

The Singleton Pattern is widely utilized across various domains in software development, including logging mechanisms, configuration settings, and resource management. This section aims to illustrate the practical usage of the Singleton Pattern through several real-world examples. These examples will demonstrate the pattern's effectiveness, discussing how it ensures single instances and centralized access in different scenarios.

Example 1: Logger

A logging framework often needs a global access point to record log entries from diverse parts of an application. Using the Singleton Pattern ensures that there is only one logger instance handling all the log requests.

```
public class Logger {
    private static Logger loggerInstance;

    private Logger() {
        // private constructor to prevent instantiation
    }

    public static Logger getInstance() {
        if (loggerInstance == null) {
            loggerInstance = new Logger();
        }
        return loggerInstance;
    }

    public void log(String message) {
        System.out.println(message);
    }
}

// Usage:
Logger logger = Logger.getInstance();
logger.log("This is a log message.");
```

In this example, the Logger class employs lazy initialization to create the unique loggerInstance only when the getInstance() method is first called. This approach ensures that all log messages within the application are handled by the same logger instance, avoiding conflicts and potential inconsistencies.

Example 2: Configuration Settings

In many applications, configuration settings need to be accessed globally and modified at runtime. The Singleton Pattern is an excellent fit for managing configuration settings.

```
import java.util.HashMap;
import java.util.Map;

public class Configuration {
    private static Configuration configInstance;
    private Map<String, String> settings;

    private Configuration() {
        settings = new HashMap<>();
    }

    public static synchronized Configuration getInstance() {
        if (configInstance == null) {
            configInstance = new Configuration();
        }
        return configInstance;
    }

    public void setSetting(String key, String value) {
        settings.put(key, value);
    }

    public String getSetting(String key) {
        return settings.get(key);
    }
}

// Usage:
Configuration config = Configuration.getInstance();
config.setSetting("url", "http://example.com");
System.out.println(config.getSetting("url"));
```

Here, the Configuration class follows the Singleton Pattern, ensuring only one instance manages the entire application's settings. The getInstance method is synchronized to maintain thread safety, guaranteeing that configInstance is initialized only once, even in multi-threaded environments.

Example 3: Database Connection Pool

Applications with high performance requirements often use a connection pool to manage database connections efficiently. Implementing a connection pool using the Singleton Pattern facilitates centralized control over connection management.

```
import java.sql.Connection;
import java.sql.DriverManager;
```

```
import java.sql.SQLException;
import java.util.LinkedList;
import java.util.Queue;

public class ConnectionPool {
    private static ConnectionPool poolInstance;
    private Queue<Connection> connectionQueue;
    private static final int MAX_CONNECTIONS = 10;

    private ConnectionPool() throws SQLException {
        connectionQueue = new LinkedList<>();
        for (int i = 0; i < MAX_CONNECTIONS; i++) {
            connectionQueue.add(createNewConnection());
        }
    }

    public static ConnectionPool getInstance() throws SQLException {
        if (poolInstance == null) {
            poolInstance = new ConnectionPool();
        }
        return poolInstance;
    }

    public synchronized Connection getConnection() {
        return connectionQueue.poll();
    }

    public synchronized void releaseConnection(Connection connection) {
        connectionQueue.offer(connection);
    }

    private Connection createNewConnection() throws SQLException {
        // Sample connection creation, adjust url, username and password as needed
        return DriverManager.getConnection("jdbc:mysql://localhost:3306/mydb", "user
                ", "password");
    }
}

// Usage:
ConnectionPool pool = ConnectionPool.getInstance();
Connection conn = pool.getConnection();
pool.releaseConnection(conn);
```

In this example, the ConnectionPool class controls the creation and management of database connections. The Singleton Pattern ensures that there is only one instance of the pool, which coordinates the connections, ensuring efficient resource usage. The thread-safe getConnection and releaseConnection methods allow the pool to be safely used in concurrent scenarios.

Example 4: Cache Manager

A caching mechanism is essential in many applications to improve performance by storing frequently accessed data. Using a Singleton Pattern for the cache manager ensures a single point of access and coherence across the application.

```
import java.util.HashMap;
import java.util.Map;

public class CacheManager {
    private static CacheManager cacheInstance;
    private Map<String, Object> cacheMap;

    private CacheManager() {
        cacheMap = new HashMap<>();
    }

    public static synchronized CacheManager getInstance() {
        if (cacheInstance == null) {
            cacheInstance = new CacheManager();
        }
        return cacheInstance;
    }

    public void put(String key, Object value) {
        cacheMap.put(key, value);
    }

    public Object get(String key) {
        return cacheMap.get(key);
    }
}

// Usage:
CacheManager cache = CacheManager.getInstance();
cache.put("data", "sample data");
System.out.println(cache.get("data"));
```

The CacheManager class uses the Singleton Pattern to manage cached data. By ensuring only one instance of CacheManager, the application maintains a consistent cache state, reducing memory usage and improving performance.

These examples demonstrate the versatility and utility of the Singleton Pattern in real-world applications, effectively addressing common requirements such as logging, configuration management, resource pooling, and caching. The pattern's ability to ensure a single instance and provide centralized access points makes it a powerful tool in a Java programmer's toolkit.

Chapter 7

Adapter Pattern: Bridging Incompatible Interfaces

This chapter explores the Adapter Pattern, which enables incompatible interfaces to work together. It covers the concepts of class adapters and object adapters, illustrating their implementation in Java. The chapter discusses when to use the Adapter Pattern, its benefits and limitations, and contrasts it with similar patterns. Best practices and common mistakes are highlighted to ensure effective utilization, and real-world examples provide practical insights into its application.

7.1 Introduction to the Adapter Pattern

The Adapter Pattern, a widely-used structural design pattern, facilitates the interaction between incompatible interfaces. This pattern acts as an intermediary, transforming an interface into another expected by a client, thereby enabling collaboration between classes that otherwise could not interoperate. By providing a unified interface, the Adapter Pattern integrates disparate components into a cohesive architecture.

In software development, it is common to encounter legacy code or third-party libraries with interfaces that differ from those required by the new system. Directly modifying such code is often impractical due to constraints like encapsulation, licensing, or simply the cost in resources and time. The Adapter Pattern offers an elegant solution by creating an adapter, a new class that translates one interface to another. This maintains the integrity of existing codebases while extending their functionality.

Consider the following scenario: a graphics application utilizes various shape classes, each implementing a draw() method. A new shape library is available, but its interface is incompatible with the application's existing design. Instead of rewriting the entire application or modifying the library, an adapter can be deployed to reconcile the differences.

```
class LegacyRectangle {
    public void draw(int x, int y, int width, int height) {
        // Drawing logic for the legacy rectangle
    }
}
```

```
interface Shape {
    void draw();
}
```

In the context above, the LegacyRectangle class must be adapted to comply with the Shape interface. The adapter achieves this by encapsulating an instance of LegacyRectangle and implementing the draw() method.

```
class RectangleAdapter implements Shape {
    private LegacyRectangle legacyRectangle;

    public RectangleAdapter(LegacyRectangle legacyRectangle) {
        this.legacyRectangle = legacyRectangle;
    }

    @Override
    public void draw() {
        legacyRectangle.draw(0, 0, 10, 20); // Example of translating the interface
    }
}
```

In this example, the RectangleAdapter class adjusts the LegacyRectangle interface to conform to the Shape interface expected by the client. This pattern encapsulates implementation details, providing a seamless method to integrate new components.

```
Client code using the adapter:
Shape shape = new RectangleAdapter(new LegacyRectangle());
shape.draw();
```

The Adapter Pattern can be classified into two types: class adapters and object adapters.

A class adapter inherits from both the target and adaptee classes. This form of adapter is used in languages that support multiple inheritance, such as C++. In Java, which does not support multiple inheritance of classes, class adapters can be implemented using interfaces. It means that the adapter class implements the target interface and extends the adaptee class.

```
class RectangleClassAdapter extends LegacyRectangle implements Shape {
    @Override
    public void draw() {
        super.draw(0, 0, 10, 20); // Example of adapting the interface
    }
}
```

In the example above, RectangleClassAdapter extends LegacyRectangle and implements the Shape interface to adapt the target interface to the existing implementation. While this approach is straightforward, it is limited by Java's single inheritance constraint. Hence, it is less flexible compared to the object adapter.

An object adapter, preferred in most scenarios, employs composition; it holds an instance of the adaptee class and delegates requests from the client to the adaptee. This method does not suffer from the limitations imposed by single inheritance and promotes better decoupling and maintainability.

```
class RectangleObjectAdapter implements Shape {
    private LegacyRectangle legacyRectangle;

    public RectangleObjectAdapter(LegacyRectangle legacyRectangle) {
        this.legacyRectangle = legacyRectangle;
    }

    @Override
    public void draw() {
        legacyRectangle.draw(0, 0, 10, 20); // Example of translating the interface
    }
}
```

With the object adapter pattern, changes to LegacyRectangle will not necessitate alterations to the Shape hierarchy, fostering scalability. The choice between class adapters and object adapters depends on specific use cases, encapsulation requirements, and language constraints.

The primary use cases for the Adapter Pattern include:

- Integrating legacy components or third-party libraries into new systems without altering their source code.
- Enabling classes with incompatible interfaces to collaborate.
- Facilitating unit testing by providing mock objects.

Understanding and implementing the Adapter Pattern is crucial for software engineers tasked with maintaining and expanding complex systems. It harmonizes components with varied interfaces, promoting reusability and flexibility while adhering to the principles of object-oriented design.

7.2 Understanding the Adapter Pattern

The Adapter Pattern is a structural design pattern that allows objects with incompatible interfaces to collaborate. By acting as a bridge between two disparate interfaces, it enables systems to integrate existing components seamlessly without modifying their source code. This methodology is particularly useful in large codebases where interface changes are undesirable or impractical.

The Adapter Pattern can be categorized into two main types: class adapters and object adapters. Both types aim to resolve incompatibility issues, but they differ in their implementation techniques and use cases.

Class adapters leverage inheritance to achieve interface compatibility. By extending both the target interface and the adaptee class, class adapters can convert one interface into another. However, the strict coupling through inheritance may limit their flexibility, especially in languages like Java, which do not support multiple inheritance.

Object adapters, on the other hand, utilize composition. An object adapter holds a reference to the adaptee and implements the target interface. It delegates requests to the adaptee, which enhances flexibility by allowing the adapter to work with any subclass of the adaptee. Object adapters are generally preferred in Java because they avoid the restrictions of inheritance and promote loose coupling.

The following example demonstrates the fundamental concepts of the Adapter Pattern. Consider a scenario where we have an existing class OldPrinter that performs printing tasks but does not conform to the new PrinterInterface.

```
class OldPrinter {
    public void printDocument(String content) {
        System.out.println("Printing: " + content);
    }
}
```

The new interface PrinterInterface specifies a single method print.

```
interface PrinterInterface {
    void print(String text);
}
```

To bridge the gap between OldPrinter and PrinterInterface, we design an adapter class. Here, we use the object adapter approach for its flexibility.

```
class PrinterAdapter implements PrinterInterface {
    private OldPrinter oldPrinter;

    public PrinterAdapter(OldPrinter oldPrinter) {
        this.oldPrinter = oldPrinter;
    }

    @Override
    public void print(String text) {
        // Translate the request to the adaptee's method
        oldPrinter.printDocument(text);
    }
}
```

In this example, PrinterAdapter implements PrinterInterface and holds an instance of OldPrinter. The print method of PrinterInterface is implemented to delegate the call to printDocument of OldPrinter. This setup enables clients to use OldPrinter objects through the PrinterInterface, achieving compatibility without modifying existing code.

To illustrate, the following client code uses the adapter to perform a printing task:

```
public class Main {
    public static void main(String[] args) {
        OldPrinter oldPrinter = new OldPrinter();
        PrinterInterface printer = new PrinterAdapter(oldPrinter);
        printer.print("Hello World");
    }
}
```

The output of this program is:

```
Printing: Hello World
```

This concise example underscores the power of the Adapter Pattern in facilitating interoperability between incompatible systems. By adhering to the established principles of delegation and composition, the object adapter approach maintains the adaptability required for complex software systems.

Flexibility in the Adapter Pattern is not limited to object adapters. Class adapters can also be effective when used judiciously. Consider the following class adapter implementation:

```
class ClassPrinterAdapter extends OldPrinter implements PrinterInterface {
    @Override
    public void print(String text) {
        // Translate the request directly to the inherited method
        printDocument(text);
    }
}
```

Here, ClassPrinterAdapter extends OldPrinter and implements PrinterInterface. The method print is overridden to directly call printDocument. While this accomplishes the same result as the object adapter, it does so by directly leveraging the inheritance mechanism.

Class adapters are simpler as they do not require an explicit reference to the adaptee. However, they are limited by Java's single inheritance constraint, which may reduce their applicability in more complex scenarios.

The Adapter Pattern is not without its limitations. Adapters introduce an additional layer of abstraction, which can increase code complexity. Careful consideration must be given to performance implications, particularly in latency-sensitive applications. Adapters can also lead to maintenance challenges if overused or applied to systems with rapidly evolving interfaces.

Nevertheless, the Adapter Pattern remains an invaluable tool for software engineers. Its ability to promote reuse and facilitate integration significantly outweighs its potential drawbacks. Through strategic application, the Adapter Pattern helps achieve modular, maintainable, and interoperable software architectures.

7.3 Implementing the Adapter Pattern in Java

The Adapter Pattern can be implemented in two forms: class adapters and object adapters. Both forms provide a means to enable two incompatible interfaces to work together.

A class adapter uses multiple inheritance to adapt one interface to another. In Java, this is achieved using inheritance and Java's ability to implement multiple interfaces. The following example illustrates the concept of a class adapter.

```
interface Target {
    void request();
```

```
}

class Adaptee {
    void specificRequest() {
        System.out.println("Called specificRequest()");
    }
}

class Adapter extends Adaptee implements Target {
    @Override
    public void request() {
        specificRequest();
    }
}

public class Client {
    public static void main(String[] args) {
        Target target = new Adapter();
        target.request();
    }
}
```

In Listing **??**, Adapter extends Adaptee and implements Target. This allows the Client to interact with the Adaptee using the Target interface.

When running the Client program, the output will be:

```
Called specificRequest()
```

An object adapter, by contrast, uses composition to forward requests from the target interface to the adaptee. This form of the adapter delegates the calls to an instance of the adaptee. The following code demonstrates an object adapter.

```
interface Target {
    void request();
}

class Adaptee {
    void specificRequest() {
        System.out.println("Called specificRequest()");
    }
}

class Adapter implements Target {
    private Adaptee adaptee;

    Adapter(Adaptee adaptee) {
        this.adaptee = adaptee;
    }

    @Override
    public void request() {
        adaptee.specificRequest();
    }
}

public class Client {
    public static void main(String[] args) {
```

```
        Adaptee adaptee = new Adaptee();
        Target target = new Adapter(adaptee);
        target.request();
    }
}
```

In Listing ??, the Adapter holds an instance of Adaptee and implements the Target interface. This way, the Client can use the Target interface to interact with Adaptee.

When executing the Client program, the output will be the same:

```
Called specificRequest()
```

When choosing between class and object adapters, it is essential to consider the following points:

- **Class Adapter:** This form is limited by the fact that Java does not support multiple inheritance of classes. It can only extend one class, so it cannot adapt a class that already has a different superclass.
- **Object Adapter:** This form is more flexible because it allows the adapter to wrap multiple adaptees. It can also adapt a class that does not have a public interface that extends a specific single class.

Both class adapters and object adapters serve to bridge incompatible interfaces, but their specific use cases and constraints must be considered to determine which form best fits a given situation.

The Adapter Pattern can be effectively utilized when integrating new functionalities into legacy codebases. It allows new systems to work with existing systems without modifying the underlying implementations. Proper use of the Adapter Pattern ensures greater modularity and extensibility in the software design.

The next section will delve into comparing class adapters and object adapters, exploring their advantages and disadvantages in different scenarios.

7.4 Class Adapter vs. Object Adapter

Class adapters and object adapters are two primary ways to implement the Adapter Pattern in Java. Each has distinct characteristics, advantages, and potential limitations that affect their suitability for specific scenarios. Understanding the differences between these two approaches is crucial for selecting the most appropriate method for a given problem.

A Class Adapter pattern utilizes multiple inheritance to adapt one interface to another. This approach is feasible in Java through the use of interface inheritance and class inheritance. Here, the adapter class inherits from the source (adaptee) class and implements the target interface.

```
interface Target {
    void request();
}

class Adaptee {
    void specificRequest() {
        System.out.println("Called specificRequest()");
    }
}

class ClassAdapter extends Adaptee implements Target {
    @Override
    public void request() {
        specificRequest();
    }
}
```

In this example, ClassAdapter inherits from Adaptee and implements the Target interface. The request() method from the Target interface is implemented to call the specificRequest() method of the Adaptee.

There are specific benefits and drawbacks associated with the class adapter approach:

- **Pros**
  - ClassAdapter can directly access Adaptee's protected members, allowing a tight coupling.
  - It facilitates overriding Adaptee's methods in the adapter, offering greater flexibility in modifying the adaptee's behavior.
  - Since it leverages inheritance, there is no need for an adaptee instance within the adapter.
- **Cons**
  - Java does not support multiple inheritance with classes, limiting the ClassAdapter to only one concrete adaptee class.
  - Tight coupling to the Adaptee class reduces flexibility and reusability of adapters.

On the other hand, the Object Adapter pattern employs composition to adapt one interface to another. In this method, the adapter contains an instance of the adaptee and implements the target interface, delegating calls to the adaptee instance.

```
interface Target {
    void request();
}

class Adaptee {
    void specificRequest() {
        System.out.println("Called specificRequest()");
    }
}

class ObjectAdapter implements Target {
    private Adaptee adaptee;

    public ObjectAdapter(Adaptee adaptee) {
        this.adaptee = adaptee;
    }

    @Override
    public void request() {
        adaptee.specificRequest();
    }
}
```

In this example, ObjectAdapter implements the Target interface and holds a reference to an Adaptee instance, which it uses to fulfill the request() method.

The Object Adapter approach also has its own set of pros and cons:

- **Pros**
  - Since adapters use composition, they can adapt multiple adaptee types, enhancing flexibility.
  - The decoupling of adapter and adaptee increases reusability and allows easy changes or substitution of adaptees.
  - Reduces the potential for tight coupling to a specific implementation.
- **Cons**
  - The adapter cannot directly access protected members of the adaptee, limiting the scope of changes.
  - Slight overhead associated with object composition, as the adapter must maintain and forward calls to the adaptee instance.

Choosing between class adapters and object adapters depends largely on the specific requirements of the system being designed. Class adapters might be preferable when inheriting mostly stable, unchanging interfaces, and where the added flexibility from accessing protected members can be beneficial. On the other hand, object adapters are more suited to environments needing greater adaptability and reduced coupling, where multiple adaptee objects might be involved, making the approach more modular and easier to manage.

Understanding both patterns equips developers with the tools to apply the Adapter Pattern effectively in diverse scenarios, ensuring that incompatible interfaces can communicate seamlessly while adhering to the principles of object-oriented design.

7.5 When to Use the Adapter Pattern

The Adapter Pattern should be employed when there is a necessity to integrate classes that otherwise would be incompatible due to differing interfaces. This pattern is particularly important in scenarios where applications must work with legacy systems, third-party libraries, or external APIs that cannot be modified directly. The Adapter Pattern serves as a bridge, allowing disparate components to communicate seamlessly.

There are several specific scenarios where the Adapter Pattern is highly useful:

- **Integrating Legacy Code:** When applications need to interact with older systems whose interfaces are outdated or incompatible with modern design paradigms, adapters can be implemented to translate these interfaces, enabling smoother integration.
- **Working with Third-Party Libraries:** Third-party libraries often have predefined interfaces that may not align with the needs of your application. An adapter can be created to convert these existing interfaces to the required client interface, facilitating the use of the library without altering its code.
- **Standardizing Interfaces:** In large projects, various subsystems might develop independently, leading to multiple variations of interfaces that perform similar functions. Adapters can standardize these interfaces, ensuring uniformity and easing integration across the system.

- **Reusing Existing Classes:** The Adapter Pattern allows the reuse of existing classes even when their interfaces are not directly usable. This avoids the overhead of rewriting code and accelerates the development process.

- **Support for Multiple Interfaces:** An application might need to support multiple interfaces for different clients. Adapters can provide the necessary flexibility by converting client-specific requests into compatible formats.

To elucidate these scenarios further, consider a Java application that needs to utilize a third-party library for file encryption. The library provides an interface Encryptor with a specific method encryptData(String input). However, your application was designed using a custom interface DataEncryptor with a method process(String data). The following example demonstrates the use of the Adapter Pattern in this context:

```
/** Third-party library class */
public class ThirdPartyEncryptor implements Encryptor {
    @Override
    public String encryptData(String input) {
        // implementation of encryption
    }
}

/** Custom application interface */
public interface DataEncryptor {
    String process(String data);
}

/** Adapter class */
public class EncryptorAdapter implements DataEncryptor {
    private Encryptor encryptor;

    public EncryptorAdapter(Encryptor encryptor) {
        this.encryptor = encryptor;
    }

    @Override
    public String process(String data) {
        return encryptor.encryptData(data);
    }
}
```

In this Java snippet, EncryptorAdapter enables the integration of ThirdPartyEncryptor with the application by adapting the Encryptor interface to DataEncryptor. This process ensures the third-party encryption functionality can be utilized without altering existing application logic.

The Adapter Pattern can be employed not only in systematic software design but also during transitional phases of software lifecycle management. For example, during refactoring, where parts of a system are being improved and modernized, adapters enable continuous operation of the system despite disparate components.

Additionally, the Adapter Pattern is critical for systems designed with a plug-in architecture. It allows developers to add new functionality through additional modules without impacting the primary system. For instance, consider a payment processing system that initially uses PayPal for transactions but needs to support Stripe without altering existing interfaces:

```
/** Existing payment interface */
public interface PaymentProcessor {
    void processPayment(double amount);
}

/** PayPal implementation */
public class PayPalProcessor implements PaymentProcessor {
    @Override
    public void processPayment(double amount) {
        // PayPal specific payment processing code
    }
}

/** Stripe implementation with different interface */
public class StripePayment {
    public void sendPayment(double money) {
        // Stripe specific payment processing code
    }
}

/** Adapter for Stripe */
public class StripeAdapter implements PaymentProcessor {
    private StripePayment stripePayment;

    public StripeAdapter(StripePayment stripePayment) {
        this.stripePayment = stripePayment;
    }

    @Override
    public void processPayment(double amount) {
        stripePayment.sendPayment(amount);
    }
}
```

In this scenario, StripeAdapter converges the StripePayment method to the PaymentProcessor interface, thereby allowing the application to process payments via Stripe without altering the existing architecture that was designed for PayPal.

Architectural resilience and flexibility are augmented by employing the Adapter Pattern. It ensures systems can evolve by integrating new components and leveraging existing ones without extensive reengineering. This compatibility is achieved seamlessly, maintaining the coherence and stability of the software system.

7.6 Advantages and Disadvantages of the Adapter Pattern

The Adapter Pattern holds significant utility in software design, enabling disparate systems to interface harmoniously. This section delves into the core advantages and potential disadvantages of adopting the Adapter Pattern in Java application development, fostering a comprehensive understanding of its impact.

Advantages of the Adapter Pattern:

- Enhanced Reusability: The Adapter Pattern promotes the reuse of existing classes, even those with interfaces that are not directly compatible with new systems. By using adapters, developers can integrate existing solutions without requiring modification of their interfaces, resulting in reduced development effort and cost.
- Improved Interoperability: In a heterogeneous computing environment, different systems often need to communicate. The Adapter Pattern facilitates communication by making incompatible interfaces work together, thus improving system interoperability and enabling seamless interaction between components.
- Separation of Concerns: Adapters clearly separate the concerns of the client interface from that of the adaptee. This separation ensures that the changes in the adaptee's interface do not affect the client of the adapter, enhancing code maintainability and flexibility.
- Ease of Implementation: The Adapter Pattern is relatively straightforward to implement in Java. By using inheritance or composition to wrap around the incompatible class interface, developers can quickly create adapters that fulfill the required contracts.
- Legacy Code Integration: Adapters provide a mechanism to integrate legacy systems or third-party libraries with new interfaces. This integration extends the lifespan of legacy codebases and allows leveraging existing investments without cumbersome refactoring.

The practical implementation of these advantages can be illustrated through the following Java code snippet, demonstrating an adapter that converts a CsvReader to a JsonReader:

```
// Target interface
public interface JsonReader {
    String readJson();
}

// Adaptee class
public class CsvReader {
    public String readCsv() {
        return "Data,from,a,CSV,source";
    }
}

// Adapter implementation using composition
public class CsvToJsonAdapter implements JsonReader {
    private final CsvReader csvReader;

    public CsvToJsonAdapter(CsvReader csvReader) {
        this.csvReader = csvReader;
    }

    @Override
    public String readJson() {
        String csvData = csvReader.readCsv();
        // Convert CSV data to JSON format
        return convertCsvToJson(csvData);
    }

    private String convertCsvToJson(String csvData) {
        // Simplistic conversion logic (for illustration)
        return "{ \"data\": \"" + csvData.replace(",", "\", \"") + "\" }";
    }
}

// Client code
public class AdapterPatternDemo {
    public static void main(String[] args) {
        CsvReader csvReader = new CsvReader();
        JsonReader adapter = new CsvToJsonAdapter(csvReader);
        System.out.println(adapter.readJson());
    }
}
```

Executing the above code will produce the following output:

```
{ "data": "Data", "from", "a", "CSV", "source" }
```

Disadvantages of the Adapter Pattern:

- Increased Complexity: Introducing an adapter adds an extra layer of abstraction, which could increase the system's complexity. This additional complexity may be unnecessary if the interfaces could be aligned through simpler means.
- Performance Overhead: The Adapter Pattern can introduce performance overhead due to the additional processing required to bridge the interfaces. This overhead may be critical in

performance-sensitive applications, where direct interaction between components is preferred.

- Proliferation of Adapters: In systems where multiple different adapters are required, there can be a proliferation of adapter classes, making the system harder to manage and understand. Each new adaptee requires an adapter, contributing to potential maintenance challenges.
- Limited functionality: Adapters often provide only a limited set of functionality from the adaptee. As a result, not all features of the original interface may be accessible through the adapter. Thus, developers may encounter constraints when trying to utilize the full potential of the adaptee's capabilities.
- Incompatibility with Future Changes: If either the target or adaptee interface undergoes significant changes, the adapter might need to be modified or replaced. This dependency on interface stability means that the Adapter Pattern can become a maintenance burden when systems evolve rapidly.

The drawbacks highlighted here necessitate careful consideration when applying the Adapter Pattern. The decision to use this pattern should be balanced against these potential complications to ascertain that the benefits outweigh the costs in the specific context of the application.

Students learning about the Adapter Pattern need to not just understand how to implement it, but also to appreciate the trade-offs involved. This awareness ensures judicious use of the pattern, optimizing software interoperability and maintainability while avoiding unnecessary complexity and performance issues.

7.7 Adapter Pattern Best Practices

To leverage the full potential of the Adapter Pattern in Java, adhering to a set of best practices is crucial. These best practices ensure that the pattern is applied effectively, maintains code maintainability, and minimizes the introduction of errors.

Clearly Define Interfaces: Before employing the Adapter Pattern, it is pivotal to clearly define the interfaces involved. This includes both the existing interface that needs to be adapted (Adaptee) and the target interface (Target). Avoid ambiguous or overly complex interfaces that may hinder the adaptability.

Minimal Interface Contract: Keep the interface methods minimal and as straightforward as possible. The purpose of an adapter is to reconcile functionality between incompatible interfaces, hence overloading the interfaces with excessive methods can result in unnecessary complexity.

Protect Encapsulation: Adapters should not expose internal state or behavior directly. Maintain the encapsulation boundaries by making sure that the adapter only exposes what's necessary to fulfill the target interface.

Favor Composition Over Inheritance: Wherever feasible, use the object adapter (composition) over the class adapter (inheritance). The object adapter pattern is more flexible and decouples the adapter from the Adaptee at the cost of potential performance overhead.

```
public interface Target {
    void request();
}

public class Adaptee {
    public void specificRequest() {
        // Implementation code
    }
}

public class Adapter implements Target {
    private Adaptee adaptee;

    public Adapter(Adaptee adaptee) {
        this.adaptee = adaptee;
    }

    public void request() {
        adaptee.specificRequest();
    }
}
```

Ensure Seamless Integration: The Adapter Pattern should provide a seamless transition between incompatible systems. This entails making sure that all functionalities are correctly delegated and that no translation errors occur. Rigorous testing is essential for ensuring that adapters translate all necessary calls and data perfectly.

Simplify Testing: Adapters add another layer of abstraction, which can complicate testing. Ensure that you utilize proper mocking and stubbing practices to isolate adapters during unit tests. Frameworks such as JUnit or Mockito can be significantly useful.

```
public class AdapterTest {
    @Test
    public void testRequest() {
        Adaptee adaptee = new Adaptee();
        Target adapter = new Adapter(adaptee);

        // Sample assertion
        assertEquals("Expected behavior", adapter.request());
    }
}
```

Document Thoroughly: Clear and comprehensive documentation is essential. Explain why an adapter is used, how it interacts with the Adaptee and Target, and any implications this might have for future extensions or modifications. Include diagrams where applicable to illustrate relationships and interactions.

Avoid Overuse: Use the Adapter Pattern judiciously. Overuse can lead to code that is difficult to follow and maintain. Assess whether adapting interfaces is the best course of action, or if refactoring the original code may yield a more elegant solution.

Consider Future Changes: Plan for future changes in either the Adaptee or Target interfaces. Design your adapter in a way that it can accommodate changes without significant rewrites. This often entails abstracting common functionalities and facilitating easy extension points.

Performance Considerations: While the adapter introduces an additional layer of abstraction, it is important to be mindful of performance implications. If the adapter is used in a performance-critical path, ensure it doesn't introduce significant overhead. Profiling and performance testing should be conducted to ensure that the system meets its performance criteria.

Adhering to these best practices makes the usage of the Adapter Pattern robust, maintainable, and efficient. It instills confidence in the design choices and facilitates smoother integration of disparate systems.

7.8 Use Cases for the Adapter Pattern

The Adapter Pattern is particularly effective when dealing with scenarios where existing code needs to be integrated with new components without altering their source. This pattern finds its utility across various contexts, facilitating the seamless interaction between incompatible interfaces. In this section, we will explore several concrete use cases that illustrate the practical application of the Adapter Pattern in Java, demonstrating its versatility and necessity.

1. Legacy Code Integration

When maintaining or upgrading software systems, developers often encounter legacy code that is cumbersome to modify. By employing the Adapter Pattern, legacy systems can be integrated with modern libraries or frameworks without significant refactoring. Consider a scenario where an old financial reporting system needs to leverage a new, sophisticated data analytics library:

```
public interface NewAnalyticsLib {
    void analyzeData(DataSet data);
}

public class LegacyReportSystem {
    public void generateReport(LegacyData legacyData) {
        // ... existing reporting logic
    }
}

public class LegacyDataAdapter implements NewAnalyticsLib {
    private LegacyReportSystem legacyReportSystem;

    public LegacyDataAdapter(LegacyReportSystem legacyReportSystem) {
        this.legacyReportSystem = legacyReportSystem;
    }

    @Override
    public void analyzeData(DataSet data) {
        LegacyData legacyData = convertToLegacyData(data);
        legacyReportSystem.generateReport(legacyData);
    }

    private LegacyData convertToLegacyData(DataSet data) {
        // Conversion logic
    }
}
```

With this adapter, the 'LegacyReportSystem' can remain untouched while still utilizing the functionalities of the 'NewAnalyticsLib'.

2. Third-Party Library Integration

Integrating third-party libraries into an existing system often requires bridging varying interfaces. The Adapter Pattern serves as an intermediary without necessitating alterations to either the existing system or the third-party library. For instance, connecting a third-party payment gateway with a predefined payment system interface:

```
public interface PaymentGateway {
    void processPayment(PaymentDetails details);
}

public class ThirdPartyPaymentProcessor {
```

```
    public void makePayment(NewPaymentDetails newDetails) {
        // ... third-party payment processing logic
    }
}

public class PaymentAdapter implements PaymentGateway {
    private ThirdPartyPaymentProcessor processor;

    public PaymentAdapter(ThirdPartyPaymentProcessor processor) {
        this.processor = processor;
    }

    @Override
    public void processPayment(PaymentDetails details) {
        NewPaymentDetails newDetails = convertToNewPaymentDetails(details);
        processor.makePayment(newDetails);
    }

    private NewPaymentDetails convertToNewPaymentDetails(PaymentDetails details)
          {
        // Conversion logic
    }
}
```

3. Multiple Framework Integration

A project may need to support multiple frameworks or libraries that conform to different interfaces. By designing adapters, a uniform interface can be presented to the client code, enabling flexibility and interchangeability. Consider an application that supports different logging frameworks:

```
public interface Logger {
    void log(String message);
}

public class Log4jLogger {
    public void logMessage(String msg) {
        // Log using Log4j
    }
}

public class Slf4jLogger {
    public void printLog(String message) {
        // Log using SLF4J
    }
}

public class Log4jAdapter implements Logger {
    private Log4jLogger log4jLogger;

    public Log4jAdapter(Log4jLogger log4jLogger) {
        this.log4jLogger = log4jLogger;
    }

    @Override
    public void log(String message) {
        log4jLogger.logMessage(message);
    }
```

```
}

public class Slf4jAdapter implements Logger {
    private Slf4jLogger slf4jLogger;

    public Slf4jAdapter(Slf4jLogger slf4jLogger) {
        this.slf4jLogger = slf4jLogger;
    }

    @Override
    public void log(String message) {
        slf4jLogger.printLog(message);
    }
}
```

4. Service Wrapping for APIs

The Adapter Pattern can be effectively employed to wrap diverse web services, ensuring that a consistent API is provided to the client. This is especially useful in scenarios involving microservices architectures where different services might evolve independently. For example, consider different user authentication services:

```
public interface AuthService {
    boolean authenticate(UserCredentials credentials);
}

public class OAuthService {
    public boolean verifyCredentials(OAuthCredentials credentials) {
        // OAuth authentication logic
    }
}

public class LdapService {
    public boolean checkLogin(LdapCredentials credentials) {
        // LDAP authentication logic
    }
}

public class OAuthAdapter implements AuthService {
    private OAuthService oauthService;

    public OAuthAdapter(OAuthService oauthService) {
        this.oauthService = oauthService;
    }

    @Override
    public boolean authenticate(UserCredentials credentials) {
        OAuthCredentials oauthCredentials = convertToOAuthCredentials(credentials);
        return oauthService.verifyCredentials(oauthCredentials);
    }

    private OAuthCredentials convertToOAuthCredentials(UserCredentials credentials)
          {
        // Conversion logic
    }
}

public class LdapAdapter implements AuthService {
```

```
    private LdapService ldapService;

    public LdapAdapter(LdapService ldapService) {
        this.ldapService = ldapService;
    }

    @Override
    public boolean authenticate(UserCredentials credentials) {
        LdapCredentials ldapCredentials = convertToLdapCredentials(credentials);
        return ldapService.checkLogin(ldapCredentials);
    }

    private LdapCredentials convertToLdapCredentials(UserCredentials credentials) {
        // Conversion logic
    }
}
```

5. Hardware and Device Integration

Bridging different hardware or device APIs in applications often necessitates the use of adapters to conform to unified interfaces. Imagine integrating various types of sensors in a monitoring system:

```
public interface SensorInterface {
    double getSensorReading();
}

public class TemperatureSensor {
    public double readTemperature() {
        // Read from temperature sensor
    }
}

public class HumiditySensor {
    public double getHumidity() {
        // Read from humidity sensor
    }
}

public class TemperatureAdapter implements SensorInterface {
    private TemperatureSensor temperatureSensor;

    public TemperatureAdapter(TemperatureSensor temperatureSensor) {
        this.temperatureSensor = temperatureSensor;
    }

    @Override
    public double getSensorReading() {
        return temperatureSensor.readTemperature();
    }
}

public class HumidityAdapter implements SensorInterface {
    private HumiditySensor humiditySensor;

    public HumidityAdapter(HumiditySensor humiditySensor) {
        this.humiditySensor = humiditySensor;
    }

    @Override
```

```
    public double getSensorReading() {
        return humiditySensor.getHumidity();
    }
}
```

These use cases exemplify the broad applicability of the Adapter Pattern, underscoring its role in enabling seamless integration between diverse components. By utilizing this pattern, developers can extend functionality, facilitate maintenance, and preserve existing investments in legacy systems without compromising system integrity or code flexibility.

7.9 Comparing Adapter Pattern with Other Patterns

The Adapter Pattern, a structural design pattern, is utilized to bridge the gap between incompatible interfaces, allowing them to work seamlessly together. In this section, we will compare the Adapter Pattern with other similar design patterns such as the Decorator Pattern, the Proxy Pattern, and the Facade Pattern. Understanding the distinctions and similarities among these patterns will enhance your ability to choose the most suitable design pattern based on the problem context.

Adapter Pattern vs. Decorator Pattern

The Adapter Pattern and the Decorator Pattern both fall under the category of structural design patterns, and they share some similarities, such as wrapping existing classes. However, their primary objectives differ significantly.

- **Objective:** The Adapter Pattern is primarily used to make two incompatible interfaces compatible, while the Decorator Pattern is used to add new behavior or responsibilities to an object dynamically.
- **Usage Example:** The Adapter Pattern might be used to allow a legacy system to interface with a new system without modifications to the legacy code. In contrast, the Decorator Pattern might be employed to add features such as logging or data validation to objects in a flexible manner.
- **Technical Implementation:**

```
interface Target {
    void request();
}

class Adaptee {
    void specificRequest() {
        System.out.println("Specific request");
    }
}

class Adapter implements Target {
    private Adaptee adaptee;

    public Adapter(Adaptee adaptee) {
        this.adaptee = adaptee;
    }

    @Override
    public void request() {
        adaptee.specificRequest();
    }
}

public class Client {
    public static void main(String[] args) {
        Adaptee adaptee = new Adaptee();
        Target target = new Adapter(adaptee);
        target.request();
    }
}
```

```
interface Component {
    void operation();
}

class ConcreteComponent implements Component {
    @Override
    public void operation() {
        System.out.println("Concrete operation");
    }
}

class Decorator implements Component {
    protected Component component;

    public Decorator(Component component) {
        this.component = component;
    }

    @Override
    public void operation() {
        component.operation();
    }
}

class ConcreteDecorator extends Decorator {
    public ConcreteDecorator(Component component) {
        super(component);
    }

    @Override
```

```
    public void operation() {
        super.operation();
        addedBehavior();
    }

    private void addedBehavior() {
        System.out.println("Added behavior");
    }
}

public class Client {
    public static void main(String[] args) {
        Component component = new ConcreteDecorator(new ConcreteComponent());
        component.operation();
    }
}
```

- **Wrapping and Extending:** The Adapter Pattern wraps the object to translate interface while the Decorator Pattern wraps the object to add new behavior.

Adapter Pattern vs. Proxy Pattern

Both the Adapter Pattern and the Proxy Pattern involve forwarding requests to an underlying object, but they serve different purposes.

- **Objective:** The Adapter Pattern's goal is to allow incompatible interfaces to work together, whereas the Proxy Pattern's goal is to control access to an object by adding a level of indirection.
- **Usage Example:** The Adapter Pattern might be used to integrate a third-party library into a system effortlessly. The Proxy Pattern might be employed to implement lazy initialization, access control, or logging.
- **Technical Implementation:**

```
interface Subject {
    void request();
}

class RealSubject implements Subject {
    @Override
    public void request() {
        System.out.println("Real subject request");
    }
}

class Proxy implements Subject {
    private RealSubject realSubject;

    @Override
```

```
    public void request() {
        if (realSubject == null) {
            realSubject = new RealSubject();
        }
        System.out.println("Proxy request");
        realSubject.request();
    }
}

public class Client {
    public static void main(String[] args) {
        Subject subject = new Proxy();
        subject.request();
    }
}
```

- **Access Control:** The Proxy Pattern involves controlling access to the underlying object, whereas the Adapter Pattern focuses on interface compatibility.

Adapter Pattern vs. Facade Pattern

The Adapter Pattern and the Facade Pattern both involve working with existing classes and interfaces, but they address different concerns.

- **Objective:** The Adapter Pattern makes two incompatible interfaces compatible to work together, whereas the Facade Pattern simplifies interactions with a complex subsystem by providing a unified interface.
- **Usage Example:** The Adapter Pattern might be used when integrating components with mismatched interfaces. The Facade Pattern, on the other hand, might be used to provide a simple interface to a complex subsystem such as a library of network protocols.
- **Technical Implementation:**

```
class ComplexSubsystem {
    void operationA() {
        System.out.println("Operation A");
    }

    void operationB() {
        System.out.println("Operation B");
    }

    void operationC() {
        System.out.println("Operation C");
    }
}
```

```
class Facade {
    private ComplexSubsystem subsystem;

    public Facade() {
        this.subsystem = new ComplexSubsystem();
    }

    public void simpleOperation() {
        subsystem.operationA();
        subsystem.operationB();
        subsystem.operationC();
    }
}

public class Client {
    public static void main(String[] args) {
        Facade facade = new Facade();
        facade.simpleOperation();
    }
}
```

- **Simplification:** The Facade Pattern simplifies the interaction with a complex subsystem, while the Adapter Pattern focuses on enabling usage of an existing interface with a different one.

Understanding the intended use and implementation of each pattern provides clarity on how to effectively apply them in various circumstances. The Adapter Pattern focuses on compatibility, the Decorator Pattern on dynamic behavior addition, the Proxy Pattern on controlled access, and the Facade Pattern on simplification of complex subsystems.

7.10 Common Mistakes with the Adapter Pattern

A thorough understanding of the Adapter Pattern is paramount for avoiding common pitfalls associated with its implementation. While the Adapter Pattern offers robust solutions for integrating incompatible interfaces, misapplication can lead to suboptimal design and maintenance challenges. The following lists details frequent mistakes to avoid when applying the Adapter Pattern in Java.

- **Overusing the Adapter Pattern**

  It is crucial to recognize when the Adapter Pattern is the appropriate design choice. Overuse of this pattern can lead to a proliferation of adapter classes, increasing the codebase complexity unnecessarily. The Adapter Pattern should be reserved for scenarios where there is a clear need to bridge incompatible interfaces, rather than becoming a default solution for any compatibility issue.

- **Ignoring Object Composition**

  The Object Adapter approach relies on composition rather than inheritance. A common mistake is to unduly prefer class adapters, which use inheritance, potentially leading to tight coupling between classes. Object adapters promote loose coupling and should be preferred, particularly in scenarios that benefit from enhanced flexibility and easier maintenance.

- **Insufficient Interface Definition**

  An adapter must correctly align the target interface with the adaptee interface. Inadequate definition of either interface can result in reduced functionality or incorrect behavior of the adapter. Ensure the interface definitions are comprehensive and encapsulate the necessary methods that the client expects.

- **Limited Scalability Consideration**

  Failing to account for future changes in either the target or adaptee interface can lead to scalability issues. Adapters should be designed with potential extensions in mind. If the underlying interfaces change, the adapter must be flexible enough to accommodate these modifications without requiring a complete overhaul.

- **Improper Exception Handling**

  Adapters must gracefully handle exceptions arising from the adaptee classes, translating these into meaningful exceptions that the client can understand and manage. Ignoring exception handling in the adapter can propagate unexpected behaviors to the client.

Listing 1 demonstrates an example of an adapter implementation where common mistakes have been avoided:

```
public interface Target {
    void request();
}

public class Adaptee {
```

```
    public void specificRequest() {
        System.out.println("Specific request processing");
    }
}

public class Adapter implements Target {
    private Adaptee adaptee;

    public Adapter(Adaptee adaptee) {
        this.adaptee = adaptee;
    }

    @Override
    public void request() {
        adaptee.specificRequest();
    }
}

public class Client {
    public static void main(String[] args) {
        Adaptee adaptee = new Adaptee();
        Target target = new Adapter(adaptee);
        target.request(); // Output: Specific request processing
    }
}
```

The implementation in Listing 1 illustrates the use of object composition, appropriate interface alignment, and direct handling of method invocations without extraneous logic. This design ensures loose coupling and maintains flexibility.

Another critical aspect involves understanding the distinctions between class adapters and object adapters. Class adapters use multiple inheritance to adapt one interface to another, which is typically impractical in Java due to its single inheritance constraint. An inappropriate class adapter might look like:

```
public interface Target {
    void request();
}

public class Adaptee {
    public void specificRequest() {
        System.out.println("Specific request processing");
    }
}

public class IncorrectAdapter extends Adaptee implements Target {

    @Override
    public void request() {
        specificRequest();
    }
}

public class Client {
    public static void main(String[] args) {
        Target target = new IncorrectAdapter();
```

```
        target.request(); // Output: Specific request processing
    }
}
```

In Listing 2, the IncorrectAdapter class inherits from Adaptee and implements Target, tightly coupling the adapter to the adaptee. This design reduces flexibility, making it harder to adapt to changes in the Adaptee class without modifying the adapter implementation.

Avoiding these common mistakes ensures that the Adapter Pattern is used effectively, promoting maintainability and scalability in the codebase. By emphasizing composition over inheritance, properly defining interfaces, handling exceptions appropriately, and planning for scalability, developers can leverage the full potential of the Adapter Pattern in their Java applications.

7.11 Real-World Examples of the Adapter Pattern in Java

To demonstrate the practical application of the Adapter Pattern, we will explore multiple real-world examples and analyze how this pattern can be utilized effectively. These examples encompass diverse scenarios, illustrating the adaptability and versatility of the Adapter Pattern in integrating incompatible interfaces.

Integrating Legacy Systems with Modern APIs

Consider a scenario where an organization has a legacy inventory management system that must interface with a modern e-commerce API. The legacy system uses a different interface for inventory management than the modern API. Using the Adapter Pattern, we can create an adapter that bridges the gap between the two systems.

The legacy inventory system interface:

```
public interface LegacyInventorySystem {
    void addItem(String itemId, int quantity);
    void removeItem(String itemId, int quantity);
    int checkStock(String itemId);
}
```

The modern e-commerce API interface:

```
public interface ModernInventoryAPI {
    void addProduct(String productId, int quantity);
    void deleteProduct(String productId, int quantity);
    int getProductStock(String productId);
```

```
}
```

The Adapter class implementation:

```
public class InventoryAdapter implements ModernInventoryAPI {
    private final LegacyInventorySystem legacyInventorySystem;

    public InventoryAdapter(LegacyInventorySystem legacyInventorySystem) {
        this.legacyInventorySystem = legacyInventorySystem;
    }

    @Override
    public void addProduct(String productId, int quantity) {
        legacyInventorySystem.addItem(productId, quantity);
    }

    @Override
    public void deleteProduct(String productId, int quantity) {
        legacyInventorySystem.removeItem(productId, quantity);
    }

    @Override
    public int getProductStock(String productId) {
        return legacyInventorySystem.checkStock(productId);
    }
}
```

By using the InventoryAdapter, the modern API can now interact seamlessly with the legacy system.

Adapting Different Logging Frameworks

Organizations often employ different logging frameworks across various modules of a software system. Suppose an organization decides to standardize on a single logging interface but has existing code that uses multiple logging frameworks. The Adapter Pattern can be used to adapt legacy logging frameworks to the new standardized interface.

The standardized logging interface:

```
public interface UnifiedLogger {
    void logInfo(String message);
    void logError(String message);
    void logDebug(String message);
}
```

An existing logging framework interface:

```
public class LegacyLogger {
    public void info(String msg) {
        System.out.println("INFO: " + msg);
    }

    public void error(String msg) {
        System.err.println("ERROR: " + msg);
    }
```

```
    public void debug(String msg) {
        System.out.println("DEBUG: " + msg);
    }
}
```

The Adapter class implementation:

```
public class LoggerAdapter implements UnifiedLogger {
    private final LegacyLogger legacyLogger;

    public LoggerAdapter(LegacyLogger legacyLogger) {
        this.legacyLogger = legacyLogger;
    }

    @Override
    public void logInfo(String message) {
        legacyLogger.info(message);
    }

    @Override
    public void logError(String message) {
        legacyLogger.error(message);
    }

    @Override
    public void logDebug(String message) {
        legacyLogger.debug(message);
    }
}
```

With the LoggerAdapter, the existing code that uses LegacyLogger can now interact with the unified logging system without modifying the legacy framework.

Adapting Different Payment Gateways

In an e-commerce application, you may need to integrate with multiple payment gateways, each providing different interfaces. The Adapter Pattern allows the creation of a consistent interface for payment processing.

The unified payment processor interface:

```
public interface PaymentProcessor {
    void processPayment(String paymentDetails);
}
```

An existing payment gateway interface:

```
public class LegacyPaymentGateway {
    public void makePayment(String details) {
        // Payment processing logic
    }
}
```

The Adapter class implementation:

```
public class PaymentGatewayAdapter implements PaymentProcessor {
    private final LegacyPaymentGateway legacyPaymentGateway;

    public PaymentGatewayAdapter(LegacyPaymentGateway legacyPaymentGateway) {

        this.legacyPaymentGateway = legacyPaymentGateway;
    }

    @Override
    public void processPayment(String paymentDetails) {
        legacyPaymentGateway.makePayment(paymentDetails);
    }
}
```

With the PaymentGatewayAdapter, the application can use various payment gateways through a unified interface without rewriting the payment processing logic.

Streamlining File System Access

Another common scenario is adapting disparate file system interfaces to a unified interface. For example, a file system abstraction layer might provide different interfaces for local and cloud-based storage.

A unified file system interface:

```
public interface FileSystem {
    void writeFile(String path, String content);
    String readFile(String path);
}
```

A local file system implementation:

```
public class LocalFileSystem {
    public void saveFile(String path, String content) {
        // Save file logic
    }

    public String loadFile(String path) {
        // Load file logic
        return "File content";
    }
}
```

The Adapter class implementation:

```
public class LocalFileSystemAdapter implements FileSystem {
    private final LocalFileSystem localFileSystem;

    public LocalFileSystemAdapter(LocalFileSystem localFileSystem) {
        this.localFileSystem = localFileSystem;
    }

    @Override
    public void writeFile(String path, String content) {
        localFileSystem.saveFile(path, content);
    }
```

```
    @Override
    public String readFile(String path) {
        return localFileSystem.loadFile(path);
    }
}
```

Through the LocalFileSystemAdapter, the application can interact with the local file system using the unified FileSystem interface, thus simplifying access to different file storage mechanisms.

These examples illustrate how the Adapter Pattern can be applied in various real-world scenarios to integrate incompatible interfaces, making legacy systems and modern components work together seamlessly.

Chapter 8

Observer Pattern: Keeping Objects In Sync

This chapter examines the Observer Pattern, which maintains consistency between related objects by ensuring that changes in one object are reflected in others. It details the roles of the Subject and Observer interfaces, and explains the implementation in Java, including both push and pull models. The chapter discusses the optimal scenarios for using the Observer Pattern, its advantages and disadvantages, and provides best practices and common mistakes to avoid. Real-world examples are included to demonstrate its practical use.

8.1 Introduction to the Observer Pattern

The Observer Pattern is a fundamental design pattern in software development, particularly in object-oriented programming. Its primary purpose is to create a one-to-many dependency between objects so that when one object changes state, all its dependents are notified and updated automatically. This pattern is particularly useful in scenarios where a change in one part of the system needs to be propagated to multiple other parts without them being tightly coupled.

The key to the Observer Pattern is to define two main components: the Subject and the Observer. The Subject is an entity that maintains a list of observers and notifies them of state changes. The Observer is an entity that needs to be updated when the state of the Subject changes.

- **Subject:** The subject keeps track of its observers and provides an interface to attach or detach observers. It is responsible for notifying the observers about any state changes.
- **Observer:** The observer defines an updating interface for objects that should be notified of changes in a subject.

To clearly understand the structure and behavior of the Observer Pattern, consider a basic representation of it in Java:

```
interface Observer {
    public void update();
}

class ConcreteObserver implements Observer {
    @Override
    public void update() {
        // Concrete implementation of update
    }
}

interface Subject {
    public void attach(Observer o);
    public void detach(Observer o);
    public void notifyObservers();
}

class ConcreteSubject implements Subject {
    private List<Observer> observers = new ArrayList<>();

    @Override
    public void attach(Observer o) {
        observers.add(o);
    }

    @Override
    public void detach(Observer o) {
        observers.remove(o);
    }

    @Override
    public void notifyObservers() {
        for (Observer o : observers) {
            o.update();
        }
    }

    // Method to change state and notify observers
    public void changeState() {
        // Change the state
        notifyObservers();
    }
}
```

In this example, the Subject interface defines the methods for attaching and detaching observers, as well as a method to notify all observers of a state change. The ConcreteSubject class implements the Subject interface and maintains a list of observers. It provides the functionality to add and remove observers and to notify them whenever its state changes.

The Observer interface defines the update() method that all observers must implement. The ConcreteObserver class provides a concrete implementation of the update() method, defining what should happen when the observer is notified of changes.

When the ConcreteSubject changes state, it calls its notifyObservers() method, which in turn calls the update() method on each of its observers. This decouples the subjects and observers, allowing them to vary independently.

The above structure can be visualized more effectively through a simple sequence of events:

<ObserverPatternSequence>
ObserverPatternSequence: A diagram or description that illustrates the process.
</ObserverPatternSequence>

Implementing the Observer Pattern provides several tangible benefits:

- **Loosely coupled design:** The subject and its observers are loosely coupled, as the subject does not need to know the concrete implementations of its observers.
- **Flexibility:** New observers can be added without modifying the subject, which promotes flexibility and scalability in the system.
- **Reusability:** Observer classes can be reused across different contexts within the application or even in different applications.

However, it is important to also recognize some potential disadvantages:

- **Memory leaks:** If observers are not properly detached from subjects when no longer needed, it can lead to memory leaks.
- **Unexpected updates:** Observers might receive updates under unexpected circumstances, leading to potential inconsistencies if not managed carefully.

Understanding the Observer Pattern's structure and implications enables developers to implement efficient one-to-many dependencies in their software applications. This pattern is particularly effective in graphical user interfaces, event handling systems, and distributed event-driven systems, where changes in one component need to be dynamically propagated to others.

8.2 Understanding the Observer Pattern

The Observer Pattern is a fundamental design pattern in software engineering, which aims to establish a one-to-many dependency between objects so that when one object changes state, all its dependents are notified and updated automatically. This pattern is pivotal in creating a decoupled and responsive architecture, particularly in scenarios where data representation needs to be synchronized across various components.

The core components of the Observer Pattern are the Subject and the Observer interfaces. The Subject interface maintains a collection of its dependents, called Observers, and provides mechanisms to attach, detach, and notify these Observers. The Observer interface, on the other hand, defines an update method which gets called by the Subject when it changes its state.

Subject Interface:

The Subject interface typically declares the following methods:

```
public interface Subject {
    void registerObserver(Observer o);
    void removeObserver(Observer o);
    void notifyObservers();
}
```

Observer Interface:

The Observer interface requires the following method:

```
public interface Observer {
    void update(Object arg);
}
```

The Subject interface contains methods to attach and detach observers, as well as a method to notify all registered observers when a significant state change occurs. The Observer interface defines the update method, which is called when the Subject notifies its observers.

To delve deeper, let us understand the key operations of the Observer Pattern through a detailed glance at the method implementations in the context of a Weather Monitoring system:

- registerObserver(Observer o): This method is used to add a new Observer to the list of subscribers.
- removeObserver(Observer o): This method removes an existing Observer from the list of subscribers.
- notifyObservers(): This method iterates through the list of registered Observers and calls their update method to propagate the state change.

Below is an implementation of a concrete Subject class, WeatherData, which tracks weather data and notifies its observers upon updates.

```
import java.util.ArrayList;

public class WeatherData implements Subject {
    private ArrayList<Observer> observers;
    private float temperature;
    private float humidity;
    private float pressure;

    public WeatherData() {
        observers = new ArrayList<Observer>();
    }

    public void registerObserver(Observer o) {
        observers.add(o);
    }

    public void removeObserver(Observer o) {
        int i = observers.indexOf(o);
        if (i >= 0) {
            observers.remove(i);
        }
    }

    public void notifyObservers() {
        for (int i = 0; i < observers.size(); i++) {
            Observer observer = (Observer)observers.get(i);
            observer.update(getTemperature(), getHumidity(), getPressure());
        }
    }

    public void measurementsChanged() {
        notifyObservers();
    }

    public void setMeasurements(float temperature, float humidity, float pressure) {
```

```
        this.temperature = temperature;
        this.humidity = humidity;
        this.pressure = pressure;
        measurementsChanged();
    }

    public float getTemperature() {
        return temperature;
    }

    public float getHumidity() {
        return humidity;
    }

    public float getPressure() {
        return pressure;
    }
}
```

In this WeatherData class, the setMeasurements method sets the latest weather data and subsequently triggers the measurementsChanged method to notify all registered Observers. Each observer then updates its state using the provided weather data.

It is crucial to note that the notifyObservers method in our example employs the push model, where the Subject pushes the state to each Observer. Alternatively, the pull model can be implemented by having the Observers pull the state from the Subject after being notified.

To demonstrate a concrete Observer, consider a CurrentConditionsDisplay which implements the Observer interface, receiving weather updates and displaying the current conditions.

```
public class CurrentConditionsDisplay implements Observer {
    private float temperature;
    private float humidity;
    private Subject weatherData;

    public CurrentConditionsDisplay(Subject weatherData) {
        this.weatherData = weatherData;
        weatherData.registerObserver(this);
    }

    public void update(Object temp, Object humidity, Object pressure) {
        this.temperature = (float) temp;
        this.humidity = (float) humidity;
        display();
    }

    public void display() {
        System.out.println("Current conditions: " +
                           temperature + "F degrees and " +
                           humidity + "% humidity");
    }
}
```

In this implementation, the CurrentConditionsDisplay subscribes to weather updates by registering itself with WeatherData. When update is called, it receives the new temperature and humidity, processes the data, and updates its display.

Through this pattern, the complexity of maintaining consistent state across various dependent components is effectively managed, with the Subject and Observer classes adhering to the principles of low coupling and high cohesion, fostering maintainability and scalability in software design.

8.3 Implementing the Observer Pattern in Java

To implement the Observer Pattern in Java, we typically follow a structured approach involving the creation of Subject and Observer interfaces and their respective implementations. This section will guide you through a meticulous implementation, ensuring that changes in the state of one object (the Subject) are reflected in other objects (the Observers).

First, we define the terms:

- **Subject**: The object that maintains a list of dependents, known as observers, and notifies them of any state changes.
- **Observer**: An interface or class that gets notified and updated by the Subject.

Step 1: Create the Subject Interface

The Subject interface declares methods for attaching, detaching, and notifying observers. Here is the Subject interface in Java:

```
public interface Subject {
    void registerObserver(Observer o);
    void removeObserver(Observer o);
    void notifyObservers();
}
```

Step 2: Create the Observer Interface

The Observer interface contains the update method that is called when the Subject's state changes:

```
public interface Observer {
    void update(float temperature, float humidity, float pressure);
}
```

Step 3: Implement the Subject Interface in a Concrete Class

For this example, we will create a WeatherData class that implements the Subject interface:

```
import java.util.ArrayList;

public class WeatherData implements Subject {
    private ArrayList<Observer> observers;
    private float temperature;
    private float humidity;
    private float pressure;

    public WeatherData() {
        observers = new ArrayList<>();
    }

    public void registerObserver(Observer o) {
        observers.add(o);
    }

    public void removeObserver(Observer o) {
        int i = observers.indexOf(o);
        if (i >= 0) {
            observers.remove(i);
        }
    }

    public void notifyObservers() {
        for (Observer observer : observers) {
            observer.update(temperature, humidity, pressure);
        }
    }

    public void measurementsChanged() {
        notifyObservers();
    }

    public void setMeasurements(float temperature, float humidity, float pressure) {
        this.temperature = temperature;
        this.humidity = humidity;
        this.pressure = pressure;
        measurementsChanged();
    }

    public float getTemperature() {
        return temperature;
    }

    public float getHumidity() {
        return humidity;
    }

    public float getPressure() {
        return pressure;
    }
```

```
}
```

Step 4: Implement the Observer Interface in Concrete Classes

The display elements that will act as Observers need to implement the Observer interface. For instance, here is an implementation of a CurrentConditionsDisplay:

```
public class CurrentConditionsDisplay implements Observer {
    private float temperature;
    private float humidity;
    private Subject weatherData;

    public CurrentConditionsDisplay(Subject weatherData) {
        this.weatherData = weatherData;
        weatherData.registerObserver(this);
    }

    public void update(float temperature, float humidity, float pressure) {
        this.temperature = temperature;
        this.humidity = humidity;
        display();
    }

    public void display() {
        System.out.println("Current conditions: " + temperature + "F degrees and " +
                humidity + "% humidity");
    }
}
```

Step 5: Integrate The System

To integrate the system, create instances of WeatherData and CurrentConditionsDisplay, and change the state in WeatherData to see how the display updates:

```
public class WeatherStation {
    public static void main(String[] args) {
        WeatherData weatherData = new WeatherData();

        CurrentConditionsDisplay currentDisplay = new CurrentConditionsDisplay(
                weatherData);
        // You can add more display elements here

        weatherData.setMeasurements(80, 65, 30.4f);
        weatherData.setMeasurements(82, 70, 29.2f);
        weatherData.setMeasurements(78, 90, 29.2f);
    }
}
```

Given the above implementation, consider the following aspects:

- **Modularity**: The Observers are decoupled from the Subject. Each observer can be added or removed dynamically.
- **Extensibility**: New types of Observers can be added without al-

tering the Subject.

- **Reusability**: The implementation can be reused in scenarios where a Subject maintains and updates multiple observers.

The pull model can be integrated by modifying the Observer interface and its implementation to request the state it needs during the update call. However, for simplicity and clarity, the push model has been used here.

8.4 Subject and Observer Interfaces

The Observer Pattern relies heavily on the interaction between two primary components: the Subject and the Observer interfaces. These interfaces define the contract for communication between objects, ensuring that observers are notified whenever the subject's state changes. Properly implementing these interfaces is crucial for maintaining the integrity and functionality of the Observer Pattern in Java.

The Subject interface typically consists of methods to register, remove, and notify observers. Here is a basic implementation in Java:

```
public interface Subject {
    void registerObserver(Observer o);
    void removeObserver(Observer o);
    void notifyObservers();
}
```

In this interface:

- registerObserver(Observer o) adds an observer to the list of observers.
- removeObserver(Observer o) removes an observer from the list.
- notifyObservers() iterates through the list of observers and calls their update methods.

To build upon this, we then define the Observer interface, which includes an update method that will be called when the subject's state changes. A simple version of the Observer interface can be like this:

```
public interface Observer {
    void update(Object arg);
}
```

In this case, the update(Object arg) method is a placeholder that expects the subject to pass some information about the state change. The arg parameter can be a detailed state object, allowing the observers to extract the necessary data.

Next, let's integrate these interfaces into a practical example. Assume we have a weather monitoring system where the WeatherData class acts as the subject, and the CurrentConditionsDisplay is one of its observers:

```
import java.util.ArrayList;

public class WeatherData implements Subject {
    private ArrayList<Observer> observers;
    private float temperature;
    private float humidity;
    private float pressure;

    public WeatherData() {
        observers = new ArrayList<>();
    }

    public void registerObserver(Observer o) {
        observers.add(o);
    }

    public void removeObserver(Observer o) {
        int i = observers.indexOf(o);
        if (i >= 0) {
            observers.remove(i);
        }
    }

    public void notifyObservers() {
        for (Observer o : observers) {
            o.update(this);
        }
    }

    public void measurementsChanged() {
        notifyObservers();
    }

    public void setMeasurements(float temperature, float humidity, float pressure) {
        this.temperature = temperature;
        this.humidity = humidity;
        this.pressure = pressure;
        measurementsChanged();
    }

    public float getTemperature() {
        return temperature;
    }

    public float getHumidity() {
        return humidity;
    }

    public float getPressure() {
```

```
        return pressure;
    }
}

public class CurrentConditionsDisplay implements Observer {
    private float temperature;
    private float humidity;
    private Subject weatherData;

    public CurrentConditionsDisplay(Subject weatherData) {
        this.weatherData = weatherData;
        weatherData.registerObserver(this);
    }

    public void update(Object arg) {
        if (arg instanceof WeatherData) {
            WeatherData weatherData = (WeatherData) arg;
            this.temperature = weatherData.getTemperature();
            this.humidity = weatherData.getHumidity();
            display();
        }
    }

    public void display() {
        System.out.println("Current conditions: " + temperature + "F degrees and " +
                humidity + "% humidity");
    }
}
```

In this example:

- The WeatherData class implements the Subject interface and maintains a list of observers.
- It provides methods to register, remove, and notify observers.
- When new weather measurements are set via setMeasurements(), the measurementsChanged() method is called, which in turn calls notifyObservers() to update all observers.
- The CurrentConditionsDisplay class implements the Observer interface.
- The CurrentConditionsDisplay class registers itself with the WeatherData subject, meaning it will receive updates.
- The update(Object arg) method extracts the relevant data from the WeatherData object and calls display() to print the current conditions.

When the observable weather data changes, the registered displays are automatically updated, reflecting the new state. The clear separation of responsibilities allows for a decoupled system, making it easy to add, remove, or modify observers without affecting the subject.

This pattern also exhibits resilience in the face of changes, as new types of displays can be created without altering the base classes. For example, another observer could be a StatisticsDisplay, focusing on summary statistics, or a ForecastDisplay, predicting future conditions based on trends.

```
public class StatisticsDisplay implements Observer {
    private float maxTemp = 0.0f;
    private float minTemp = 200;
    private float tempSum= 0.0f;
    private int numReadings;
    private Subject weatherData;

    public StatisticsDisplay(Subject weatherData) {
        this.weatherData = weatherData;
        weatherData.registerObserver(this);
    }

    public void update(Object arg) {
        if (arg instanceof WeatherData) {
            WeatherData weatherData = (WeatherData) arg;
            float temp = weatherData.getTemperature();
            tempSum += temp;
            numReadings++;

            if (temp > maxTemp) {
                maxTemp = temp;
            }

            if (temp < minTemp) {
                minTemp = temp;
            }

            display();
        }
    }

    public void display() {
        System.out.println("Avg/Max/Min temperature = " + (tempSum /
            numReadings) + "/" + maxTemp + "/" + minTemp);
    }
}
```

This new observer, StatisticsDisplay, also registers with WeatherData and receives updates. It calculates and displays the average, maximum, and minimum temperatures over time.

Maintaining clean and comprehensive interfaces between subjects and observers is fundamental to the effective application of the Observer Pattern. This ensures flexibility and scalability, while reducing the potential for tight coupling and promoting a robust design in software systems.

8.5 Push vs Pull Models

In the Observer Pattern, two primary models describe how information is communicated between the Subject and Observer: the Push model and the Pull model. Understanding these models is pivotal to implementing the Observer Pattern efficiently and effectively.

Push Model

In the Push model, the Subject sends detailed updates to the Observers whenever a change occurs. This model proactively pushes all necessary data to the Observers without prompting. The Observers receive data whether or not they need the full set of information at the given time.

A typical implementation in Java would look like this:

```
public interface Observer {
    void update(Object data);
}
```

```
public class ConcreteObserver implements Observer {
    private Object observerState;

    @Override
    public void update(Object data) {
        this.observerState = data;
        display();
    }

    public void display() {
        System.out.println("Updated Observer State: " + observerState);
    }
}
```

```
public class ConcreteSubject {
    private List<Observer> observers = new ArrayList<>();
    private Object subjectState;

    public void addObserver(Observer observer) {
        observers.add(observer);
    }

    public void removeObserver(Observer observer) {
        observers.remove(observer);
    }

    public void setState(Object state) {
        this.subjectState = state;
        notifyObservers();
    }

    private void notifyObservers() {
        for (Observer observer : observers) {
            observer.update(subjectState);
```

```
        }
    }
}
```

Every time the state changes in ConcreteSubject, it notifies all registered Observers by calling their update method with the new state as the argument. This results in immediate and uniform data push to all Observers.

Pull Model

In the Pull model, the Subject only sends a minimal notification to the Observers to indicate that a change has occurred. It then becomes the responsibility of the Observers to pull the required data from the Subject. This model is more reactive, where Observers must request data, potentially leading to more efficient use of resources since Observers can decide what specific information to retrieve based on their current need.

A typical implementation in Java would appear as follows:

```
public interface Observer {
    void update(); // No data is pushed
}
```

```
public class ConcreteObserver implements Observer {
    private ConcreteSubject subject;

    public ConcreteObserver(ConcreteSubject subject) {
        this.subject = subject;
    }

    @Override
    public void update() {
        Object updatedState = subject.getState();
        System.out.println("Pulled Observer State: " + updatedState);
    }
}
```

```
public class ConcreteSubject {
    private List<Observer> observers = new ArrayList<>();
    private Object subjectState;

    public void addObserver(Observer observer) {
        observers.add(observer);
    }

    public void removeObserver(Observer observer) {
        observers.remove(observer);
    }

    public void setState(Object state) {
        this.subjectState = state;
        notifyObservers();
    }
```

```
    private void notifyObservers() {
        for (Observer observer : observers) {
            observer.update();
        }
    }

    public Object getState() {
        return subjectState; // Observers pull this data when needed
    }
}
```

In this implementation, ConcreteSubject calls the update method of Observers without passing any data. Observers then invoke the getState method of ConcreteSubject to pull the required data.

Choosing between the Push and Pull models depends on specific requirements such as the amount of data, timeliness, and system performance. The Push model is suitable for scenarios where frequent and detailed updates are necessary, and Observers cannot afford the overhead of pulling data repeatedly. The Pull model, on the other hand, is preferred when updates are infrequent, or Observers require only certain parts of the state at a time, reducing unnecessary data transmission and potentially improving performance. Be diligent in analyzing application needs to choose the model that offers the best trade-offs in terms of resource usage, simplicity, and responsiveness.

8.6 When to Use the Observer Pattern

The Observer Pattern is primarily used when an application must ensure that changes in one object, referred to as the Subject, are reported to and reflected in other dependent objects, called Observers. This pattern promotes a one-to-many dependency between objects, enabling state consistency across multiple entities. Certain conditions and scenarios make the Observer Pattern particularly advantageous.

- **State Change Propagation:** When there is a need to propagate changes in the state of one object (the Subject) to multiple dependent objects (Observers) without tightly coupling them. For example, in a Model-View-Controller (MVC) architecture, the model can act as the Subject to notify the views (Observers) when data has changed.
- **Dynamic Dependents:** When the list of dependents can change dynamically, i.e., you need to add or remove dependents at run-

time. The Observer Pattern provides an elegant mechanism for such scenarios by allowing Observers to register and deregister dynamically with the Subject.

- **Decoupling:** When promoting loose coupling between Subject and Observers is essential. The Subject does not require explicit knowledge of who its Observers are, only that they implement a certain interface. This promotes flexibility and reusability within the application.
- **Event Handling Systems:** When implementing systems that rely extensively on events or state changes, such as graphical user interface (GUI) frameworks, notification services, etc. By adopting the Observer Pattern, these systems can manage event listeners and handlers in a clean and modular fashion.
- **Data Binding:** When developing applications that require data binding features. For instance, in a two-way data binding scenario often seen in web applications and frameworks, the Observer Pattern ensures that updates to the data model are reflected in the UI components and vice versa.

```
import java.util.ArrayList;
import java.util.List;

// Subject interface
interface Subject {
    void registerObserver(Observer o);
    void removeObserver(Observer o);
    void notifyObservers();
}

// Concrete subject
class WeatherData implements Subject {
    private List<Observer> observers;
    private float temperature;
    private float humidity;
    private float pressure;

    public WeatherData() {
        observers = new ArrayList<>();
    }

    public void registerObserver(Observer o) {
        observers.add(o);
    }

    public void removeObserver(Observer o) {
        observers.remove(o);
    }

    public void notifyObservers() {
        for (Observer observer : observers) {
```

```
            observer.update(temperature, humidity, pressure);
        }
    }

    public void measurementsChanged() {
        notifyObservers();
    }

    public void setMeasurements(float temperature, float humidity, float pressure) {
        this.temperature = temperature;
        this.humidity = humidity;
        this.pressure = pressure;
        measurementsChanged();
    }
}

// Observer interface
interface Observer {
    void update(float temp, float humidity, float pressure);
}

// Concrete observer
class CurrentConditionsDisplay implements Observer {
    private float temperature;
    private float humidity;

    public void update(float temperature, float humidity, float pressure) {
        this.temperature = temperature;
        this.humidity = humidity;
        display();
    }

    public void display() {
        System.out.println("Current conditions: " + temperature + "F degrees and " +
                humidity + "% humidity");
    }
}

// Main method usage
public class WeatherStation {
    public static void main(String[] args) {
        WeatherData weatherData = new WeatherData();

        CurrentConditionsDisplay currentDisplay = new CurrentConditionsDisplay();
        weatherData.registerObserver(currentDisplay);

        weatherData.setMeasurements(80, 65, 30.4f);
        weatherData.setMeasurements(82, 70, 29.2f);
    }
}
```

In the above Java example, WeatherData acts as the Subject, while CurrentConditionsDisplay is an Observer. The WeatherData object notifies the CurrentConditionsDisplay whenever its state changes.

Some factors to consider to determine if the Observer Pattern fits include:

- **Simplicity vs. Flexibility:** While the Observer Pattern introduces a simple way to manage dependencies, it may add complexity if used inappropriately. The flexibility it provides should outweigh the additional complexity.

- **Performance Overhead:** The added layer of communication between the Subject and Observers may lead to performance overhead, especially if the number of Observers is large or the update mechanism is frequent. Evaluating the performance impact is essential.

- **Notification Granularity:** Determine the granularity of notifications required by the application. Using the Observer Pattern for too granular notifications might lead to inefficiencies, while too coarse notifications may miss out on critical updates.

In systems where maintaining object synchronization and state consistency is paramount, and where the coupling between components needs to be minimized while allowing for dynamic interactions, the Observer Pattern is an invaluable design choice. The pattern ensures that your system remains both modular and scalable, facilitating easier maintenance and potential extension in the future.

8.7 Advantages and Disadvantages of the Observer Pattern

The Observer Pattern offers a structured way to maintain consistency among related objects. It establishes a one-to-many dependency between objects such that a state change in one object (the Subject) is automatically reflected in the dependent objects (the Observers). While this pattern brings numerous benefits, it also introduces certain challenges and trade-offs.

Advantages:

- **Promotes Loose Coupling:** The Observer Pattern reduces the dependencies between the Subject and Observers. Observers only need to conform to a common interface to be notified of changes, which decouples the Subject from knowing specific details about the Observers.

- **Facilitates Scalability:** New Observers can be added to the system without modifying the Subject. This allows the system to scale easily, accommodating additional Observers with minimal changes to existing code.

- **Improves Responsiveness:** By offering a mechanism for automatic and timely updates, the Observer Pattern ensures that changes are propagated quickly through the system. This enhances the responsiveness of applications, especially in real-time systems.

- **Encapsulates Change Propagation:** The logic for propagating changes is encapsulated within the Subject, reducing redundancy and centralizing the mechanism that ensures consistency.

- **Simplifies Maintenance:** The pattern centralizes update logic within the Subject, which simplifies maintenance and debugging. When issues arise, developers can focus on the Subject to diagnose and resolve problems.

- Supports Broadcast Communication: The Observer Pattern inherently supports broadcasting, where a single Subject can notify multiple Observers simultaneously, which is effective for event-driven systems.

Disadvantages:

- **Memory Leaks:** A common issue in the Observer Pattern is the potential for memory leaks, particularly if Observer objects are not unregistered properly. Java's weak references (via WeakReference class) can mitigate this problem but add complexity.

- **Unexpected Updates:** If not managed carefully, the order and timing of updates can lead to inconsistencies or unexpected behavior. It's essential to design update mechanisms that are predictable and well-understood.

- **Performance Overheads:** The need to notify all Observers can introduce significant performance overheads, especially when the number of Observers is large or when updates are frequent.

- **Complex Debugging:** Because the Observer Pattern can generate numerous interactions among objects, debugging can become complex. Tracing the source of updates and understanding the sequence of notifications can be challenging.

- **Excessive Notifications:** In scenarios where Observers don't filter updates effectively or the Subject sends updates too frequently, the system may suffer from excessive notifications, leading to performance bottlenecks or unnecessary processing.

- Concurrency Issues: Handling notifications in a multi-threaded environment requires careful synchronization. Failure to do so can result in race conditions, deadlocks, or other concurrency-related problems.

To illustrate these points, consider the following implementation snippet of an Observer pattern in Java:

```
import java.util.ArrayList;
import java.util.List;

interface Observer {
    void update(String message);
}

class Subject {
    private List<Observer> observers = new ArrayList<>();

    public void addObserver(Observer observer) {
        observers.add(observer);
    }

    public void removeObserver(Observer observer) {
        observers.remove(observer);
    }

    public void notifyObservers(String message) {
        for (Observer observer : observers) {
            observer.update(message);
        }
    }
}

class ConcreteObserver implements Observer {
    private String name;

    public ConcreteObserver(String name) {
        this.name = name;
    }

    @Override
    public void update(String message) {
        System.out.println(name + " received: " + message);
    }
}
```

Execution result:

```
Observer1 received: State Changed
Observer2 received: State Changed
```

This code demonstrates how the Subject can notify multiple Observers of a state change. However, if we neglect to remove Observers when they are no longer needed, it may lead to memory leaks. Similarly, if we had a large number of Observers or frequent updates, the performance overhead could become noticeable.

The Observer Pattern's benefits must be carefully weighed against its disadvantages. By understanding both sides, developers can apply this pattern effectively, ensuring robust and maintainable code.

8.8 Observer Pattern Best Practices

Understanding how to implement the Observer Pattern correctly can significantly enhance the efficiency and maintainability of your code. This section outlines best practices that can help you avoid common pitfalls and leverage the full benefits of the Observer Pattern.

1. Minimizing Dependencies:

Aim to minimize the dependencies between the Subject and Observer classes. One of the core ideas behind the Observer Pattern is to promote loose coupling. Avoid implementing functionality in the Subject that depends heavily on the concrete implementation of the Observer. Utilize abstract interfaces to ensure that the Subject only knows about the general capabilities of the Observer and not its specific implementation details.

```
public interface Observer {
    void update();
}

public interface Subject {
    void attach(Observer o);
    void detach(Observer o);
    void notifyObservers();
}
```

2. Defining Clear Contracts:

Ensure clearly defined contracts for both Subject and Observer interfaces. The methods attach(), detach(), and notifyObservers() in the Subject interface should be well-documented and consistent. Similarly, the update() method in the Observer should clearly describe what changes should be expected and any assumptions the Observer can make.

3. Managing Observer Lifecycle:

Carefully manage the lifecycle of Observers. Ensure that Observers are removed when they are no longer needed to prevent memory leaks. Utilize appropriate data structures to manage the list of Observers efficiently. For example, a CopyOnWriteArrayList can be useful in a multi-threaded environment, as it provides thread-safe iteration with minimal locking overhead.

```
import java.util.concurrent.CopyOnWriteArrayList;

public class ConcreteSubject implements Subject {
    private List<Observer> observers = new CopyOnWriteArrayList<>();

    public void attach(Observer o) {
        observers.add(o);
    }

    public void detach(Observer o) {
        observers.remove(o);
    }

    public void notifyObservers() {
        for (Observer o : observers) {
            o.update();
        }
    }
}
```

4. Handling Excessive Notifications:

Be cautious of excessive notifications. Frequent updates can lead to performance bottlenecks if not properly managed. Implementing a threshold for change notifications, aggregating changes, or using a scheduling mechanism to batch notify Observers can mitigate this issue.

```
public class BatchNotifierSubject extends ConcreteSubject {
    private boolean changed = false;

    public void setState(Object newState) {
        this.state = newState;
        changed = true;
    }

    public void notifyObservers() {
        if (changed) {
            super.notifyObservers();
            changed = false;
        }
    }
}
```

5. Using the Right Notification Approach:

Choose between the push and pull models based on your application's needs. The push model immediately sends state information to Observers, while the pull model requires Observers to request state information. The choice can impact performance and complexity.

Push Model Example:

```
public interface Observer {
    void update(Object newState);
}
```

```
public class ConcreteSubject implements Subject {
    private List<Observer> observers = new CopyOnWriteArrayList<>();
    private Object state;

    public void notifyObservers() {
        for (Observer o : observers) {
            o.update(state);
        }
    }

    public void setState(Object state) {
        this.state = state;
        notifyObservers();
    }
}
```

Pull Model Example:

```
public interface Observer {
    void update();
}
```

```
public class ConcreteObserver implements Observer {
    private ConcreteSubject subject;

    public ConcreteObserver(ConcreteSubject subject) {
        this.subject = subject;
    }

    public void update() {
        Object state = subject.getState();
        // process state
    }
}
```

6. Ensuring Update Consistency:

Ensure consistency of updates in multi-threaded environments. The Subject should handle concurrent modifications carefully to avoid race conditions. Using thread-safe collections and synchronization mechanisms is crucial for maintaining data integrity.

7. Decoupling Using Event Buses or Message Queues:

In scenarios requiring high decoupling, consider using event buses or message queues. These patterns further decouple Subjects and Observers, allowing asynchronous communication and reducing direct dependencies.

8. Testing Observers and Subjects Separately:

Isolate tests for Subjects and Observers to ensure they function correctly independently. Use mock objects to test the interactions, verifying that Subjects properly notify Observers and that Observers correctly handle updates.

```
import static org.mockito.Mockito.*;

public class ObserverTest {
    @Test
    public void testObserverUpdate() {
        Subject subject = new ConcreteSubject();
        Observer observer = mock(Observer.class);
        subject.attach(observer);

        subject.notifyObservers();
        verify(observer).update();
    }
}
```

9. Documenting Assumptions and Operations:

Document the assumptions and operations clearly, particularly if the Subject and Observers are part of a library or an API. Proper documentation aids in understanding the expected behavior and reduces the risk of incorrect usage.

Applying these best practices can enhance the scalability, maintainability, and performance of your Observer Pattern implementations, making them more robust and easier to manage in complex applications.

8.9 Use Cases for the Observer Pattern

The Observer Pattern is employed in various scenarios where a one-to-many relationship is needed between objects, so that if one object changes state, all its dependents are notified and updated automatically. This section delves into several typical use cases where the Observer Pattern proves to be highly effective.

- **Event Management Systems:**
  Event management systems often need to notify multiple subscribers about certain events. For instance, a GUI framework with buttons and text fields can utilize the Observer Pattern to notify observers when an event like a button click or text change occurs. Here, the button or text field acts as the *Subject*, whereas the various parts of the application interested in the event (observers)

will implement the Observer interface.

- **Data Modeling:**
In applications dealing with data models, such as spreadsheets, dashboards, or simulations, keeping views synchronized with the underlying data model is crucial. For example, in a financial application that tracks stock prices, a change in the stock price should automatically update any graphs, tables, or other visual representations of that data. In this scenario, the stock price data serves as the *Subject*, and the visual components act as Observers.

- **Distributed Systems:**
In distributed systems, components often interact through events. For example, in a microservices architecture, one service might need to notify other services about specific changes. The Observer Pattern can be employed to manage these notifications efficiently. Suppose a user management service updates user information, and other services such as billing, email, and logging need to be notified. The user management service acts as the *Subject*, whereas the other services play the roles of Observers.

- **Notification Services:**
Notification services or alerting systems can leverage the Observer Pattern to disseminate alerts to multiple subscribers. For instance, an alert system might monitor servers for downtime. Once downtime is detected, it notifies all registered services, which might include administrators' applications, logging services, and recovery systems. Here, the alert system is the *Subject*, and the entities receiving the alerts are the *Observers*.

- **Real-time Systems:**
Real-time systems, such as gaming or simulation platforms, often need multiple components to stay in sync with changes occurring in real-time. For example, in an online multiplayer game, changing the state of an avatar should automatically update all other players' views to reflect those changes. The game server can act as the *Subject*, and the individual player clients can be the *Observers*.

- **Social Media Applications:**
Social media applications use the Observer Pattern to implement the "following" feature. When a user posts an update, all followers are notified about this update. The user in this case acts as the *Subject*, and the followers are the *Observers* who receive the

updates. This can be elegantly implemented using the Observer Pattern to manage the relationships and notifications efficiently.

- **Publishing-Subscriber Systems:**
  In publish-subscribe systems, the Observer Pattern forms the backbone by providing a way for publishers to notify subscribers about updates or new content. For instance, news feed applications where different users are interested in different news categories employ this pattern. The news category acts as the *Subject*, and the users subscribing to those categories act as the Observers.

To illustrate a concrete implementation in a GUI framework, consider the following pseudocode that models the behavior of an event management system:

```
// Subject interface
public interface Subject {
    void registerObserver(Observer o);
    void removeObserver(Observer o);
    void notifyObservers();
}

// Observer interface
public interface Observer {
    void update();
}

// Concrete Subject
public class Button implements Subject {
    private List<Observer> observers;

    public Button() {
        this.observers = new ArrayList<>();
    }

    @Override
    public void registerObserver(Observer o) {
        observers.add(o);
    }

    @Override
    public void removeObserver(Observer o) {
        observers.remove(o);
    }

    @Override
    public void notifyObservers() {
        for(Observer observer : observers) {
            observer.update();
        }
    }

    // Simulating a button click
    public void click() {
        System.out.println("Button clicked.");
```

```
        notifyObservers();
    }
}

// Concrete Observer
public class ButtonClickHandler implements Observer {
    @Override
    public void update() {
        System.out.println("Button was clicked! Handling event...");
    }
}

// Usage
public class EventManager {
    public static void main(String[] args) {
        Button button = new Button();
        ButtonClickHandler handler = new ButtonClickHandler();

        button.registerObserver(handler);

        button.click();
    }
}
```

The output for the above implementation would be:

```
Button clicked.
Button was clicked! Handling event...
```

This example illustrates how an event management system can use the Observer Pattern to notify multiple observers about events. The Button class acts as the Subject, and the ButtonClickHandler class acts as the Observer. When the button receives a click event, it notifies all its observers.

Analyzing these diverse use cases helps in understanding that the Observer Pattern is versatile and can be suited to a wide range of applications where synchronization and automatic updates are crucial. The pattern's implementation ensures low coupling between the Subject and Observers, allowing for extendibility and scalability in complex software systems.

8.10 Comparing Observer Pattern with Other Patterns

When considering the implementation of the Observer Pattern, it is essential to compare it with other design patterns to understand its unique characteristics and application scenarios better. This comparative analysis highlights the structural and behavioral nuances of the Observer Pattern in contrast with other common design patterns, such as the

Mediator Pattern, the Event-Driven Pattern, and Model-View-Controller (MVC) Architecture.

- **Observer Pattern vs. Mediator Pattern**

  The Observer Pattern promotes one-to-many dependencies between objects. In this pattern, a single subject (or publisher) updates multiple observers (or subscribers) whenever a change in state occurs. This direct but loosely-coupled relationship ensures that the subject is unaware of the specific observers attached to it, focusing instead on the general notification mechanism.

  In contrast, the Mediator Pattern encapsulates how objects interact, promoting many-to-many relationships. It centralizes complex communication and control logic in a mediator object, altering interactions between colleagues (objects) by having them communicate only with the mediator rather than directly with each other. This minimizes direct references among colleagues, reducing the interdependency.

  Here is a simplified code illustration in Java to exemplify the distinction:

```
public interface Subject {
    void registerObserver(Observer o);
    void removeObserver(Observer o);
    void notifyObservers();
}
```

```
public interface Mediator {
    void registerColleague(Colleague c);
    void colleagueChanged(Colleague c);
}
```

  The critical difference lies in how these patterns manage dependencies and communication, making them suited for different kinds of complex systems.

- **Observer Pattern vs. Event-Driven Pattern**

  Both the Observer Pattern and Event-Driven Pattern revolve around notification mechanisms, yet they differ fundamentally in their architectures. The Observer Pattern uses tight coupling where the subject holds references to observers. Notifications are made through a direct call to the observer's update method.

  Conversely, the Event-Driven Pattern employs a more decoupled approach using event dispatchers or event buses. Listeners register with an event bus without a direct reference to the event source. The event processing happens asynchronously, handled by an event queue or an event loop, which enhances scalability.

Consider an example illustrating the syntax of event registration:

```
public class ConcreteSubject implements Subject {
    private List<Observer> observers;

    public void notifyObservers() {
        for (Observer observer : observers) {
            observer.update(this);
        }
    }
}
```

```
public class EventBus {
    private Map<Class<?>, List<Consumer<Object>>> listeners =
        new HashMap<>();

    public <T> void register(Class<T> eventClass, Consumer<T>
        listener) {
        listeners.computeIfAbsent(eventClass, k -> new ArrayList<>()).
            add((Consumer<Object>) listener);
    }

    public void post(Object event) {
        List<Consumer<Object>> consumers = listeners.get(event.
            getClass());
        if (consumers != null) {
            consumers.forEach(listener -> listener.accept(event));
        }
    }
}
```

This structural difference means that while the Observer Pattern might be simpler and more straightforward, the Event-Driven Pattern offers more flexibility and scalability, particularly in larger, distributed systems.

- **Observer Pattern vs. Model-View-Controller (MVC)**

  The MVC architecture pattern divides an application into three interconnected components: Model, View, and Controller. The Observer Pattern is often used within MVC to synchronize the View and the Model. Here, the View acts as an observer; it subscribes to the Model to get notified about changes and update itself accordingly.

  The fundamental concept remains the same: a one-to-many relationship. However, MVC encompasses more than just notification; it deals with the overall structuring of application logic.

  Consider the following MVC-inspired setup:

```
public interface Model {
```

```
    void addObserver(Observer o);
    void removeObserver(Observer o);
    void notifyObservers();
}
```

```
public class ConcreteView implements Observer {
    @Override
    public void update(Model m) {
        // Update view based on model changes
    }
}
```

Here we can see how MVC leverages the Observer Pattern within its broad architecture, incorporating additional structure and roles.

Understanding these differences assists developers in making informed decisions about which pattern best addresses the specific requirements of their software system, whether it be focusing on flexible communication through the Mediator Pattern, enhanced scalability with the Event-Driven approach, or structured application design with MVC.

8.11 Common Mistakes with the Observer Pattern

Implementing the Observer Pattern, though conceptually straightforward, comes with a number of common pitfalls that can undermine its effectiveness. Understanding these mistakes can help in developing more robust and maintainable systems. Below, we explore some prevalent errors and how to avoid them.

1. Memory Leaks Due to Unsubscribed Observers: One of the most common issues with the Observer Pattern is failing to properly manage the life cycle of Observers. If Observers are not removed from the list of the Subject's subscribers, they may persist even when they are no longer needed, leading to memory leaks.

To avoid this problem, ensure that Observers are unsubscribed when they are no longer required. This can be achieved by providing a method in the Subject to remove Observers. For example:

```
public class Subject {
    private List<Observer> observers = new ArrayList<>();

    public void addObserver(Observer observer) {
```

```
        observers.add(observer);
    }

    public void removeObserver(Observer observer) {
        observers.remove(observer);
    }

    public void notifyObservers() {
        for (Observer observer : observers) {
            observer.update();
        }
    }
}
```

2. Inefficient Notification Mechanism: Another common mistake is implementing an inefficient notification mechanism where the Subject notifies all Observers regardless of the changes that have occurred. This can lead to performance degradation, especially when dealing with a large number of Observers or frequent updates.

To optimize the notification process, consider the following strategies:

- State Change Filtering: Notify only those Observers that have registered interest in specific types of changes.
- Batch Updates: Aggregate multiple changes and send a single update notification rather than multiple notifications.

State Change Filtering example:

```
public class SpecificObserver implements Observer {
    private String interest;

    public SpecificObserver(String interest) {
        this.interest = interest;
    }

    @Override
    public void update(String changeType) {
        if (interest.equals(changeType)) {
            // Process the update
        }
    }
}
```

Batch Updates example:

```
public class Subject {
    private List<Observer> observers = new ArrayList<>();
    private List<String> changes = new ArrayList<>();

    public void addObserver(Observer observer) {
        observers.add(observer);
    }
```

```
    public void removeObserver(Observer observer) {
        observers.remove(observer);
    }

    public void addChange(String change) {
        changes.add(change);
    }

    public void notifyObservers() {
        for (Observer observer : observers) {
            observer.update(changes);
        }
        changes.clear();
    }
}
```

3. Cyclic Dependencies: Poor design can lead to cyclic dependencies where Observers and Subjects are mutually dependent on each other, resulting in infinite update loops. This problem can be mitigated by designing clear and unidirectional communication paths.

One way to address this is by introducing a mediator that controls the communication between the Subject and Observers, thus breaking the direct dependency:

```
public class Mediator {
    private Subject subject;
    private List<Observer> observers = new ArrayList<>();

    public Mediator(Subject subject) {
        this.subject = subject;
    }

    public void addObserver(Observer observer) {
        observers.add(observer);
    }

    public void notifyObservers() {
        for (Observer observer : observers) {
            observer.update();
        }
    }
}
```

4. Overloading the Subject: Another mistake is overloading the Subject with too many responsibilities, such as business logic, managing state, and notifying Observers. This violates the Single Responsibility Principle (SRP) and makes the code harder to maintain.

To adhere to SRP, separate the responsibilities by using additional components where appropriate. For example, delegate the state management to a different class, and let the Subject focus solely on notification logic.

State Management class:

```
public class StateManager {
    private String state;

    public String getState() {
        return state;
    }

    public void setState(String state) {
        this.state = state;
    }
}
```

Modified Subject class:

```
public class Subject {
    private List<Observer> observers = new ArrayList<>();
    private StateManager stateManager;

    public Subject(StateManager stateManager) {
        this.stateManager = stateManager;
    }

    public void addObserver(Observer observer) {
        observers.add(observer);
    }

    public void removeObserver(Observer observer) {
        observers.remove(observer);
    }

    public void changeState(String newState) {
        stateManager.setState(newState);
        notifyObservers();
    }

    public void notifyObservers() {
        for (Observer observer : observers) {
            observer.update();
        }
    }
}
```

5. Lack of Synchronization: In multi-threaded environments, failing to properly synchronize access to shared resources can lead to race conditions. Both the Subject and the Observers need to handle synchronization to ensure thread safety.

Using synchronized blocks or appropriate concurrency utilities from the java.util.concurrent package can alleviate this issue.

Example with synchronized blocks:

```
public class Subject {
    private List<Observer> observers = Collections.synchronizedList(new ArrayList
        <>());

    public synchronized void addObserver(Observer observer) {
        observers.add(observer);
```

```
    }

    public synchronized void removeObserver(Observer observer) {
        observers.remove(observer);
    }

    public void notifyObservers() {
        synchronized (observers) {
            for (Observer observer : observers) {
                observer.update();
            }
        }
    }
}
```

To avoid common mistakes when implementing the Observer Pattern, it is vital to pay close attention to observer lifecycle management, optimize notification mechanisms, design clear communication flows to prevent cyclic dependencies, adhere to the Single Responsibility Principle, and ensure proper synchronization in multi-threaded environments. These practices will help in achieving a sound and efficient Observer Pattern implementation.

8.12 Real-World Examples of the Observer Pattern in Java

One of the most potent ways to internalize the Observer Pattern is to examine its application in real-world scenarios. This section provides two detailed examples to elucidate how the Observer Pattern is employed in professional Java programming. The first example involves a simple weather monitoring system, while the second one explores a more complex case in a stock market application.

Weather Monitoring System

In a weather monitoring system, we need to update multiple display elements whenever there are changes in weather data such as temperature, humidity, and pressure. The weather stations act as the Subject, and various displays act as Observers.

```
public interface Subject {
    void registerObserver(Observer o);
    void removeObserver(Observer o);
    void notifyObservers();
}
```

```
public interface Observer {
    void update(float temp, float humidity, float pressure);
```

```
}
```

```
import java.util.ArrayList;

public class WeatherData implements Subject {
    private ArrayList<Observer> observers;
    private float temperature;
    private float humidity;
    private float pressure;

    public WeatherData() {
        observers = new ArrayList<>();
    }

    public void registerObserver(Observer o) {
        observers.add(o);
    }

    public void removeObserver(Observer o) {
        int i = observers.indexOf(o);
        if (i >= 0) {
            observers.remove(i);
        }
    }

    public void notifyObservers() {
        for (Observer observer : observers) {
            observer.update(temperature, humidity, pressure);
        }
    }

    public void measurementsChanged() {
        notifyObservers();
    }

    public void setMeasurements(float temperature, float humidity, float pressure) {
        this.temperature = temperature;
        this.humidity = humidity;
        this.pressure = pressure;
        measurementsChanged();
    }
}
```

```
public class CurrentConditionsDisplay implements Observer {
    private float temperature;
    private float humidity;
    private Subject weatherData;

    public CurrentConditionsDisplay(Subject weatherData) {
        this.weatherData = weatherData;
        weatherData.registerObserver(this);
    }

    public void update(float temperature, float humidity, float pressure) {
        this.temperature = temperature;
        this.humidity = humidity;
        display();
    }

    public void display() {
        System.out.println("Current conditions: " + temperature + "F degrees and " +
```

```
            humidity + "% humidity");
    }
}
```

Here, WeatherData functions as our Subject and CurrentConditionsDisplay acts as our Observer. The CurrentConditionsDisplay automatically updates and displays the current weather conditions whenever the WeatherData measurements change.

Output:
Current conditions: 78.0F degrees and 65.0% humidity

Stock Market Application

In a stock market application, multiple observers monitor changes in stock prices. Here, the stock data acts as the Subject, and various elements such as dashboards or alert systems function as Observers.

```
public interface StockSubject {
    void registerObserver(StockObserver o);
    void removeObserver(StockObserver o);
    void notifyObservers();
}
```

```
public interface StockObserver {
    void update(String stockSymbol, float stockPrice);
}
```

```
import java.util.*;

public class StockData implements StockSubject {
    private Map<String, Float> stockPrices;
    private ArrayList<StockObserver> observers;

    public StockData() {
        stockPrices = new HashMap<>();
        observers = new ArrayList<>();
    }

    public void registerObserver(StockObserver o) {
        observers.add(o);
    }

    public void removeObserver(StockObserver o) {
        observers.remove(o);
    }

    public void notifyObservers(String stockSymbol, float stockPrice) {
        for (StockObserver observer : observers) {
            observer.update(stockSymbol, stockPrice);
        }
    }

    public void setStockPrice(String stockSymbol, float stockPrice) {
        stockPrices.put(stockSymbol, stockPrice);
        notifyObservers(stockSymbol, stockPrice);
    }
```

```
    public float getStockPrice(String stockSymbol) {
        return stockPrices.get(stockSymbol);
    }
}
```

```
public class StockDisplay implements StockObserver {
    private String stockSymbol;
    private float stockPrice;

    public StockDisplay(StockSubject stockData) {
        stockData.registerObserver(this);
    }

    public void update(String stockSymbol, float stockPrice) {
        this.stockSymbol = stockSymbol;
        this.stockPrice = stockPrice;
        display();
    }

    public void display() {
        System.out.println("Stock: " + stockSymbol + " is now at price: " + stockPrice)
            ;
    }
}
```

In this scenario, StockData is our Subject, while StockDisplay acts as our Observer. Whenever a stock price changes, the StockDisplay updates to reflect the latest price.

Output:
Stock: AAPL is now at price: 150.00

These examples underscore the versatility and utility of the Observer Pattern in real-world applications, ensuring data consistency and automated updates across multiple components.

Chapter 9

Strategy Pattern: Defining a Family of Algorithms

This chapter delves into the Strategy Pattern, which defines a family of algorithms, encapsulates each one, and makes them interchangeable. It explains the implementation in Java, detailing the Strategy and Context classes. The chapter discusses when to utilize the Strategy Pattern, its benefits and drawbacks, and contrasts it with other design patterns. Best practices and common pitfalls are outlined to ensure effective use, and real-world examples illustrate its application in solving diverse algorithmic problems.

9.1 Introduction to the Strategy Pattern

The Strategy Pattern is a behavioral design pattern that allows an algorithm's behavior to be selected at runtime. It defines a family of algorithms, encapsulates each algorithm, and makes the algorithms interchangeable within that family. This pattern promotes the use of composition over inheritance and allows a client to choose an algorithm from a family of related algorithms.

The primary participants in the Strategy Pattern are the *Strategy*, *Context*, and *Concrete Strategy* classes/interfaces. Understanding each component is crucial to implementing and utilizing this pattern effectively.

A Strategy typically defines a common interface for algorithms. This interface is implemented by different ConcreteStrategy classes, each encapsulating a particular algorithm. The Context class contains a reference to a Strategy object and interacts with the Strategy through this interface.

```
public interface Strategy {
    void executeAlgorithm();
}
```

In the above listing, the Strategy interface has a method executeAlgorithm(), which must be implemented by all concrete strategy classes. This allows the Context class to call the executeAlgorithm() method without knowing which specific algorithm is being used.

```
public class ConcreteStrategyA implements Strategy {
    @Override
    public void executeAlgorithm() {
        // Algorithm A implementation
        System.out.println("Executing Algorithm A");
    }
}
```

```
public class ConcreteStrategyB implements Strategy {
    @Override
    public void executeAlgorithm() {
        // Algorithm B implementation
        System.out.println("Executing Algorithm B");
    }
}
```

In Listings **??** and **??**, ConcreteStrategyA and ConcreteStrategyB provide different implementations of the executeAlgorithm() method. These classes can be exchanged at runtime to change the algorithm that the Context employs.

```
public class Context {
    private Strategy strategy;

    public Context(Strategy strategy) {
        this.strategy = strategy;
    }

    public void setStrategy(Strategy strategy) {
        this.strategy = strategy;
    }

    public void executeStrategy() {
        strategy.executeAlgorithm();
    }
}
```

The Context class, as shown in Listing **??**, maintains a reference to a Strategy object. The executeStrategy() method delegates the call to the encapsulated Strategy object's executeAlgorithm() method.

By using the Strategy Pattern, the Context class can operate independently of the algorithm it uses, allowing the algorithm to vary independently from the clients that use it. Clients interact with the Context class and can change the strategy at runtime by passing a different strategy to the setStrategy() method.

```
public class StrategyPatternDemo {
    public static void main(String[] args) {
        Context context = new Context(new ConcreteStrategyA());
        context.executeStrategy(); // Outputs: Executing Algorithm A

        context.setStrategy(new ConcreteStrategyB());
        context.executeStrategy(); // Outputs: Executing Algorithm B
    }
}
```

In Listing **??**, a simple demonstration of the Strategy Pattern is provided. By instantiating the Context with ConcreteStrategyA, Algorithm A is executed. When the strategy is changed to ConcreteStrategyB, Algorithm B is executed instead.

```
Output:
Executing Algorithm A
Executing Algorithm B
```

The Strategy Pattern allows developers to define a family of algorithms, encapsulate each one as a separate class, and make them easily interchangeable. Clients using the Context class are insulated from the implementation details of these algorithms, leading to more modular and maintainable code.

The flexibility provided by the Strategy Pattern is invaluable in situations where multiple algorithms could be applied but the decision on which to use might depend on runtime conditions or user input. By decoupling the algorithm from the context, the Strategy Pattern adheres to the Open/Closed Principle, one of the key SOLID principles, which states that software entities should be open for extension but closed for modification. This means that new algorithms can be introduced without altering the existing system, thus enhancing its robustness and scalability.

9.2 Understanding the Strategy Pattern

The Strategy Pattern is a behavioral design pattern that enables selecting an algorithm's behavior at runtime. This pattern encapsulates algorithm families into distinct classes, making algorithms interchangeable within a context. The core idea is to define a family of algorithms, encapsulate each one, and make them interchangeable to allow the algorithm to vary independently from the clients that use it.

Key Concepts

The Strategy Pattern involves the following key concepts:

- Strategy Interface: This interface defines a common set of methods that each algorithm must implement.
- Concrete Strategies: These are classes that implement the Strategy Interface, providing specific algorithm implementations.
- Context Class: This class interacts with the Strategy Interface and is configured with a Concrete Strategy. The Context does not know the specific algorithm but delegates the task to the strategy object.

Design Structure

The Strategy Pattern involves a composition structure where the Context maintains a reference to a Strategy object. The usage of composition instead of inheritance ensures that the Context can vary its behavior by changing its associated Strategy object.

```
+-------------------+ +--------------------+
| Context |<---->| Strategy |
+-------------------+ +--------------------+
| - strategy:Strategy | | + algorithmMethod() |
| + setStrategy() | +--------------------+
| + executeStrategy()| /_\
+-------------------+ |
| --------+
| |
+----------------+ +--------------------+
| ConcreteStrategyA | | ConcreteStrategyB |
+-----------------+ +--------------------+
| algorithmMethod()| | algorithmMethod() |
+-----------------+ +--------------------+
```

Implementation Mechanics

The Strategy Interface declares common operations, which all concrete strategies must implement. Below is an example in Java:

```
public interface Strategy {
    void algorithmMethod();
}
```

Each concrete strategy class implements the Strategy interface:

```
public class ConcreteStrategyA implements Strategy {
    @Override
    public void algorithmMethod() {
        // Implementation of algorithm A
        System.out.println("Algorithm A implementation");
    }
}

public class ConcreteStrategyB implements Strategy {
    @Override
    public void algorithmMethod() {
        // Implementation of algorithm B
        System.out.println("Algorithm B implementation");
    }
}
```

The context class interacts with the strategy through the Strategy interface:

```
public class Context {
    private Strategy strategy;

    // Constructor to set the strategy
    public Context(Strategy strategy) {
        this.strategy = strategy;
    }

    // Method to change the strategy
    public void setStrategy(Strategy strategy) {
        this.strategy = strategy;
    }

    // Method to execute the current strategy
    public void executeStrategy() {
        strategy.algorithmMethod();
    }
}
```

Behavioral Change at Runtime

The Strategy Pattern's flexibility comes from the ability to change the strategy object, allowing the context's behavior to be modified dynamically:

```
public class StrategyPatternDemo {
    public static void main(String[] args) {
        // Creating concrete strategy objects
        Strategy strategyA = new ConcreteStrategyA();
        Strategy strategyB = new ConcreteStrategyB();

        // Creating context with initial strategy
```

```
        Context context = new Context(strategyA);
        context.executeStrategy(); // Outputs: Algorithm A implementation

        // Changing strategy at runtime
        context.setStrategy(strategyB);
        context.executeStrategy(); // Outputs: Algorithm B implementation
    }
}
```

This demonstration shows that the Context can change its algorithm by plugging in different strategy objects, promoting decoupling and enhancing scalability.

Principles and Benefits

The Strategy Pattern adheres to several design principles:

- Open/Closed Principle: Strategies can be introduced without altering the Context class or existing strategies.
- Single Responsibility Principle: The Context object delegates tasks to strategy objects, ensuring a single focus.
- Liskov Substitution Principle: The Context operates seamlessly regardless of which specific Strategy implementation it contains.

The flexibility in algorithm selection provides maintainability and extensibility, facilitating modifications without affecting the broader system.

9.3 Implementing the Strategy Pattern in Java

The implementation of the Strategy Pattern in Java entails defining a Strategy interface, multiple concrete implementations, and a Context class that utilizes these strategies. This section will provide a meticulous walkthrough, ensuring clarity in the execution and understanding of the pattern.

Step 1: Define the Strategy Interface

The Strategy interface declares the operation that various concrete strategies will implement. This interface is abstract and allows the context class to interact with different algorithms uniformly.

```
public interface Strategy {
    void executeAlgorithm();
}
```

Step 2: Create Concrete Strategy Classes

Concrete strategy classes implement the Strategy interface. Each class encapsulates a specific algorithm, facilitating interchangeability and adherence to the open/closed principle.

```
public class ConcreteStrategyA implements Strategy {
    @Override
    public void executeAlgorithm() {
        System.out.println("Executing Algorithm A");
    }
}
```

```
public class ConcreteStrategyB implements Strategy {
    @Override
    public void executeAlgorithm() {
        System.out.println("Executing Algorithm B");
    }
}
```

```
-- Output from ConcreteStrategyA.executeAlgorithm() --
Executing Algorithm A

-- Output from ConcreteStrategyB.executeAlgorithm() --
Executing Algorithm B
```

Step 3: Implement the Context Class

The context class utilizes a Strategy object, which can be dynamically changed. It contains a reference to the strategy and a method to execute the strategy's algorithm.

```
public class Context {
    private Strategy strategy;

    public void setStrategy(Strategy strategy) {
        this.strategy = strategy;
    }

    public void executeStrategy() {
        strategy.executeAlgorithm();
    }
}
```

Context class can now interact with various strategies polymorphically, allowing for dynamic algorithm selection.

Step 4: Client Code

The client code demonstrates how to set different strategies to a context instance and execute them. This highlights the flexibility and ease of interchangeability inherent in the Strategy Pattern.

```
public class StrategyPatternDemo {
```

```
    public static void main(String[] args) {
        Context context = new Context();

        Strategy strategyA = new ConcreteStrategyA();
        context.setStrategy(strategyA);
        context.executeStrategy(); // Output: Executing Algorithm A

        Strategy strategyB = new ConcreteStrategyB();
        context.setStrategy(strategyB);
        context.executeStrategy(); // Output: Executing Algorithm B
    }
}
```

StrategyPatternDemo showcases the dynamic nature of strategy selection and the seamless interchangeability of algorithms.

Algorithm Representation Using algorithm2e Package

For a more formal algorithm representation, consider the following utilization of the algorithm2e package, encapsulating the dynamic strategy selection process:

Algorithm 1: Strategy Pattern Dynamic Selection

Data: Context, Strategy
Result: Execution of the selected strategy
1 initialize Context;
2 initialize StrategyA, StrategyB;
3 Context.setStrategy(StrategyA);
4 Context.executeStrategy();
5 Context.setStrategy(StrategyB);
6 Context.executeStrategy();

This algorithm outlines the procedural steps taken for dynamic strategy selection and execution within the context class.

Throughout this implementation, it is crucial to ensure that the Strategy interface is robust and well-defined, facilitating ease of extension and maintenance. Extending the family of algorithms merely entails adding new implementations of the Strategy interface, enhancing modularity and flexibility without modifying existing code.

9.4 Defining Strategy Interfaces

The Strategy Pattern fundamentally relies on defining a family of algorithms that can be easily interchanged. This is accomplished by creating one or more interfaces that represent these algorithms. Each concrete implementation of a strategy will implement this interface, thus allowing the context to utilize different algorithms interchangeably.

In Java, interfaces play a crucial role in the Strategy Pattern by ensuring that each strategy adheres to a common protocol. An interface in Java is essentially a reference type, similar to a class, that can contain only constants, method signatures, default methods, static methods, and nested types. Interfaces cannot contain instance fields or constructors, making them suitable for defining a set of methods that various classes can implement.

To illustrate, consider an example where we need to define an interface for a family of algorithms that perform different sorting operations. The general steps to define a strategy interface are as follows:

- Define an interface with a method or set of methods that represent the algorithm(s) to be implemented.
- Ensure that the methods defined in the interface encapsulate the core operations of the algorithm.
- Implement the interface in different classes, each providing a specific implementation of the algorithm.

The following is an example of a strategy interface for sorting algorithms in Java:

```
public interface SortingStrategy {
    void sort(int[] numbers);
}
```

This SortingStrategy interface declares a single method, sort, which takes an array of integers as input. Any sorting algorithm can be encapsulated by creating a class that implements this interface and provides a concrete implementation of the sort method.

Consider two different sorting algorithms: Bubble Sort and Quick Sort. Each of these can be implemented as a strategy by creating classes that implement the SortingStrategy interface.

Bubble Sort implementation:

```
public class BubbleSort implements SortingStrategy {
    @Override
    public void sort(int[] numbers) {
        int n = numbers.length;
        boolean swapped;
        for (int i = 0; i < n - 1; i++) {
            swapped = false;
```

```
            for (int j = 0; j < n - i - 1; j++) {
                if (numbers[j] > numbers[j + 1]) {
                    int temp = numbers[j];
                    numbers[j] = numbers[j + 1];
                    numbers[j + 1] = temp;
                    swapped = true;
                }
            }
            if (!swapped) break;
        }
    }
}
```

Quick Sort implementation:

```
public class QuickSort implements SortingStrategy {
    @Override
    public void sort(int[] numbers) {
        quickSort(numbers, 0, numbers.length - 1);
    }

    private void quickSort(int[] array, int low, int high) {
        if (low < high) {
            int pi = partition(array, low, high);
            quickSort(array, low, pi - 1);
            quickSort(array, pi + 1, high);
        }
    }

    private int partition(int[] array, int low, int high) {
        int pivot = array[high];
        int i = (low - 1);
        for (int j = low; j < high; j++) {
            if (array[j] <= pivot) {
                i++;
                int temp = array[i];
                array[i] = array[j];
                array[j] = temp;
            }
        }
        int temp = array[i + 1];
        array[i + 1] = array[high];
        array[high] = temp;
        return i + 1;
    }
}
```

In this example, BubbleSort and QuickSort are two concrete implementations of the SortingStrategy interface. These classes implement the sort method in different ways: BubbleSort uses the bubble sort algorithm, while QuickSort uses the quicksort algorithm.

This flexibility allows the context class to utilize different sorting strategies interchangeably without altering its own implementation. The context class can be designed to hold a reference to the SortingStrategy interface and use the strategy interface method to perform the algorithm.

For instance, consider the following context class:

```
public class SorterContext {
    private SortingStrategy strategy;

    public SorterContext(SortingStrategy strategy) {
        this.strategy = strategy;
    }

    public void setStrategy(SortingStrategy strategy) {
        this.strategy = strategy;
    }

    public void executeStrategy(int[] numbers) {
        strategy.sort(numbers);
    }
}
```

The SorterContext class maintains a reference to the SortingStrategy and delegates the sort operation to the current strategy. This design allows the SorterContext to change its sorting behavior at runtime by setting a different SortingStrategy.

To use the SorterContext with different strategies:

```
public class StrategyPatternDemo {
    public static void main(String[] args) {
        int[] numbers = {34, 7, 23, 32, 5, 62};

        SorterContext context = new SorterContext(new BubbleSort());
        context.executeStrategy(numbers);
        System.out.println("BubbleSorted: " + Arrays.toString(numbers));

        context.setStrategy(new QuickSort());
        context.executeStrategy(numbers);
        System.out.println("QuickSorted: " + Arrays.toString(numbers));
    }
}
```

Output:

```
BubbleSorted: [5, 7, 23, 32, 34, 62]
QuickSorted: [5, 7, 23, 32, 34, 62]
```

In this demonstration, the SorterContext uses the BubbleSort strategy to sort the array first. Then, it switches to the QuickSort strategy and sorts the same array again. The interchangeable nature of the strategies is evident, as the context can change its sorting strategy without any changes to its own structure.

Defining strategy interfaces is a crucial step in implementing the Strategy Pattern. It establishes a contract for different algorithms, ensuring that they are interchangeable within the context class. Through interfaces, Java provides a robust mechanism to define and enforce this contract, thus facilitating the Strategy Pattern's core principle of algorithm interchangeability.

9.5 Context Class in Strategy Pattern

The Context class is a pivotal component of the Strategy Pattern. It maintains a reference to a Strategy object and delegates the algorithm's execution to the encapsulated Strategy object. This section explores the structure, purpose, and implementation details of the Context class, ensuring a robust understanding of its role within the Strategy Pattern.

Structure of the Context Class

The Context class is designed to interact with clients, managing the selected Strategy instance and forwarding client requests to the encapsulated algorithm variant. The primary responsibilities of the Context class are:

- Maintaining a reference to a Strategy object.
- Providing a method for clients to set or change the Strategy object at runtime.
- Delegating algorithm execution to the current Strategy object.

Implementation in Java

To illustrate the implementation of the Context class, consider the following Java code snippet:

```
public class Context {
    private Strategy strategy;

    // Constructor to set default strategy
    public Context(Strategy strategy) {
        this.strategy = strategy;
    }

    // Method to set a new strategy
    public void setStrategy(Strategy strategy) {
        this.strategy = strategy;
    }

    // Method to execute the strategy
    public void executeStrategy() {
        strategy.execute();
    }
}
```

In this example, the Context class is designed to work with any Strategy implementation that conforms to the Strategy interface. The constructor initializes the context with a specific Strategy, and the setStrategy method allows the strategy to be changed dynamically at runtime. The executeStrategy method delegates the execution to the encapsulated Strategy instance.

Example Usage

The following example demonstrates how to utilize the Context class with different Strategy implementations. Assume we have two concrete strategies: ConcreteStrategyA and ConcreteStrategyB.

```
public class ConcreteStrategyA implements Strategy {
    @Override
    public void execute() {
        System.out.println("Executing Strategy A");
    }
}

public class ConcreteStrategyB implements Strategy {
    @Override
    public void execute() {
        System.out.println("Executing Strategy B");
    }
}
```

To use these strategies with the Context class:

```
public class StrategyPatternDemo {
    public static void main(String[] args) {
        // Create context with ConcreteStrategyA
        Context context = new Context(new ConcreteStrategyA());
        context.executeStrategy(); // Output: Executing Strategy A

        // Change context to use ConcreteStrategyB
        context.setStrategy(new ConcreteStrategyB());
        context.executeStrategy(); // Output: Executing Strategy B
    }
}
```

In this example, the Context instance is first initialized with ConcreteStrategyA. When executeStrategy is called, it outputs "Executing Strategy A". The strategy is then dynamically changed to ConcreteStrategyB, and subsequent calls to executeStrategy reflect this change, outputting "Executing Strategy B".

Benefits of the Context Class

The Context class offers several benefits:

- Encapsulation of algorithm selection, promoting modularity and separation of concerns.
- Flexibility to change behavior dynamically at runtime by altering the current strategy.

- Simplification of client code, as clients interact with the context rather than individual strategies.

Common Pitfalls and Considerations

While the Context class greatly improves flexibility and modularity, certain pitfalls must be avoided:

- Ensure thread safety when the Context class is used in a concurrent environment. Use synchronization techniques if necessary.
- Avoid tight coupling between the Context class and concrete strategies. Depend on the abstract Strategy interface.
- Consider the overhead of switching strategies dynamically, especially in performance-critical applications.

Thorough understanding and diligent implementation of the Context class equip developers to leverage the full potential of the Strategy Pattern, addressing diverse algorithmic challenges with interchangeable strategies. Effective use of the Context class fosters modular, maintainable, and flexible codebases.

9.6 When to Use the Strategy Pattern

The Strategy Pattern is particularly useful in situations where multiple algorithms are applicable for a problem, and the best choice of algorithm varies based on the context in which it is applied. Several scenarios justify the use of this pattern, reflecting its ability to provide flexibility, enhance code modularity, and ensure maintainability.

One should consider the Strategy Pattern when an object requires the ability to select from multiple algorithms. Consider a sorting mechanism where different sorting algorithms, such as QuickSort, MergeSort, or BubbleSort, may be applied depending on the size or nature of the data. By encapsulating these sorting algorithms within separate classes that share a common strategy interface, each sorting algorithm can be interchanged without affecting the client code that utilizes them.

The Strategy Pattern facilitates the adherence to the Open/Closed Principle by allowing behavior to be extended without modifying existing code. For instance, if an application requires new or improved algorithms in the future, they can be integrated with minimal changes to the client code. This principle underscores the design pattern's utility in scenarios where algorithmic variations are common, making it a valuable pattern in evolving systems.

The Strategy Pattern is also advantageous in removing conditional statements from the client code, which enhances its readability and maintainability. Traditionally, one might use if-else or switch-case statements to select an algorithm based on certain conditions. With the Strategy Pattern, these conditionals are encapsulated within strategy objects, leading to cleaner and more maintainable code. For example:

```
if (sortingType.equals("QuickSort")) {
    sorter = new QuickSort();
} else if (sortingType.equals("MergeSort")) {
    sorter = new MergeSort();
} else if (sortingType.equals("BubbleSort")) {
    sorter = new BubbleSort();
}
sorter.sort(data);
```

This can be refactored using the Strategy Pattern to read:

```
sorter.setStrategy(new QuickSort()); // Strategy chosen at runtime
sorter.sort(data);
```

Such refactoring not only simplifies the client code but also consolidates algorithm-specific logic within their respective strategy classes, fostering stronger adherence to the Single Responsibility Principle.

Another pertinent scenario is when different classes share a similar algorithm, which diverges in some details. Here, the Strategy Pattern centralizes the core algorithm logic. Consider the context of a payment processing system where various payment methods (credit card, PayPal, Bitcoin) share a common interface but differ in implementation details. Using strategy classes encapsulates these distinct payment processing algorithms, while the core payment processing logic remains consistent.

When algorithmic behavior needs to be selected at runtime, the Strategy Pattern provides the required flexibility. In contexts where users can dynamically change preferences, or where external conditions define the optimal algorithm, the Strategy Pattern facilitates runtime selection. For example, a graphics rendering application might switch between rendering algorithms based on hardware capabilities detected at runtime.

The Strategy Pattern is instrumental when an algorithm requires access to data that is impractical to pass through method parameters.

Strategy objects can maintain state, simplifying the interaction between algorithm and data. This characteristic is particularly beneficial in simulation and game development, where stateful algorithms often govern character behaviors or physics simulations.

Consider also the requirement for testing multiple algorithm implementations in isolation. The Strategy Pattern allows each strategy to be unit tested independently, as each algorithm encapsulated in a strategy class can be instantiated and tested separately, reducing dependencies and improving test coverage.

Lastly, the Strategy Pattern can mitigate the risk of code duplication. In scenarios where similar algorithms spread across multiple client classes, employing the Strategy Pattern condenses these algorithms into reusable strategy classes. This consolidation enhances consistency and reduces the potential for errors.

By allowing the dynamic selection and integration of algorithms at runtime, promoting code modularity, enhancing maintainability, and aligning with critical object-oriented principles, the Strategy Pattern proves its merit across diverse application contexts.

9.7 Advantages and Disadvantages of the Strategy Pattern

The Strategy Pattern presents both advantages and disadvantages depending on the context in which it is employed. Its proper application can lead to more maintainable and flexible code, while improper use may introduce needless complexity. This section details these considerations to offer a balanced perspective.

Advantages

- **Eliminates Conditional Statements**: By encapsulating behaviors within strategy classes, the Strategy Pattern eradicates the need for conditional statements (if-else or switch-case) that would otherwise swamp the Context class. This supports the *Single Responsibility Principle*, keeping the responsibilities of the Context centralized.
- **Promotes Code Reusability**: Individual strategy implementations can be reused across different parts of an application. By

defining a set of strategies, developers can compose new behaviors for different contexts without rewriting common logic.

- **Enhances Maintainability**: Modifying or extending the behavior of an application becomes streamlined. To introduce a new algorithm, one needs only to add a new concrete strategy class without altering existing code. This significantly reduces the risk of introducing bugs.
- **Adheres to Open/Closed Principle**: The Strategy Pattern aligns with the *Open/Closed Principle*, part of SOLID principles, which asserts that software entities should be open for extension but closed for modification. Adding new strategies does not require modifying existing ones or the context, thereby reducing potential errors.
- **Improves Testing**: Strategy classes can be individually tested. As behavior encapsulation is clear and discrete, unit testing becomes more straightforward, affording precise and exhaustive testing of each strategy.

Disadvantages

- **Increased Number of Classes**: The Strategy Pattern necessitates the creation of numerous strategy classes for varying behaviors. In scenarios with numerous algorithms, this can lead to a proliferation of classes, introducing an overhead in management and navigation.
- **Complexity in Understanding**: New developers or those unfamiliar with the pattern may find the system's design more complex to understand initially. The separation of concerns, while beneficial, requires developers to grasp the interaction between multiple strategy and context classes.
- **Possible Overhead**: In certain scenarios, switching strategies dynamically at runtime can introduce overhead, especially if the strategy's selection logic is non-trivial or if the instantiation of strategy objects is computationally expensive.
- **Tight Coupling with Context**: Although the goal of the Strategy Pattern is to decouple the algorithm from its context, a context still needs to retain references to relevant strategies. This can create a form of coupling, particularly if strategies depend heavily on the internal state of the context.

When determining whether to utilize the Strategy Pattern, it is crucial to weigh these factors carefully. By examining the current needs of the application and its expected evolution, one can make an informed decision on the utility of applying the Strategy Pattern. Proper application maximizes the benefits while mitigating the drawbacks inherent to this pattern.

9.8 Strategy Pattern Best Practices

When implementing the Strategy Pattern, it is critical to adhere to best practices to derive maximum benefits from its flexibility and maintainability. The following guidelines will ensure that the use of the Strategy Pattern is both effective and efficient:

- **Define Clear Strategy Interfaces:** Each algorithm should be encapsulated in a distinct strategy interface. These interfaces should be purposefully designed to clearly state the required inputs and expected outputs of the algorithms. Consider the following Java example:

```
public interface SortingStrategy {
    void sort(int[] numbers);
}
```

  Here, SortingStrategy provides a clear contract for sorting algorithms, ensuring that any class implementing this interface can substitute for another.

- **Favor Composition Over Inheritance:** One of the fundamental principles behind the Strategy Pattern is the preference for composition over inheritance. By composing objects with different strategies, you gain greater flexibility and can change behavior at runtime. For instance:

```
public class Sorter {
    private SortingStrategy strategy;

    public Sorter(SortingStrategy strategy) {
        this.strategy = strategy;
    }

    public void setStrategy(SortingStrategy strategy) {
        this.strategy = strategy;
    }

    public void sort(int[] numbers) {
        strategy.sort(numbers);
```

```
    }
}
```

In this example, the Sorter class can change its sorting strategy dynamically via the setStrategy method.

- **Ensure Strategies Are Interchangeable:** To maintain the utility of the Strategy Pattern, each strategy should conform to the interface and be interchangeable. Strategies should implement the appropriate interface without relying on specific details of the context. Consider the following additional implementations of the SortingStrategy:

```
public class BubbleSortStrategy implements SortingStrategy {
    public void sort(int[] numbers) {
        // Implementation of Bubble Sort
    }
}

public class QuickSortStrategy implements SortingStrategy {
    public void sort(int[] numbers) {
        // Implementation of Quick Sort
    }
}
```

Both BubbleSortStrategy and QuickSortStrategy are interchangeable within the Sorter context, allowing the sorting algorithm to be adjusted without modifying client code.

- **Utilize Dependency Injection:** Injecting strategies using a dependency injection framework can automate and simplify the management of strategy objects. This approach ensures that the correct strategy instance is used without explicitly hardcoding it in the client class. In a Spring framework context, this might look like:

```
@Service
public class SorterService {
    private final SortingStrategy sortingStrategy;

    @Autowired
    public SorterService(SortingStrategy sortingStrategy) {
        this.sortingStrategy = sortingStrategy;
    }

    public void sort(int[] numbers) {
        sortingStrategy.sort(numbers);
    }
}
```

Here, the SorterService class gets its SortingStrategy injected by the Spring framework, decoupling strategy selection from the business logic.

- **Manage Strategy Lifecycles Appropriately:** Strategies may have their own lifecycle requirements. If a strategy is stateful or expensive to create, ensure it is appropriately managed, potentially using pooling or caching techniques. Stateless strategies, on the other hand, can often be shared and reused without concern.

- **Document Strategy Behavior:** Each strategy's behavior should be thoroughly documented to make it clear what its purpose is and how it should be used. Proper documentation ensures that future maintainers understand the intent and requirements of each strategy, which is particularly important when behavior is complex or application-specific nuances are involved.

- **Maintain Single Responsibility Principle:** Each strategy should have a single responsibility, focusing solely on the algorithm it encapsulates. This adherence to the Single Responsibility Principle enhances the clarity and maintainability of each strategy and ensures coherent and cohesive modularization of behavior.

- **Test Strategies Independently:** Automated tests should be developed for each strategy to ensure they perform as expected. Unit tests can verify the correctness of the algorithms independent of the context in which they are used. For instance, using JUnit for the BubbleSortStrategy:

```
@Test
public void bubbleSortStrategyShouldSortArray() {
    SortingStrategy strategy = new BubbleSortStrategy();
    int[] numbers = {5, 3, 8, 4, 2};
    strategy.sort(numbers);
    assertArrayEquals(new int[]{2, 3, 4, 5, 8}, numbers);
}
```

  This unit test ensures that the BubbleSortStrategy performs correctly independent of its context.

- **Avoid Overusing Strategies:** While the Strategy Pattern provides substantial flexibility, it should not be used excessively or inappropriately. Employ the pattern judiciously when multiple algorithms are likely to change or need to coexist.

- **Consider Performance Impacts:** Some strategies may have different performance characteristics. Be mindful of these differences, especially if strategies are executed frequently or in performance-critical sections of the application. It may be necessary to benchmark and profile strategies to ensure acceptable performance levels.

Correctly implementing the Strategy Pattern with these best practices will ensure that the solution remains modular, flexible, and maintainable, promoting high cohesion and low coupling within your codebase.

9.9 Use Cases for the Strategy Pattern

The Strategy Pattern is a powerful tool for designing software systems that require the dynamic selection of algorithms at runtime. It is particularly useful in scenarios where multiple algorithms can solve the same problem, but the choice of the algorithm might vary based on contextual data or user preference. In this section, we will explore several use cases for the Strategy Pattern, highlighting its versatility and practical applications.

One classic use case for the Strategy Pattern is in the implementation of sorting algorithms. Consider a program that needs to sort a collection of objects. Depending on the size of the collection and specific requirements, different sorting algorithms such as QuickSort, MergeSort, or BubbleSort might be more efficient. By employing the Strategy Pattern, we can encapsulate each sorting algorithm within its own class and interchange them seamlessly.

```
public interface SortStrategy {
    void sort(int[] numbers);
}

public class BubbleSortStrategy implements SortStrategy {
    public void sort(int[] numbers) {
        // Bubble sort logic
    }
}

public class QuickSortStrategy implements SortStrategy {
    public void sort(int[] numbers) {
        // Quick sort logic
    }
}

public class Context {
    private SortStrategy strategy;

    public void setStrategy(SortStrategy strategy) {
        this.strategy = strategy;
    }
```

```
    public void executeSort(int[] numbers) {
        strategy.sort(numbers);
    }
}
```

In this example, the SortStrategy interface defines a common method for sorting. Concrete strategy classes like BubbleSortStrategy and QuickSortStrategy implement different sorting algorithms. The Context class can dynamically change the sorting strategy by using the setStrategy method, allowing for flexible algorithm selection without altering the client code.

Another practical application of the Strategy Pattern is in gaming, where various AI behaviors can be modeled as strategies. For instance, consider a game where non-player characters (NPCs) can exhibit different movement behaviors such as aggressive, defensive, or evasive maneuvers. Each behavior can be encapsulated within its own strategy class, enabling the game to switch behaviors dynamically based on game state or player actions.

```
public interface MovementStrategy {
    void move();
}

public class AggressiveMovementStrategy implements MovementStrategy {
    public void move() {
        // Aggressive movement logic
    }
}

public class DefensiveMovementStrategy implements MovementStrategy {
    public void move() {
        // Defensive movement logic
    }
}

public class EvasiveMovementStrategy implements MovementStrategy {
    public void move() {
        // Evasive movement logic
    }
}

public class NPC {
    private MovementStrategy strategy;

    public void setStrategy(MovementStrategy strategy) {
        this.strategy = strategy;
    }

    public void performMove() {
        strategy.move();
    }
}
```

Here, the MovementStrategy interface defines a common movement method. The AggressiveMovementStrategy, DefensiveMovementStrategy, and EvasiveMovementStrategy classes implement different movement algorithms. The NPC class can switch between these strategies at runtime, allowing for adaptable and unpredictable NPC behavior.

In financial software, the Strategy Pattern can be utilized to implement various algorithms for calculating interest rates or different investment strategies. For example, a financial application may need to calculate interest differently based on the type of account (e.g., savings, checking, or fixed deposit). Each calculation method can be encapsulated within its own strategy class.

```
public interface InterestStrategy {
    double calculateInterest(double amount, double rate);
}

public class SavingsInterestStrategy implements InterestStrategy {
    public double calculateInterest(double amount, double rate) {
        return amount * rate;
    }
}

public class CheckingInterestStrategy implements InterestStrategy {
    public double calculateInterest(double amount, double rate) {
        return amount * rate * 0.5;
    }
}

public class FixedDepositInterestStrategy implements InterestStrategy {
    public double calculateInterest(double amount, double rate) {
        return amount * rate * 1.5;
    }
}

public class Account {
    private InterestStrategy strategy;

    public void setStrategy(InterestStrategy strategy) {
        this.strategy = strategy;
    }

    public double getInterest(double amount, double rate) {
        return strategy.calculateInterest(amount, rate);
    }
}
```

In this scenario, the InterestStrategy interface defines a method for interest calculation. Concrete strategy classes like SavingsInterestStrategy, CheckingInterestStrategy, and FixedDepositInterestStrategy implement different interest calculation algorithms. The Account class can change its strategy based on the account type, facilitating a flexible and extensible interest calculation model.

Lastly, the Strategy Pattern is highly applicable in text formatting and conversion tools. Consider an application that converts text into different formats such as HTML, Markdown, or plain text. Each conversion process can be encapsulated within its own strategy class, allowing the application to switch between different formats as needed.

```
public interface TextFormatStrategy {
    String format(String text);
}

public class HTMLFormatStrategy implements TextFormatStrategy {
    public String format(String text) {
        return "<html><body>" + text + "</body></html>";
    }
}

public class MarkdownFormatStrategy implements TextFormatStrategy {
    public String format(String text) {
        return "**" + text + "**";
    }
}

public class PlainTextFormatStrategy implements TextFormatStrategy {
    public String format(String text) {
        return text;
    }
}

public class TextFormatter {
    private TextFormatStrategy strategy;

    public void setStrategy(TextFormatStrategy strategy) {
        this.strategy = strategy;
    }

    public String formatText(String text) {
        return strategy.format(text);
    }
}
```

In this example, the TextFormatStrategy interface defines a method for text formatting. The HTMLFormatStrategy, MarkdownFormatStrategy, and PlainTextFormatStrategy classes implement different text formatting strategies. The TextFormatter class can dynamically change its formatting strategy, providing flexibility in text conversion operations.

These use cases illustrate the Strategy Pattern's ability to promote flexibility, reusability, and maintainability in software design. By encapsulating algorithms and making them interchangeable at runtime, developers can create systems that are easier to extend and modify, reducing the impact of changes and fostering a more robust and adaptable codebase.

9.10 Comparing Strategy Pattern with Other Patterns

The Strategy Pattern is a versatile and widely applicable design pattern within the context of object-oriented design. To fully grasp its utility and nuances, it is beneficial to compare and contrast it with other commonly used design patterns. This comparison helps not only in understanding the Strategy Pattern's strengths and limitations but also in discerning when it is more appropriate to use alternative patterns.

Strategy Pattern vs. Template Method Pattern

The primary distinction between the Strategy Pattern and the Template Method Pattern lies in how the algorithm is defined and varied.

- **Algorithm Encapsulation:**
  - **Strategy Pattern:** Encapsulates the family of algorithms, allowing them to be interchangeable. Concrete strategies implement a common interface, providing specific algorithm implementations.
  - **Template Method Pattern:** Utilizes inheritance to define the skeleton of an algorithm in a base class. Subclasses override specific steps of the algorithm without altering its structure.
- **Method Overriding vs. Composition:**
  - **Strategy Pattern:** Favors composition over inheritance. The context class uses composition to maintain a reference to a strategy object.
  - **Template Method Pattern:** Relies on method overriding within an inheritance hierarchy to allow subclass-specific behavior.
- **Flexibility:**
  - **Strategy Pattern:** More flexible in that it can switch strategies at runtime, enhancing the adaptability of the context class.
  - **Template Method Pattern:** More rigid as the algorithm's structure is defined once in the base class and modifying that structure requires changes to the base class.

Strategy Pattern vs. State Pattern

Both the Strategy and State Patterns utilize composition, but they serve different purposes.

- **Intent:**
  - **Strategy Pattern:** Defines a family of interchangeable algorithms that a context can use.
  - **State Pattern:** Allows an object to alter its behavior when its internal state changes, encapsulating the state-specific behavior.
- **Behavioral Change:**
  - **Strategy Pattern:** Behavior can be changed by switching between strategy objects, independent of the object's state.
  - **State Pattern:** Behavior changes dynamically as the internal state of the context object changes.
- **Object Interaction:**
  - **Strategy Pattern:** Strategies are typically stateless and do not depend on the context's state.
  - **State Pattern:** States are stateful and dependent on or altered by other states or the context's state.

Strategy Pattern vs. Factory Method Pattern

The comparison between the Strategy and Factory Method Patterns lies in their domain of use and how they handle object creation and behavior definition.

- **Object Creation:**
  - **Strategy Pattern:** Does not concern itself with the instantiation of strategies. Strategies may be passed from external sources.
  - **Factory Method Pattern:** Centralizes the object creation process, allowing subclasses to offer specific implementations.
- **Behavioral Composition:**

  - **Strategy Pattern:** Focuses on defining interchangeable behaviors or algorithms and is used at runtime.
  - **Factory Method Pattern:** Used mainly at object creation time to decide the concrete class of the object being instantiated.

- **Design Goals:**
  - **Strategy Pattern:** Aims to enable an object to change its executed behavior by switching between strategy objects.
  - **Factory Method Pattern:** Aims to delegate the instantiation of objects to subclasses, promoting loose coupling and ensuring that client code depends more on abstract classes.

Strategy Pattern vs. Command Pattern

While both the Strategy and Command Patterns encapsulate behavior, they serve different purposes.

- **Encapsulation:**
  - **Strategy Pattern:** Encapsulates algorithms to be used interchangeably.
  - **Command Pattern:** Encapsulates requests or operations as command objects, allowing the parameterization of clients with different requests and support for undoable operations.
- **Reusability and Flexibility:**
  - **Strategy Pattern:** Promotes reusability and flexibility of algorithms with dynamically changeable behavior.
  - **Command Pattern:** Promotes reusability of commands and flexibility in queuing, logging, and supporting undoable operations.
- **Structural Differences:**
  - **Strategy Pattern:** Consists of a context that exchanges strategy objects.
  - **Command Pattern:** Encompasses invokers, commands, and receivers where a command mediates between the invoker and the receiver.

The aforementioned comparisons elucidate that the Strategy Pattern's key advantage is its ability to define a family of interchangeable algorithms with minimal effort to modify the context class to change its behavior dynamically.

9.11 Common Mistakes with the Strategy Pattern

Overlooking proper encapsulation can lead to brittle implementations. Each Strategy implementation should encapsulate a distinct algorithm. Mixing logic or dependencies between different Strategy classes contradicts the pattern's principle. Proper encapsulation ensures that changes to one algorithm do not affect others.

```
public interface SortingStrategy {
    void sort(int[] numbers);
}

public class BubbleSortStrategy implements SortingStrategy {
    public void sort(int[] numbers) {
        // Bubble sort logic
    }
}

public class QuickSortStrategy implements SortingStrategy {
    public void sort(int[] numbers) {
        // Quick sort logic
    }
}
```

Failure to define a clear and consistent interface for the Strategy can result in code that is hard to maintain and extend. The interface should be coherent and provide the methods necessary for all concrete strategies. Inconsistent interfaces force client code to incorporate unnecessary checks and can lead to errors.

Context class misuse arises when it houses logic specific to a particular Strategy. The primary role of the Context is to delegate the execution of an algorithm to the selected Strategy. Moving algorithm-specific logic into the Context class diminishes the flexibility and scalability of the pattern.

```
public class SortingContext {
    private SortingStrategy strategy;

    public void setStrategy(SortingStrategy strategy) {
        this.strategy = strategy;
    }
```

```
    public void sort(int[] numbers) {
        strategy.sort(numbers);
    }
}
```

Switching logic based on conditions within the Strategy is a common indication that the pattern was incorrectly applied. Each Strategy should operate independently without needing to know about other strategies. Conditionals within Strategy methods increase coupling and reduce the pattern's effectiveness.

Using the Strategy Pattern when algorithms do not vary can unnecessarily complicate the design. The primary indicator for employing this pattern is the necessity of interchangeable algorithms. Premature use, without clear benefits of algorithm variation, leads to unwarranted complexity.

Exposing internal details of Strategy through the Context class is another frequently encountered error. The Context should serve as an abstraction layer, enabling or disabling strategies without altering the client's perspective. This maintains the encapsulation principle and ensures that client code remains unaffected by specific algorithm changes.

Dependence on client code to manage transitions between different strategies can compromise the design. The Context class should provide mechanisms for safe and proper transitions, reducing errors and enhancing robustness. For instance, if a sorting Strategy requires certain preconditions, it should be managed within the Context.

```
public class Client {
    public static void main(String[] args) {
        SortingContext context = new SortingContext();

        // Choosing BubbleSort
        context.setStrategy(new BubbleSortStrategy());
        int[] numbers = {5, 3, 1, 4, 2};
        context.sort(numbers);

        // Transitioning to QuickSort
        // This should be managed internally instead of relying on the client
        context.setStrategy(new QuickSortStrategy());
        context.sort(numbers);
    }
}
```

Neglecting to consider performance implications can lead to suboptimal applications of the Strategy Pattern. Each Strategy may have different performance characteristics. Understanding these differences ensures the most appropriate Strategy is used in context. Profiling and benchmarking can aid in this assessment.

9.12 Real-World Examples of the Strategy Pattern in Java

The Strategy Pattern, a behavioral design pattern, is particularly useful in scenarios where multiple algorithms are applicable and can be interchanged based on specific requirements. By defining a family of algorithms, encapsulating each one, and making them interchangeable, this pattern increases flexibility and checks complexity in the code.

Consider a robust e-commerce application requiring different shipping strategies for its global customers. For such an application, the Strategy Pattern enables dynamic algorithm selection, providing a cleaner and more maintainable codebase.

Example Scenario: Shipping Cost Calculation

In our example, we will develop a shipping cost calculation system. The objective is to apply different shipping cost strategies like StandardShipping, ExpressShipping, and FreeShipping based on user choice or requirements.

```
// Strategy Interface
public interface ShippingStrategy {
    double calculateShippingCost(double weight);
}

// Concrete Strategy: Standard Shipping
public class StandardShipping implements ShippingStrategy {
    @Override
    public double calculateShippingCost(double weight) {
        return weight * 0.5;
    }
}

// Concrete Strategy: Express Shipping
public class ExpressShipping implements ShippingStrategy {
    @Override
    public double calculateShippingCost(double weight) {
        return weight * 1.0;
    }
}

// Concrete Strategy: Free Shipping
public class FreeShipping implements ShippingStrategy {
    @Override
    public double calculateShippingCost(double weight) {
        return 0.0;
    }
}
```

```
// Context Class
public class ShippingContext {
    private ShippingStrategy strategy;

    public void setShippingStrategy(ShippingStrategy strategy) {
        this.strategy = strategy;
    }

    public double calculateCost(double weight) {
        return strategy.calculateShippingCost(weight);
    }
}

// Client Code
public class StrategyPatternExample {
    public static void main(String[] args) {
        ShippingContext context = new ShippingContext();

        // Standard Shipping
        context.setShippingStrategy(new StandardShipping());
        System.out.println("Standard Shipping Cost: $" + context.calculateCost(10));

        // Express Shipping
        context.setShippingStrategy(new ExpressShipping());
        System.out.println("Express Shipping Cost: $" + context.calculateCost(10));

        // Free Shipping
        context.setShippingStrategy(new FreeShipping());
        System.out.println("Free Shipping Cost: $" + context.calculateCost(10));
    }
}
```

```
Standard Shipping Cost: $5.0
Express Shipping Cost: $10.0
Free Shipping Cost: $0.0
```

In this example, the ShippingStrategy interface defines the method calculateShippingCost, which is implemented by various concreted strategies (StandardShipping, ExpressShipping, FreeShipping). The ShippingContext class holds a reference to a ShippingStrategy and is responsible for interacting with the chosen strategy to calculate the cost.

This design allows the addition of new shipping strategies without modifying existing code, thus adhering to the Open/Closed Principle. Furthermore, the client code in the StrategyPatternExample class demonstrates how the strategy can be dynamically changed at runtime.

Example Scenario: Payment Processing System

Consider a payment processing system that supports multiple payment methods like CreditCardPayment, PayPalPayment, and BitcoinPayment. This can be effectively implemented using the Strategy Pattern to enable switching between different payment algorithms dynamically.

```
// Strategy Interface
```

```
public interface PaymentStrategy {
    void pay(double amount);
}

// Concrete Strategy: Credit Card Payment
public class CreditCardPayment implements PaymentStrategy {
    private String cardNumber;
    private String cardHolderName;

    public CreditCardPayment(String cardNumber, String cardHolderName) {
        this.cardNumber = cardNumber;
        this.cardHolderName = cardHolderName;
    }

    @Override
    public void pay(double amount) {
        System.out.println("Paid $" + amount + " using Credit Card.");
    }
}

// Concrete Strategy: PayPal Payment
public class PayPalPayment implements PaymentStrategy {
    private String email;
    private String password;

    public PayPalPayment(String email, String password) {
        this.email = email;
        this.password = password;
    }

    @Override
    public void pay(double amount) {
        System.out.println("Paid $" + amount + " using PayPal.");
    }
}

// Concrete Strategy: Bitcoin Payment
public class BitcoinPayment implements PaymentStrategy {
    private String walletAddress;

    public BitcoinPayment(String walletAddress) {
        this.walletAddress = walletAddress;
    }

    @Override
    public void pay(double amount) {
        System.out.println("Paid $" + amount + " using Bitcoin.");
    }
}

// Context Class
public class PaymentContext {
    private PaymentStrategy strategy;

    public void setPaymentStrategy(PaymentStrategy strategy) {
        this.strategy = strategy;
    }

    public void pay(double amount) {
        strategy.pay(amount);
    }
}
```

```
// Client Code
public class StrategyPatternExamplePayment {
    public static void main(String[] args) {
        PaymentContext context = new PaymentContext();

        // Credit Card Payment
        context.setPaymentStrategy(new CreditCardPayment("1234-5678-9012-3456", "
            John Doe"));
        context.pay(100.0);

        // PayPal Payment
        context.setPaymentStrategy(new PayPalPayment("john.doe@example.com", "
            securepassword"));
        context.pay(100.0);

        // Bitcoin Payment
        context.setPaymentStrategy(new BitcoinPayment("1
            A1zP1eP5QGefi2DMPTfTL5SLmv7DivfNv"));
        context.pay(100.0);
    }
}
```

```
Paid $100.0 using Credit Card.
Paid $100.0 using PayPal.
Paid $100.0 using Bitcoin.
```

For implementing different payment methods, the PaymentStrategy interface is defined with a pay method. This method is customized in the concrete strategies (CreditCardPayment, PayPalPayment, BitcoinPayment). The PaymentContext class maintains a reference to a PaymentStrategy, allowing for dynamic selection of a payment method during the runtime.

Using the Strategy Pattern for a payment processing system makes it easy to add support for new payment methods. The existing system remains unchanged, enhancing code maintainability and scalability.

These real-world examples underscore the adaptability and utility of the Strategy Pattern in scenarios requiring dynamic and flexible algorithm selection. By encapsulating algorithms and rendering them interchangeable, the Strategy Pattern facilitates a clean, extensible, and maintainable codebase across diverse applications.

Chapter 10

Decorator Pattern: Extending Functionality Dynamically

This chapter covers the Decorator Pattern, which allows for dynamically extending the functionality of objects without altering their structure. It explains how to implement the pattern in Java, focusing on the roles of component interfaces, concrete components, and decorators. The chapter examines when to use the Decorator Pattern, its pros and cons, and compares it with alternative approaches. Best practices and common pitfalls are discussed, and real-world examples are provided to demonstrate its practical application.

10.1 Introduction to the Decorator Pattern

The Decorator Pattern is a structural design pattern that provides a flexible alternative to subclassing for extending functionality. This pattern is instrumental in adding responsibilities to objects dynamically without altering their structure. The concept revolves around four core components: the $\mathrm{Component}$ interface, $\mathrm{ConcreteComponent}$ class, $\mathrm{Decorator}$ abstract class, and $\mathrm{ConcreteDecorator}$ classes.

The $\mathrm{Component}$ interface defines the interface for objects that can have responsibilities added to them. Importantly, it is common for the interface to represent generic functionality that both concrete components and decorators will share.

```
public interface Component {
    void operation();
}
```

The ConcreteComponent class is a straightforward implementation of the Component interface. It represents objects to which additional responsibilities can be attached, meaning that it operates normally until a decorator modifies its behavior.

```
public class ConcreteComponent implements Component {
    public void operation() {
        // Primary behavior of the ConcreteComponent
        System.out.println("Performing operation in ConcreteComponent.");
    }
}
```

The Decorator abstract class implements the Component interface and holds a reference to a component object. The Decorator class itself does not alter the interface's behavior but delegates the responsibility to the component. This provides the scaffolding necessary for concrete decorators to enhance functionality.

```
public abstract class Decorator implements Component {
    protected Component component;

    public Decorator(Component component) {
        this.component = component;
    }

    public void operation() {
        component.operation();
    }
}
```

Concrete decorators extend Decorator and add behaviors before or after invoking the method on the wrapped object. Multiple decorators can layer functionality in a manner that is both transparent and configurable at runtime.

```
public class ConcreteDecoratorA extends Decorator {

    public ConcreteDecoratorA(Component component) {
        super(component);
    }

    @Override
    public void operation() {
        super.operation();
        addedBehavior();
    }
```

```
    private void addedBehavior() {
        System.out.println("Additional behavior from ConcreteDecoratorA.");
    }
}
```

Consider a simplistic example where we have a core component responsible for rendering text. By applying different decorators, we might add functionalities such as scrolling, border rendering, or shadowing. Each decorator augments the base component's behavior, enabling modular and reusable enhancements. This dynamic extension capability makes the decorator pattern a robust alternative to static subclass inheritance.

```
public class TextView implements Component {
    public void operation() {
        System.out.println("Rendering TextView content.");
    }
}

public class ScrollDecorator extends Decorator {

    public ScrollDecorator(Component component) {
        super(component);
    }

    @Override
    public void operation() {
        super.operation();
        scroll();
    }

    private void scroll() {
        System.out.println("Adding scroll functionality.");
    }
}
public class BorderDecorator extends Decorator {

    public BorderDecorator(Component component) {
        super(component);
    }

    @Override
    public void operation() {
        super.operation();
        addBorder();
    }

    private void addBorder() {
        System.out.println("Adding border functionality.");
    }
}

public class DecoratorPatternDemo {

    public static void main(String[] args) {
        Component textView = new TextView();
```

```
        System.out.println("Plain TextView:");
        textView.operation();

        Component textViewWithScroll = new ScrollDecorator(new TextView());
        System.out.println("\nTextView with Scroll:");
        textViewWithScroll.operation();

        Component textViewWithBorder = new BorderDecorator(new TextView());
        System.out.println("\nTextView with Border:");
        textViewWithBorder.operation();

        Component decoratedTextView = new BorderDecorator(new ScrollDecorator(
             new TextView()));
        System.out.println("\nTextView with Scroll and Border:");
        decoratedTextView.operation();
    }
}
```

The output of the above demonstration would be:

```
Plain TextView:
Rendering TextView content.

TextView with Scroll:
Rendering TextView content.
Adding scroll functionality.

TextView with Border:
Rendering TextView content.
Adding border functionality.

TextView with Scroll and Border:
Rendering TextView content.
Adding scroll functionality.
Adding border functionality.
```

Through this example, patterns like these illustrate the powerful capability of the decorator pattern to enhance object behavior dynamically. The decomposition of aspects like scrolling and border rendering into separate decorators provides cleaner, more manageable code, avoiding the exponential growth of subclasses that a static inheritance model would necessitate.

By utilizing the Decorator Pattern, developers ensure that each additional functionality remains encapsulated within its own class. This supports the Single Responsibility Principle, making individual aspects easier to modify, test, and extend. The pattern facilitates better control over the composition of behaviors, promoting greater flexibility and scalability in software design.

10.2 Understanding the Decorator Pattern

The Decorator Pattern is a structural design pattern that allows for the extension of an object's behavior dynamically without modifying its code structure. Understanding this pattern requires comprehending the fundamental concepts of object-oriented principles, such as composition, abstraction, and polymorphism.

At its core, the Decorator Pattern facilitates the addition of responsibilities to objects transparently and flexibly. This pattern is particularly useful in scenarios where inheritance would lead to an impractical number of subclasses to cover various combinations of behaviors.

In the UML diagram shown in Figure, several key components illustrate the roles and relationships in the Decorator Pattern:

- Component: An abstract class or interface that defines the behavior that can be dynamically extended.
- ConcreteComponent: A class that implements the Component interface. This is the object whose functionality will be extended dynamically.
- Decorator: An abstract class that also implements the Component interface. It holds a reference to a Component object and delegates all operations to this object, providing a mechanism to enhance behavior.
- ConcreteDecorator: A class that extends Decorator and overrides behavior of the Component it decorates. Additional functionalities are added here.

To elucidate, let us explore each part of this structure with illustrative Java code examples.

```
public interface Component {
    void operation();
}
```

The Component interface defines the standard behavior (in this example, a single method operation) that will be implemented by both the concrete component and decorators.

```
public class ConcreteComponent implements Component {
    @Override
    public void operation() {
```

```
        System.out.println("Performing operation in ConcreteComponent.");
    }
}
```

The ConcreteComponent class implements the Component interface. It represents the core functionality: an object that clients will interact with. When additional behaviors are needed, decorators will be applied to this object.

```
public abstract class Decorator implements Component {
    protected Component component;

    public Decorator(Component component) {
        this.component = component;
    }

    @Override
    public void operation() {
        component.operation();
    }
}
```

The Decorator class is abstract and implements the Component interface. It holds a reference to a Component object through composition. The Decorator class delegates the operation to this internal component object, ensuring that additional behavior can be layered on top via subclassing.

```
public class ConcreteDecorator extends Decorator {
    public ConcreteDecorator(Component component) {
        super(component);
    }

    @Override
    public void operation() {
        super.operation();
        addedBehavior();
    }

    public void addedBehavior() {
        System.out.println("Adding behavior in ConcreteDecorator.");
    }
}
```

The ConcreteDecorator class extends the Decorator class and overrides the operation method to augment it with additional behavior. Here, it calls the super.operation() and then adds its own new behavior via the addedBehavior() method.

To instantiate and utilize these classes in a client application, the pattern is applied as follows:

```
public class Client {
    public static void main(String[] args) {
```

```
        Component component = new ConcreteComponent();
        Component decoratedComponent = new ConcreteDecorator(component);
        decoratedComponent.operation();
    }
}
```

When executed, the output demonstrates the extended behavior provided by the decorator:

```
Performing operation in ConcreteComponent.
Adding behavior in ConcreteDecorator.
```

By carefully composing these classes, the Decorator Pattern enables flexible and modular extensions of behavior. The pattern avoids the pitfalls of complex and rigid inheritance hierarchies, allowing behaviors to be mixed and matched as needed.

Common implementations of this pattern in the Java API include I/O streams (java.io.InputStream, java.io.OutputStream) where streams can be wrapped in various decorators to provide additional functionalities such as buffering, filtering, or compression.

Careful application of the Decorator Pattern enhances system extensibility and maintainability, making it an invaluable tool for architects aiming to build adaptive software solutions. The principles learned here will aid in making informed design decisions in various contexts where dynamic augmentation of object behavior is required.

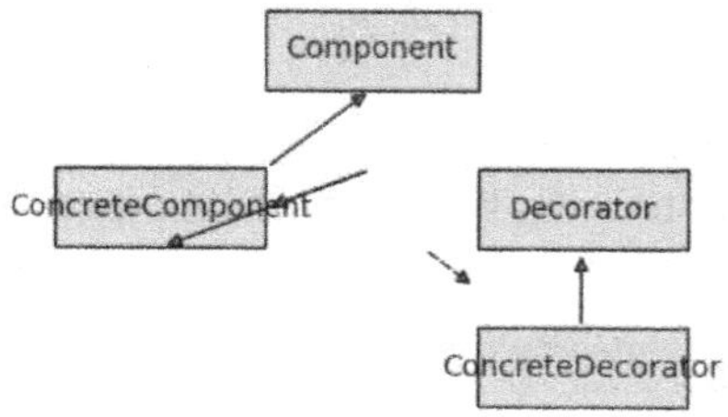

10.3 Implementing the Decorator Pattern in Java

To implement the Decorator Pattern in Java, the first step involves defining the component interface that represents the core functionality. Following this, we introduce concrete components that provide the basic operations. Decorators, which extend functionality, are then developed either as abstract decorators or as concrete implementations. This section presents a comprehensive example illustrating each aspect, ensuring clarity in the practical application of the Decorator Pattern.

The component interface is defined as follows:

```
public interface Component {
    void operation();
}
```

In this example, Component is the interface that all concrete components and decorators will implement. It contains a single method, operation, representing the core functionality to be extended.

Next, we define a concrete component that implements this interface:

```
public class ConcreteComponent implements Component {
    @Override
    public void operation() {
        System.out.println("Executing operation in ConcreteComponent.");
    }
}
```

In the code above, the ConcreteComponent provides a basic implementation of the operation method. This forms the component that decorators will extend.

Abstract decorators are designed to extend the functionality of concrete components while adhering to the same interface. Here is an example of an abstract decorator:

```
public abstract class Decorator implements Component {
    protected Component component;

    public Decorator(Component component) {
        this.component = component;
    }

    @Override
    public void operation() {
        component.operation();
    }
}
```

The Decorator class holds a reference to a Component object and implements the operation method by delegating it to the wrapped component. This allows additional functionality to be added by subclasses.

Concrete decorators extend the Decorator class to enhance or modify the behavior of the operation method. Below is an example of a concrete decorator:

```
public class ConcreteDecoratorA extends Decorator {
    public ConcreteDecoratorA(Component component) {
        super(component);
    }

    @Override
    public void operation() {
        super.operation();
        additionalOperation();
    }

    private void additionalOperation() {
        System.out.println("Adding additional functionality in ConcreteDecoratorA.");
    }
}
```

In ConcreteDecoratorA, the operation method calls the superclass method to maintain the chain of responsibility. After that, it adds extra behavior through additionalOperation.

Another concrete decorator can be created to further extend the functionality:

```
public class ConcreteDecoratorB extends Decorator {
    public ConcreteDecoratorB(Component component) {
        super(component);
    }

    @Override
    public void operation() {
        super.operation();
        additionalBehavior();
    }

    private void additionalBehavior() {
        System.out.println("Enhancing functionality in ConcreteDecoratorB.");
    }
}
```

Similar to ConcreteDecoratorA, ConcreteDecoratorB enhances the operation method by introducing new behavior.

To demonstrate how decorators can be combined at runtime, consider the following client code:

```
public class DecoratorPatternDemo {
    public static void main(String[] args) {
        Component component = new ConcreteComponent();
```

```
        Component decoratorA = new ConcreteDecoratorA(component);
        Component decoratorB = new ConcreteDecoratorB(decoratorA);

        System.out.println("Executing decorated component:");
        decoratorB.operation();
    }
}
```

The client code shows the creation of a ConcreteComponent object, which is then wrapped by ConcreteDecoratorA. Subsequently, the decorated component is further wrapped by ConcreteDecoratorB. Executing decoratorB.operation() results in the enhanced functionality provided by both decorators.

Output from the program execution:

```
Executing decorated component:
Executing operation in ConcreteComponent.
Adding additional functionality in ConcreteDecoratorA.
Enhancing functionality in ConcreteDecoratorB.
```

This output demonstrates that the decorators ConcreteDecoratorA and ConcreteDecoratorB successfully extend the behavior of the ConcreteComponent, following the structure and principles of the Decorator Pattern. Through the flexible combination of these decorators, functionality can be dynamically extended without modifying the underlying component structure.

10.4 Component Interface and Concrete Component

In the context of the Decorator Pattern, it is imperative to understand the foundational structures that facilitate the dynamic extension of object functionalities. Central to this pattern are the Component Interface and the Concrete Component. These elements serve as the core building blocks upon which decorators can operate.

The Component Interface acts as a contract that defines the behaviors that both the Concrete Component and any decorators must adhere to. Essentially, it ensures uniformity and consistency, allowing decorators to assume that any object they extend will meet these predefined behaviors.

Defining the Component Interface

The Component Interface is typically expressed in Java as an interface, although an abstract class could be used in scenarios where some shared code or default behavior should be provided. The primary purpose is to declare the methods that the concrete components and decorators need to implement.

```
public interface Component {
    void operation();
}
```

In this example, the Component interface declares a single method, operation. This method will be implemented by all concrete components and decorators. This ensures that decorators can call operation on the objects they wrap, irrespective of the underlying concrete implementation.

Implementing the Concrete Component

The Concrete Component is the class that implements the Component Interface. This class contains the actual business logic and represents the core functionality that may be extended dynamically by decorators. It's crucial that the Concrete Component adheres to the contract stipulated by the Component Interface.

```
public class ConcreteComponent implements Component {
    @Override
    public void operation() {
        System.out.println("ConcreteComponent operation performed.");
    }
}
```

In the above example, the ConcreteComponent class implements the operation method, which includes specific functionality—in this case, printing a message. This method can be extended or modified by decorators without altering the original ConcreteComponent class.

Interaction between Component Interface and Concrete Component

Once the Component Interface and Concrete Component are defined, they establish the foundation for applying decorators. The decorators will wrap objects that implement the Component Interface, enhancing or modifying their behaviors dynamically. This interaction ensures that the core functionality provided by the Concrete Component remains intact while allowing flexible extensions.

Consider the following sequence to illustrate the creation and utilization of a Concrete Component:

```
public class Main {
    public static void main(String[] args) {
        Component component = new ConcreteComponent();
        component.operation(); // Output: ConcreteComponent operation performed.
```

```
    }
}
```

The Main class contains the main method, which instantiates a ConcreteComponent and calls its operation method. The output will confirm that the Concrete Component's method was executed as expected.

Key Considerations
Several key considerations must be taken into account to effectively implement the Component Interface and Concrete Component:

- **Uniform Interface**: Ensuring that both the Concrete Component and all decorators implement a common interface is vital for seamless integration and polymorphic behavior.
- **Extensibility**: The primary goal of the Decorator Pattern is to extend functionality dynamically. The Component Interface and Concrete Component should be designed with this flexibility in mind.
- **Transparency**: Decorators should modify the behavior of the components transparently, without requiring changes to the underlying component or client code that uses the component.

Adhering to these considerations ensures a robust and flexible design, making it easier to add new functionalities without disrupting existing structures.

Example of Adding a New Operation To demonstrate adding a decorator, consider the following scenario where we want to add logging functionality to the Concrete Component.

First, define a decorator class that implements the Component interface:

```
public class LoggerDecorator implements Component {
    private final Component wrappedComponent;

    public LoggerDecorator(Component wrappedComponent) {
        this.wrappedComponent = wrappedComponent;
    }

    @Override
    public void operation() {
        System.out.println("Logging: Before operation");
        wrappedComponent.operation();
        System.out.println("Logging: After operation");
    }
}
```

Next, demonstrate the use of the decorator in the main method:

```
public class Main {
    public static void main(String[] args) {
        Component component = new ConcreteComponent();
        Component loggerComponent = new LoggerDecorator(component);
        loggerComponent.operation();
    }
}
```

Executing this program would yield:

```
Logging: Before operation
ConcreteComponent operation performed.
Logging: After operation
```

This demonstrates how the LoggerDecorator enhances the behavior of the ConcreteComponent by adding logging before and after the core operation. This approach preserves the original contract defined by the Component Interface while allowing for flexible and dynamic enhancements. The ability to add such functionalities without modifying the existing code base is one of the prime advantages of employing the Decorator Pattern.

10.5 Creating Decorators: Concrete and Abstract

In the Decorator Pattern, decorators play a pivotal role by dynamically extending the functionality of objects. They achieve this without altering the original object's structure, making them immensely powerful for enhancing flexibility and scalability in software design. This section delves into the process of creating decorators, discerning between concrete and abstract decorators, and provides comprehensive examples implemented in Java.

Abstract Decorator

An abstract decorator serves as the base class for all concrete decorators. It generally implements the component interface and holds a reference to an instance of the component interface. This reference allows the decorator to delegate operations to the component it decorates. This mechanism facilitates the seamless chaining of multiple decorators.

Here is an example of an abstract decorator in Java:

```
// Component interface
public interface Component {
```

```
    void operation();
}

// Concrete Component implementing the Component interface
public class ConcreteComponent implements Component {
    @Override
    public void operation() {
        System.out.println("ConcreteComponent operation");
    }
}

// Abstract Decorator implementing the Component interface and containing a
      reference to a Component
public abstract class AbstractDecorator implements Component {
    protected Component component;

    public AbstractDecorator(Component component) {
        this.component = component;
    }

    @Override
    public void operation() {
        component.operation();
    }
}
```

In this example, AbstractDecorator implements the Component interface and maintains a reference to a Component object. The constructor of AbstractDecorator initializes this reference. The operation method is overridden to delegate the call to the referenced Component object, ensuring the basic operation functionality is preserved.

Concrete Decorator

Concrete decorators extend the AbstractDecorator and enrich the behavior of the component they decorate. Each concrete decorator adds specific functionality, and multiple decorators can be layered to bundle various functionalities.

Consider the following example of concrete decorators:

```
// Concrete Decorator A adds additional functionality to the component
public class ConcreteDecoratorA extends AbstractDecorator {

    public ConcreteDecoratorA(Component component) {
        super(component);
    }

    @Override
    public void operation() {
        super.operation();
        addedBehaviorA();
    }

    private void addedBehaviorA() {
        System.out.println("ConcreteDecoratorA additional behavior");
    }
}
```

```
// Concrete Decorator B adds more functionality to the component
public class ConcreteDecoratorB extends AbstractDecorator {

    public ConcreteDecoratorB(Component component) {
        super(component);
    }

    @Override
    public void operation() {
        super.operation();
        addedBehaviorB();
    }

    private void addedBehaviorB() {
        System.out.println("ConcreteDecoratorB additional behavior");
    }
}
```

In this example:

- ConcreteDecoratorA and ConcreteDecoratorB both extend AbstractDecorator.
- Each override the operation method to maintain the invocation of the base operation and then add their specific functionalities through addedBehaviorA and addedBehaviorB, respectively.

This structure allows each decorator to add independent enhancements to the component while leveraging the existing behavior.

Testing Concrete Decorators

To illustrate how these decorators can be used together, consider the following client code:

```
// Client code demonstrating the use of decorators
public class DecoratorTest {
    public static void main(String[] args) {
        Component component = new ConcreteComponent();

        // Decorate the component with ConcreteDecoratorA
        Component decoratedComponentA = new ConcreteDecoratorA(component);

        // Decorate the component further with ConcreteDecoratorB
        Component decoratedComponentB = new ConcreteDecoratorB(
            decoratedComponentA);

        // Execute the operation
        decoratedComponentB.operation();
    }
}
```

Executing this code yields the following output:

```
ConcreteComponent operation
ConcreteDecoratorA additional behavior
ConcreteDecoratorB additional behavior
```

Here, the sequence in which decorators are applied is crucial. The ConcreteComponent is initially wrapped by ConcreteDecoratorA, which is then further decorated by ConcreteDecoratorB. This chain of decorators ensures that all added behaviors are executed in the precise order of decoration.

Creating effective decorators involves adhering to the principle of least knowledge and ensuring each decorator class has a single responsibility. This allows for maximized flexibility and minimized interdependencies, fostering maintainable and scalable object-oriented designs.

10.6 When to Use the Decorator Pattern

The Decorator Pattern is especially useful in scenarios where the functionality of objects needs to be extended dynamically without modifying their source code. This pattern is beneficial in several specific situations:

- **Adding Responsibilities to Objects Dynamically:** When the goal is to assign additional responsibilities to objects at runtime, the Decorator Pattern provides an efficient approach. Unlike the subclassing mechanism, which requires anticipating all possible extensions at design time, decorators offer the flexibility to combine behaviors transparently and flexibly.

- **Enhancing Object Functionality without Subclass Explosion:** In cases where subclassing would result in a complex and bulky hierarchy with numerous classes, each representing a combination of functionalities, decorators help to mitigate such explosion. By encapsulating additional behaviors in distinct classes, they promote a more manageable and structured design.

- **Adhering to the Open/Closed Principle:** The Open/Closed Principle (OCP) states that software entities should be open for extension but closed for modification. Decorators perfectly align with this principle, allowing new functionalities to be added without altering existing code, thus maintaining system integrity and reducing the risk of introducing bugs.

- **Combining Multiple Independent Behaviors:** In scenarios where objects need to exhibit multiple behaviors that can exist independently of each other, decorators offer a way to mix and match these behaviors at runtime. This composition over inheritance strategy ensures that each piece of behavior is encapsulated within its own decorator class, reducing interdependencies and improving maintainability.
- **Modifying or Augmenting Object Behavior:** If there is a need to modify or augment an object's behavior in a consistent manner across the application, decorators provide a reusable solution. Behaviors encapsulated in decorators can be easily applied to various object instances without duplicating the code.

Consider a graphical user interface (GUI) framework where visual components such as windows, buttons, and text fields may require varying functionalities, such as borders, scroll bars, or shadows. Subclassing each component to create combinations of these functionalities would lead to an explosion of subclasses. In this context, the Decorator Pattern provides a more elegant solution by allowing such functionalities to be attached at runtime using decorators.

To illustrate this with a more concrete example, consider a text editing application where text can be bolded, italicized, or both. Using the Decorator Pattern, you can create a base Text component and individual decorators that add bold or italic styles. These decorators can then be dynamically composed to achieve the desired formatting without modifying the core Text class or creating numerous subclasses for each combination of styles.

```
interface Text {
    String render();
}

class PlainText implements Text {
    private String text;

    public PlainText(String text) {
        this.text = text;
    }

    public String render() {
        return text;
    }
}

abstract class TextDecorator implements Text {
    protected Text decoratedText;

    public TextDecorator(Text decoratedText) {
```

```
        this.decoratedText = decoratedText;
    }

    public String render() {
        return decoratedText.render();
    }
}

class BoldTextDecorator extends TextDecorator {
    public BoldTextDecorator(Text decoratedText) {
        super(decoratedText);
    }

    public String render() {
        return "<b>" + super.render() + "</b>";
    }
}

class ItalicTextDecorator extends TextDecorator {
    public ItalicTextDecorator(Text decoratedText) {
        super(decoratedText);
    }

    public String render() {
        return "<i>" + super.render() + "</i>";
    }
}

// Usage
Text myText = new PlainText("Hello, World!");
myText = new BoldTextDecorator(myText);
myText = new ItalicTextDecorator(myText);

System.out.println(myText.render());
```

The output generated by this code example demonstrates how multiple decorators can be composed together to add functionalities dynamically:

```
<i><b>Hello, World!</b></i>
```

This example highlights the utility of the Decorator Pattern in avoiding subclass proliferation by enabling behavior composition. Decorators such as BoldTextDecorator and ItalicTextDecorator extend the functionality of PlainText in a flexible and reusable manner.

Overall, the Decorator Pattern is a powerful and versatile tool in a developer's arsenal, particularly for cases where system behavior needs to be extended dynamically and in adherence to fundamental design principles. This pattern's proper application results in clean, maintainable, and scalable code architectures that adapt well to evolving requirements.

10.7 Advantages and Disadvantages of the Decorator Pattern

The Decorator Pattern provides a flexible and powerful way to add behavior to objects dynamically. Understanding the benefits and drawbacks of this design pattern is essential for making informed design decisions. This section delves into the core advantages and disadvantages of implementing the Decorator Pattern in Java.

Advantages:

- **Open/Closed Principle Compliance:** The Decorator Pattern adheres to the *Open/Closed Principle* by allowing objects to be extended without modifying their code. This principle states that software entities (classes, modules, functions, etc.) should be open for extension but closed for modification. By using decorators, you can create new functionalities by extending existing ones, ensuring that the original code remains unchanged and reducing the risk of introducing new bugs.

- **Greater Flexibility:** Decorators provide high flexibility as they can be combined in various ways, allowing multiple behaviors to be added independently to an object. This compositional approach avoids the combinatorial explosion typically associated with inheritance, where subclassing every possible combination of behaviors leads to an impractical number of classes.

- **Single Responsibility Principle:** By using the Decorator Pattern, you can isolate specific behaviors into separate classes, each with a single responsibility. This adheres to the *Single Responsibility Principle*, making the system easier to understand, maintain, and debug.

- **Dynamic Behavior Changes:** The Decorator Pattern allows the behavior of an object to be changed at runtime. This ability to modify the behavior dynamically, without altering the object's class, is beneficial in scenarios where the behavior needs to be adjusted based on the object's state or context.

- **Enhanced Reusability:** Decorators encapsulate behaviors that can be reused across different contexts in the application. This modularity facilitates the reuse of code, reducing redundancy and enhancing maintainability.

Disadvantages:

- **Increased Number of Objects:** One potential drawback of the Decorator Pattern is that it can lead to an increase in the number of objects created. Each additional behavior requires its decorator class, which can result in a proliferation of small classes. Managing these classes can become cumbersome, and object instantiation could impose performance overhead.

- **Complex Debugging:** Debugging in a system that heavily uses decorators can be more challenging. Since the behavior of objects is distributed across multiple classes, tracing the flow of execution through these layers can be complex. This added complexity requires more sophisticated debugging tools and techniques.

- **Tight Coupling via Decorator Dependencies:** While the Decorator Pattern promotes loose coupling between the core component and the extended functionalities, it can introduce tight coupling between decorators themselves. If decorators are not designed carefully, they may depend on specific behaviors of preceding decorators in the decoration chain, potentially leading to fragile and less-maintainable code.

- **Potential Performance Overheads:** Due to the additional layer of decorators, there may be a performance penalty. Each decorator wraps around the existing object, leading to multiple passes through the method calls. This additional overhead can be non-trivial, especially in performance-critical applications.

- **Dependency Management:** Keeping track of the different instances and types of decorators can be challenging, especially in large-scale systems. Ensuring that the correct sequence of decorators is applied and managing their dependencies requires careful planning.

Understanding these advantages and disadvantages will enable developers to weigh the benefits against the potential drawbacks when deciding to implement the Decorator Pattern. This evaluation helps in ensuring that the pattern is applied judiciously and effectively within the broader context of system design.

10.8 Decorator Pattern Best Practices

When applying the Decorator Pattern in Java, adherence to best practices ensures not only the successful implementation of the pattern but also its maintainability and scalability over time. This section delves into key principles and recommendations that help refine the use of decorators in software design.

Primary guidelines include the following points:

- **Maintain the Interface Consistency:** Ensure that decorators conform to the original component interface. By doing so, decorated and undecorated objects can be treated uniformly, facilitating smooth integration and interaction within the system. For instance:

```
// Component Interface
public interface Widget {
    void draw();
}

// Concrete Component
public class TextBox implements Widget {
    @Override
    public void draw() {
        System.out.println("Drawing TextBox");
    }
}

// Decorator
public abstract class WidgetDecorator implements Widget {
    protected Widget widget;

    public WidgetDecorator(Widget widget) {
        this.widget = widget;
    }

    @Override
    public void draw() {
        widget.draw();
    }
}
```

- **Composition Over Inheritance:** Leverage composition rather than inheritance to add new functionalities. Decorators should encapsulate components and potentially other decorators, thereby enabling the dynamic extension of behavior without altering component classes directly.

- **Design for Transparency:** Strive to keep the decorator's presence as transparent as possible from the client's perspective. Ideally, the client code should interact with the decorated object in the same way as it would with the original object, allowing the added behavior to remain unobtrusive.

- **Avoid Redundant Decorators:** Ensure that each decorator adds distinct functionality. Applying multiple decorators that perform identical or similar operations can lead to redundancy, increasing complexity without tangible benefits. For example, do not stack multiple decorators that achieve the same outcome, such as multiple instances adding logging capabilities:

```
// Inefficient redundant decorators
public class LoggingDecorator extends WidgetDecorator {
    public LoggingDecorator(Widget widget) {
        super(widget);
    }

    @Override
    public void draw() {
        System.out.println("Logging before drawing");
        super.draw();
        System.out.println("Logging after drawing");
    }
}

public class AnotherLoggingDecorator extends WidgetDecorator {
    public AnotherLoggingDecorator(Widget widget) {
        super(widget);
    }

    @Override
    public void draw() {
        System.out.println("Another log before drawing");
        super.draw();
        System.out.println("Another log after drawing");
    }
}

// Only one logging decorator should be sufficient
```

- **Documentation and Code Comments:** Clearly document the purpose and behavior of each decorator. Given that decorators can be stacked in various combinations, explicit documentation assists developers in understanding the overall effect any stacking will have, and what behavior each decorator contributes.

- **Use Abstract Decorators for Reusability:** Implement abstract decorators when there's a need to inherit common functionality among multiple concrete decorators. This approach ensures code reuse, reducing duplication, and facilitating maintainability:

```
// Abstract Decorator
public abstract class BorderDecorator extends WidgetDecorator {
    public BorderDecorator(Widget widget) {
```

```
        super(widget);
    }

    public abstract void addBorder();
}

// Concrete Decorator
public class SolidBorderDecorator extends BorderDecorator {
    public SolidBorderDecorator(Widget widget) {
        super(widget);
    }

    @Override
    public void draw() {
        super.draw();
        addBorder();
    }

    @Override
    public void addBorder() {
        System.out.println("Adding solid border");
    }
}
```

- **Prefer Interfaces to Abstract Classes:** Wherever possible, use interfaces over abstract classes for defining decorators. This keeps the design more flexible and less constrained by a specific class hierarchy, thereby enabling different combinations and hierarchies of decorators.

- **Monitoring and Performance:** Profile the system for performance bottlenecks, especially when multiple decorators are applied. Decorations add a layer of wrapping and can introduce additional overhead. Careful consideration is required to ensure that the performance remains within acceptable limits.

- **Testing Decorators Independently:** Individual decorators should be tested in isolation to guarantee that each decorator adds its specific functionality correctly without negative interference with other decorators. Afterward, combinations of decorators should also be tested to ensure cohesive functionality:

```
Widget simpleTextBox = new TextBox();
Widget decoratedTextBox = new SolidBorderDecorator(new TextBox());
decoratedTextBox.draw();

// Expected Output:
// Drawing TextBox
// Adding solid border
```

- **Single Responsibility Principle:** Each decorator should adhere to the Single Responsibility Principle by focusing on extending a single aspect of behavior. Avoid coupling multiple responsibilities within a single decorator, which can lead to harder maintenance and lower reusability.

Attentive implementation of these best practices enhances the robustness, flexibility, and readability of systems making use of the Decorator Pattern, ensuring high code quality and ease of future enhancements. Ensuring these principles are closely followed allows the Decorator Pattern to achieve its full potential in a diverse range of applications.

10.9 Use Cases for the Decorator Pattern

The Decorator Pattern is particularly advantageous in scenarios where objects need to be dynamically extended with new functionalities without modifying their structure or the underlying class definitions. Its primary utility arises in applications demanding flexible and reusable modifications. Understanding these use cases is critical for selecting the appropriate design pattern for your software architecture. Below, we enumerate several fundamental situations where the Decorator Pattern proves to be beneficial.

Graphical User Interfaces (GUIs): In GUI applications, components such as text boxes, buttons, and panels often need to support various extended functionalities, like borders, scrollbars, and tooltips. The Decorator Pattern allows these additional features to be applied dynamically. For example, consider a text box that may need to have a border, shadow, or both. Without changing the text box class, decorators can be used to add these features:

```
public interface VisualComponent {
    void draw();
}

public class TextBox implements VisualComponent {
    public void draw() {
        // Code to draw text box
    }
}

public abstract class ComponentDecorator implements VisualComponent {
    protected VisualComponent component;

    public ComponentDecorator(VisualComponent component) {
        this.component = component;
    }

    public void draw() {
        component.draw();
```

```
    }
}

public class BorderDecorator extends ComponentDecorator {
    public BorderDecorator(VisualComponent component) {
        super(component);
    }

    public void draw() {
        super.draw();
        drawBorder();
    }

    private void drawBorder() {
        // Code to draw border
    }
}

public class ShadowDecorator extends ComponentDecorator {
    public ShadowDecorator(VisualComponent component) {
        super(component);
    }

    public void draw() {
        super.draw();
        drawShadow();
    }

    private void drawShadow() {
        // Code to draw shadow
    }
}
```

```
VisualComponent textBox = new TextBox();
VisualComponent borderedTextBox = new BorderDecorator(textBox);
borderedTextBox.draw();

VisualComponent shadowedTextBox = new ShadowDecorator(textBox);
shadowedTextBox.draw();

VisualComponent decoratedTextBox = new BorderDecorator(new ShadowDecorator(textBox));
decoratedTextBox.draw();
```

Input/Output (I/O) Streams: The Java I/O library extensively employs the Decorator Pattern. Various decorators like BufferedInputStream, DataInputStream, and FilterInputStream allow for flexible construction of different functionalities around a core InputStream. For instance, one can attach buffering and data conversion features to a file input stream:

```
FileInputStream fileInputStream = new FileInputStream("file.txt");
BufferedInputStream bufferedInputStream = new BufferedInputStream(fileInputStream
    );
DataInputStream dataInputStream = new DataInputStream(bufferedInputStream);

int data = dataInputStream.readInt();
```

Responsibilities and Behaviors: When objects need to be assigned responsibilities or behaviors dynamically, the Decorator Pattern fits aptly. For example, an email notification system might require emails to be sent with varying levels of logging, encryption, or additional headers depending on the context:

```
public interface Email {
    void send();
}

public class BasicEmail implements Email {
    public void send() {
        // Code to send a basic email
    }
}

public abstract class EmailDecorator implements Email {
    protected Email email;

    public EmailDecorator(Email email) {
        this.email = email;
    }

    public void send() {
        email.send();
    }
}

public class EncryptedEmailDecorator extends EmailDecorator {
    public EncryptedEmailDecorator(Email email) {
        super(email);
    }

    public void send() {
        encrypt();
        super.send();
    }

    private void encrypt() {
        // Code to encrypt email
    }
}

public class LoggedEmailDecorator extends EmailDecorator {
    public LoggedEmailDecorator(Email email) {
        super(email);
    }

    public void send() {
        log();
        super.send();
    }

    private void log() {
        // Code to log email details
    }
}
```

```
Email email = new BasicEmail();
Email encryptedEmail = new EncryptedEmailDecorator(email);
encryptedEmail.send();

Email loggedAndEncryptedEmail = new LoggedEmailDecorator(new EncryptedEmailDecorator(email));
loggedAndEncryptedEmail.send();
```

Middleware in Data Processing Pipelines: The Decorator Pattern is beneficial in constructing data processing pipelines or middleware stacks. This is seen in web servers and message queues where each part of the pipeline can add additional processing steps dynamically. For example, a message processing system could utilize decorators to add compression, encryption, and logging to messages:

```
public interface Message {
    void process();
}

public class BasicMessage implements Message {
    public void process() {
        // Code to process a basic message
    }
}

public abstract class MessageDecorator implements Message {
    protected Message message;

    public MessageDecorator(Message message) {
        this.message = message;
    }

    public void process() {
        message.process();
    }
}

public class CompressedMessageDecorator extends MessageDecorator {
    public CompressedMessageDecorator(Message message) {
        super(message);
    }

    public void process() {
        compress();
        super.process();
    }

    private void compress() {
        // Code to compress the message
    }
}

public class EncryptedMessageDecorator extends MessageDecorator {
    public EncryptedMessageDecorator(Message message) {
        super(message);
    }

    public void process() {
        encrypt();
        super.process();
    }
```

```
    private void encrypt() {
        // Code to encrypt the message
    }
}

public class LoggedMessageDecorator extends MessageDecorator {
    public LoggedMessageDecorator(Message message) {
        super(message);
    }

    public void process() {
        log();
        super.process();
    }

    private void log() {
        // Code to log the message processing
    }
}
```

```
Message message = new BasicMessage();
Message compressedMessage = new CompressedMessageDecorator(message);
compressedMessage.process();

Message encryptedAndLoggedMessage = new LoggedMessageDecorator(new EncryptedMessageDecorator(message));
encryptedAndLoggedMessage.process();
```

In production-grade systems, utilizing the Decorator Pattern can significantly ramp up the configurability and extendibility of objects. Proper comprehension of when and how to apply this pattern facilitates the development of robust, maintainable, and flexible code bases, adapting seamlessly to evolving requirements.

10.10 Comparing Decorator Pattern with Other Patterns

The Decorator Pattern, by definition, provides a flexible alternative to extending an object's functionality without modifying its structure, which is achieved through composition rather than inheritance. This section aims to compare the Decorator Pattern with several other design patterns, highlighting the distinct situations in which each is appropriate and contrasting their structural and behavioral differences. Specifically, we will compare the Decorator Pattern with the following design patterns: the Adapter Pattern, the Proxy Pattern, and the Composite Pattern.

Adapter Pattern

The Adapter Pattern enables two incompatible interfaces to work together. Essentially, it allows for existing classes to cooperate without altering their source code. The primary intention is to convert the interface of a class into another interface that clients expect. This pattern involves a single-object transformation, whereas the Decorator Pattern focuses on enhancing object functionality.

To illustrate, consider the following Java code for an Adapter:

```
public interface Target {
    void request();
}

public class Adaptee {
    public void specificRequest() {
        System.out.println("Called specificRequest()");
    }
}

public class Adapter implements Target {
    private Adaptee adaptee;

    public Adapter(Adaptee adaptee) {
        this.adaptee = adaptee;
    }

    @Override
    public void request() {
        adaptee.specificRequest();
    }
}
```

The output of request() through an Adapter is redirected to specificRequest() of the Adaptee. This contrasts with the Decorator Pattern, where the goal is not to adapt interfaces, but to wrap objects with additional behavior selectively.

Proxy Pattern

The Proxy Pattern involves creating a surrogate or placeholder for another object to control access to it. The core purpose of the Proxy Pattern is to control, manage, or check access to another object, as opposed to the Decorator Pattern's aim of adding responsibilities.

Consider a typical virtual proxy example:

```
public interface Image {
    void display();
}

public class RealImage implements Image {
    private String filename;

    public RealImage(String filename) {
        this.filename = filename;
        loadImageFromDisk();
    }

    private void loadImageFromDisk() {
```

```
        System.out.println("Loading " + filename);
    }

    @Override
    public void display() {
        System.out.println("Displaying " + filename);
    }
}

public class ProxyImage implements Image {
    private RealImage realImage;
    private String filename;

    public ProxyImage(String filename) {
        this.filename = filename;
    }

    @Override
    public void display() {
        if (realImage == null) {
            realImage = new RealImage(filename);
        }
        realImage.display();
    }
}
```

The ProxyImage controls the creation and access to RealImage only when display() is called. Here, the focus is on controlling access rather than adding functionalities dynamically as seen in the Decorator Pattern.

Composite Pattern

The Composite Pattern is used to treat individual objects and compositions of objects uniformly. It allows a tree structure to represent part-whole hierarchies. While the Decorator Pattern deals with adding behavior, the Composite Pattern focuses on part-whole relationships.

Here is a simplified example in Java:

```
public interface Graphic {
    void draw();
}

public class CompositeGraphic implements Graphic {
    private List<Graphic> graphics = new ArrayList<>();

    public void add(Graphic graphic) {
        graphics.add(graphic);
    }

    public void remove(Graphic graphic) {
        graphics.remove(graphic);
    }

    @Override
    public void draw() {
        for (Graphic graphic : graphics) {
```

```
            graphic.draw();
        }
    }
}

public class Circle implements Graphic {
    @Override
    public void draw() {
        System.out.println("Drawing Circle");
    }
}

public class Square implements Graphic {
    @Override
    public void draw() {
        System.out.println("Drawing Square");
    }
}
```

In this scenario, a CompositeGraphic can contain Circle and Square objects, and draw() will invoke their respective draw() methods. The key difference is the hierarchical composition with Composite versus the layer-based functionality aggregation of the Decorator.

Observer Pattern

The Observer Pattern defines a one-to-many dependency between objects so that when one object changes state, all its dependents are notified and updated automatically. This pattern contrasts with the Decorator, which weaves additional functionalities without disturbing the existing structure of the object.

A simple notification system example:

```
public interface Observer {
    void update(String message);
}

public interface Subject {
    void attach(Observer o);
    void detach(Observer o);
    void notifyObservers();
}

public class ConcreteSubject implements Subject {
    private List<Observer> observers = new ArrayList<>();
    private String state;

    @Override
    public void attach(Observer o) {
        observers.add(o);
    }

    @Override
    public void detach(Observer o) {
        observers.remove(o);
    }
```

```
    @Override
    public void notifyObservers() {
        for (Observer o : observers) {
            o.update(state);
        }
    }

    public void setState(String state) {
        this.state = state;
        notifyObservers();
    }
}

public class ConcreteObserver implements Observer {
    private String name;

    public ConcreteObserver(String name) {
        this.name = name;
    }

    @Override
    public void update(String message) {
        System.out.println(name + " received update: " + message);
    }
}
```

In this case, once the ConcreteSubject's state changes, all attached ConcreteObserver instances are alerted. The Observer Pattern's role is event notification, while the Decorator Pattern's role is to provide enhanced behavior.

By understanding these comparisons, developers can discern when to use the Decorator Pattern versus other patterns, recognizing each pattern's unique advantages and appropriate use cases. The decision of which pattern to implement should align with the problem's requirements and constraints, ensuring the design remains flexible, maintainable, and scalable.

10.11 Common Mistakes with the Decorator Pattern

The Decorator Pattern is a powerful tool for extending the functionality of objects dynamically, but its misuse can lead to complex, hard-to-maintain code. In this section, we will explore several common mistakes developers make when implementing the Decorator Pattern in Java, providing detailed examples to illustrate each point.

1. Not Using an Interface or Abstract Class for Components

One of the fundamental principles of the Decorator Pattern is that both the concrete components and decorators should adhere to a common interface or abstract class. Skipping this step can lead to inconsistencies and tightly coupled code. Consider the following flawed implementation:

```
class SimpleCoffee {
    public double getCost() {
        return 1.0;
    }
}

class MilkDecorator {
    private SimpleCoffee coffee;

    public MilkDecorator(SimpleCoffee coffee) {
        this.coffee = coffee;
    }

    public double getCost() {
        return coffee.getCost() + 0.5;
    }
}
```

Since SimpleCoffee and MilkDecorator do not share a common interface, the latter cannot be used interchangeably with other concrete component types. A more appropriate implementation involves defining a common interface or abstract class:

```
interface Coffee {
    double getCost();
}

class SimpleCoffee implements Coffee {
    public double getCost() {
        return 1.0;
    }
}

class MilkDecorator implements Coffee {
    private Coffee coffee;

    public MilkDecorator(Coffee coffee) {
        this.coffee = coffee;
    }

    public double getCost() {
        return coffee.getCost() + 0.5;
    }
}
```

2. Overloading Constructors Unnecessarily

While constructors in decorators are essential for establishing the connection to the component they wrap, overloading constructors without necessity introduces additional complexity. The purpose of the decorator is to enhance the existing component's functionality dynamically, not create multiple variations. The preferred design includes a single constructor that takes a component interface:

```
class SugarDecorator implements Coffee {
    private Coffee coffee;

    public SugarDecorator(Coffee coffee) {
        this.coffee = coffee;
    }

    public double getCost() {
        return coffee.getCost() + 0.2;
    }
}
```

3. Not Wrapping Components Correctly

Neglecting the proper wrapping of components within decorators can lead to incorrect behavior. This occurs when a decorator does not delegate to the wrapped component's methods correctly. Always ensure that each decorator calls the necessary methods on the wrapped component to maintain correct functionality.

```
class WhippedCreamDecorator implements Coffee {
    private Coffee coffee;

    public WhippedCreamDecorator(Coffee coffee) {
        this.coffee = coffee;
    }

    public double getCost() {
        return coffee.getCost() + 0.7;
    }
}
```

4. Too Many Layers of Decorators

The Decorator Pattern enables stacking of multiple decorators. However, excessive layering can result in performance degradation and increased complexity. Each additional decorator adds another layer of indirection.

Consider such chain:

```
Coffee coffee = new WhippedCreamDecorator(
                    new SugarDecorator(
                        new MilkDecorator(
                            new SimpleCoffee())));
```

While this maintains flexibility, careful consideration of performance and readability should guide the number of layers used. Aim for a balanced approach to avoid unnecessarily deep decorator stacks.

5. Ignoring the Single Responsibility Principle

Decorators should focus singularly on adding specific functionality without overstepping into responsibilities beyond their remit. Violating the Single Responsibility Principle leads to bloated decorators that are hard to manage and maintain.

```
class CaramelDecorator implements Coffee {
    private Coffee coffee;

    public CaramelDecorator(Coffee coffee) {
        this.coffee = coffee;
    }

    public double getCost() {
        return coffee.getCost() + 0.3;
    }
}
```

In contrast, a poorly designed decorator could handle unrelated duties, diverging from its primary objective.

6. Failing to Maintain Open/Closed Principle

The Decorator Pattern should adhere to the Open/Closed Principle, allowing extensions through new decorators rather than changing existing ones. This principle ensures scalability and maintenance of the codebase.

If a need arises to add new behaviors, implement an additional decorator rather than modifying an existing one.

Following these guidelines ensures that the Decorator Pattern remains a useful technique for adding dynamic functionality while maintaining code clarity and performance.

10.12 Real-World Examples of the Decorator Pattern in Java

To elucidate the practical applications of the Decorator Pattern in Java, we will inspect several real-world examples that demonstrate its effective use. These examples span multiple domains, showcasing the pattern's versatility.

Example 1: Java I/O Streams

One of the most prominent and frequently encountered implementations of the Decorator Pattern in Java is found within the java.io package, particularly in the handling of I/O Streams. Here, the pattern is utilized to add responsibilities such as buffering, data filtering, and character encoding to base stream classes.

Below is a simplified illustration highlighting the core concepts:

```
import java.io.*;

public class FileStreamExample {
    public static void main(String[] args) {
        try {
            InputStream fileStream = new FileInputStream("example.txt");
            InputStream bufferedStream = new BufferedInputStream(fileStream);
            InputStream dataStream = new DataInputStream(bufferedStream);

            // Reading from the file
            int data = dataStream.read();
            while(data != -1) {
                System.out.print((char) data);
                data = dataStream.read();
            }
            dataStream.close();
        } catch (IOException e) {
            e.printStackTrace();
        }
    }
}
```

In this code, FileInputStream is the basic I/O stream that reads bytes from a file. We then wrap it with BufferedInputStream to add buffering capabilities. Finally, DataInputStream extends the functionality to read Java primitive data types. Each decorator adds its own responsibility while delegating the core byte-reading task to the underlying component.

Example 2: Graphical User Interfaces (GUIs)

In GUI design, decorating components dynamically to change appearance or behavior is a common use case. The following example uses the Java Swing framework to demonstrate how the Decorator Pattern can be applied to enhance visual elements of a GUI.

```
import javax.swing.*;
import java.awt.*;

public class BorderDecoratorExample {
    public static void main(String[] args) {
        JFrame frame = new JFrame();
        frame.setDefaultCloseOperation(JFrame.EXIT_ON_CLOSE);
        frame.setSize(400, 300);

        JButton simpleButton = new JButton("Simple Button");

        // Decorating the button with an EmptyBorder
        JButton decoratedButton = new JButton("Decorated Button");
        decoratedButton.setBorder(BorderFactory.createEmptyBorder(10, 10, 10, 10));

        // Panel to hold buttons
```

```
        JPanel panel = new JPanel();
        panel.add(simpleButton);
        panel.add(decoratedButton);

        frame.add(panel);
        frame.setVisible(true);
    }
}
```

Here, the BorderFactory.createEmptyBorder method is used to add an empty border around the JButton, demonstrating a visual extension to the component's appearance. This approach allows for flexible and reusable styling enhancements without modifying the core button class.

Example 3: Message Encryption

In security-focused applications, decorators can be used to add encryption to message objects. Suppose we have a system that sends messages over a network and we want to add encryption as an optional feature.

```
abstract class Message {
    public abstract String getContent();
}

class TextMessage extends Message {
    private String content;

    public TextMessage(String content) {
        this.content = content;
    }

    @Override
    public String getContent() {
        return content;
    }
}

abstract class MessageDecorator extends Message {
    protected Message message;

    public MessageDecorator(Message message) {
        this.message = message;
    }
}

class EncryptedMessage extends MessageDecorator {
    public EncryptedMessage(Message message) {
        super(message);
    }

    @Override
    public String getContent() {
        // Simple encryption logic (e.g., base64 encoding)
        return Base64.getEncoder().encodeToString(message.getContent().getBytes());
    }
}
```

```
class SecureMessageExample {
    public static void main(String[] args) {
        Message message = new TextMessage("Hello, World!");
        System.out.println("Original: " + message.getContent());

        Message encryptedMessage = new EncryptedMessage(message);
        System.out.println("Encrypted: " + encryptedMessage.getContent());
    }
}
```

In this example, TextMessage represents the core component, while EncryptedMessage is a decorator that adds encryption functionality. By adhering to the Decorator Pattern, additional features such as compression or secondary encryption can be easily added in the future without altering the original message structure.

Example 4: Notification System

A notification system that supports various notification types (e.g., email, SMS) can benefit from the Decorator Pattern to dynamically add new notification channels.

```
interface Notifier {
    void send(String message);
}

class EmailNotifier implements Notifier {
    public void send(String message) {
        System.out.println("Sending email: " + message);
    }
}

abstract class NotifierDecorator implements Notifier {
    protected Notifier notifier;

    public NotifierDecorator(Notifier notifier) {
        this.notifier = notifier;
    }
}

class SMSNotifier extends NotifierDecorator {
    public SMSNotifier(Notifier notifier) {
        super(notifier);
    }

    @Override
    public void send(String message) {
        notifier.send(message);
        System.out.println("Sending SMS: " + message);
    }
}

class NotificationSystemExample {
    public static void main(String[] args) {
        Notifier emailNotifier = new EmailNotifier();
        Notifier emailAndSmsNotifier = new SMSNotifier(emailNotifier);

        emailNotifier.send("Hello, this is a basic email.");
```

```
        emailAndSmsNotifier.send("Hello, this message includes SMS.");
    }
}
```

In this notification system, EmailNotifier sends notifications via email, and SMSNotifier extends this capability by adding SMS notifications. Decorators like SMSNotifier enable chaining multiple notification types dynamically, enhancing system flexibility.

These examples highlight the practical advantages and diverse applications of the Decorator Pattern, reinforcing its suitability for scenarios requiring dynamic and flexible feature augmentation.

Made in United States
Orlando, FL
04 November 2026

90207103R00226